The Color Companion of

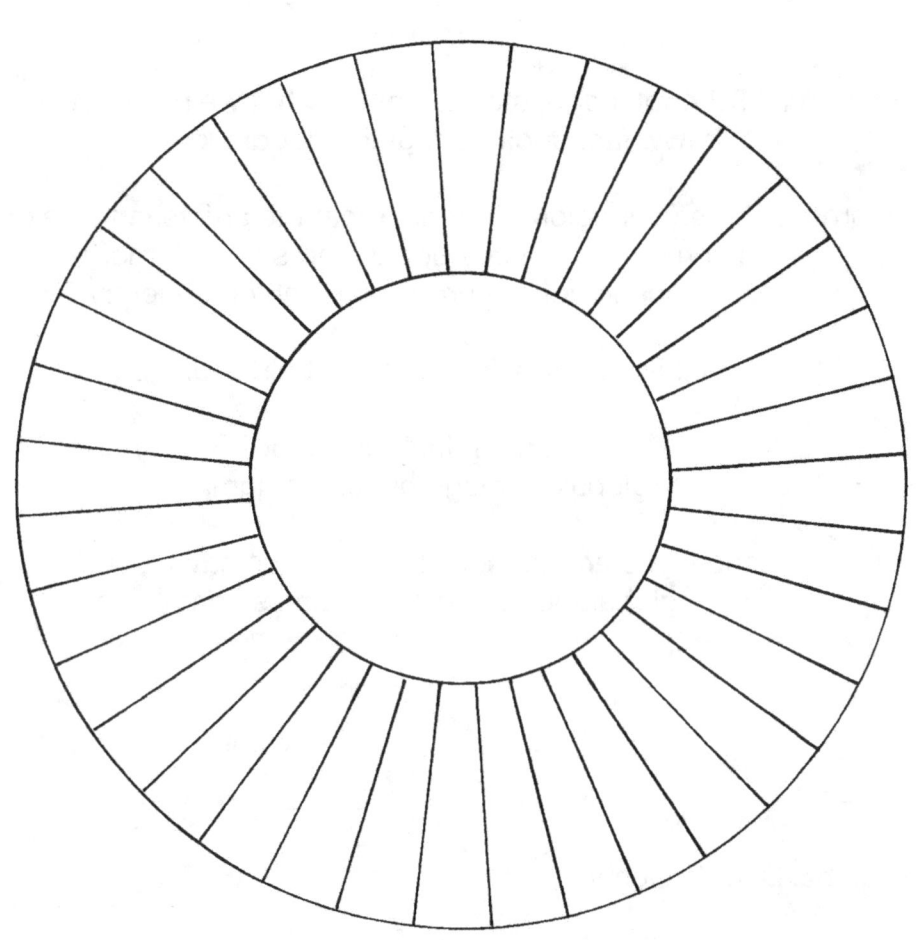

"My Colors, my style, my way!"

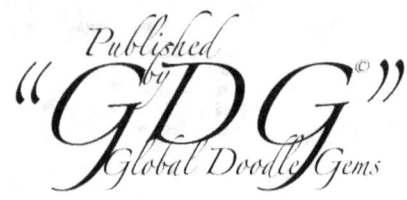

Share your colored versions with us ! We love seeing your results and hearing from you we are social !

The Official FB book page, stay on top of what we have in the works !
www.facebook.com/globaldoodlegems

The Community group, share your colored pages, meet the artists, enjoy exclusive freebies, take part in community Charity books and so much more......
www.facebook.com/groups/globaldoodlegems/

Follow us on Twitter.... @GlobalDoodlegem

We are on Instagram too
@globaldoodlegems for instagram

...and if you are not social like that we have a blog
globaldoodlegems.wordpress.com

Copyright © 2016 Global Doodle Gems

All rights are reserved by Global Doodle Gems.

Duplication of pages for personal use are allowed. You are invited to color the pages then scan/post your coloured versions to social networks, mentioning the book title and author/artist (Global Doodle Gems).

All artwork and images are protected by copyright laws. This book or any portion thereof may not, otherwise, be reproduced and/or distributed or transmitted without the express written permission of the artist/publisher of Global Doodle Gems.

All of us from the Global Doodle Gems wish you a colortastic time and look forward to seeing your wonderful color results online !

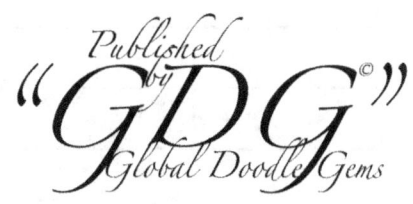

My Color Companion, the idea for this book
comes from my own need, to always keep
records of my colors, it is the first thing I do, when I get new pencils,
markers or pens, as an artist I also test fineliners and pencils, I have
handdrawn the 30 different templates inside this book (each template
is repeated 4 times in the book) , I recommend that you use a piece of
cardstock between the pages when you test markers.
The book is printed on the same paper as 90 % of most of the coloring books you will find on Amazon, which means it is a great place
to test how your colors will work in the books, and create your own
unique color palettes that are your style.
Also check out the pocket edition with 15 different templates (also repeated 4 times, giving you a whole 60 single pages to work with your
colors on).
The Pocket edition is thought to be your companion on the go, a
smaller size, easier to bring along on short trips !

A big Thank you to my friend Johanna Ans for her great help with the
creation of My Color Companion, be sure to follow our blog to get
unique tips and ideas of how to use your color companion, and Please
do share your own tips with us ! We would love to see and hear how
you use your Color Companion....
globaldoodlegems.wordpress.com

Maria Wedel

Template 1
6 rows of 8 circles = 48 circles x 4 spaces each = a total of 192 spaces

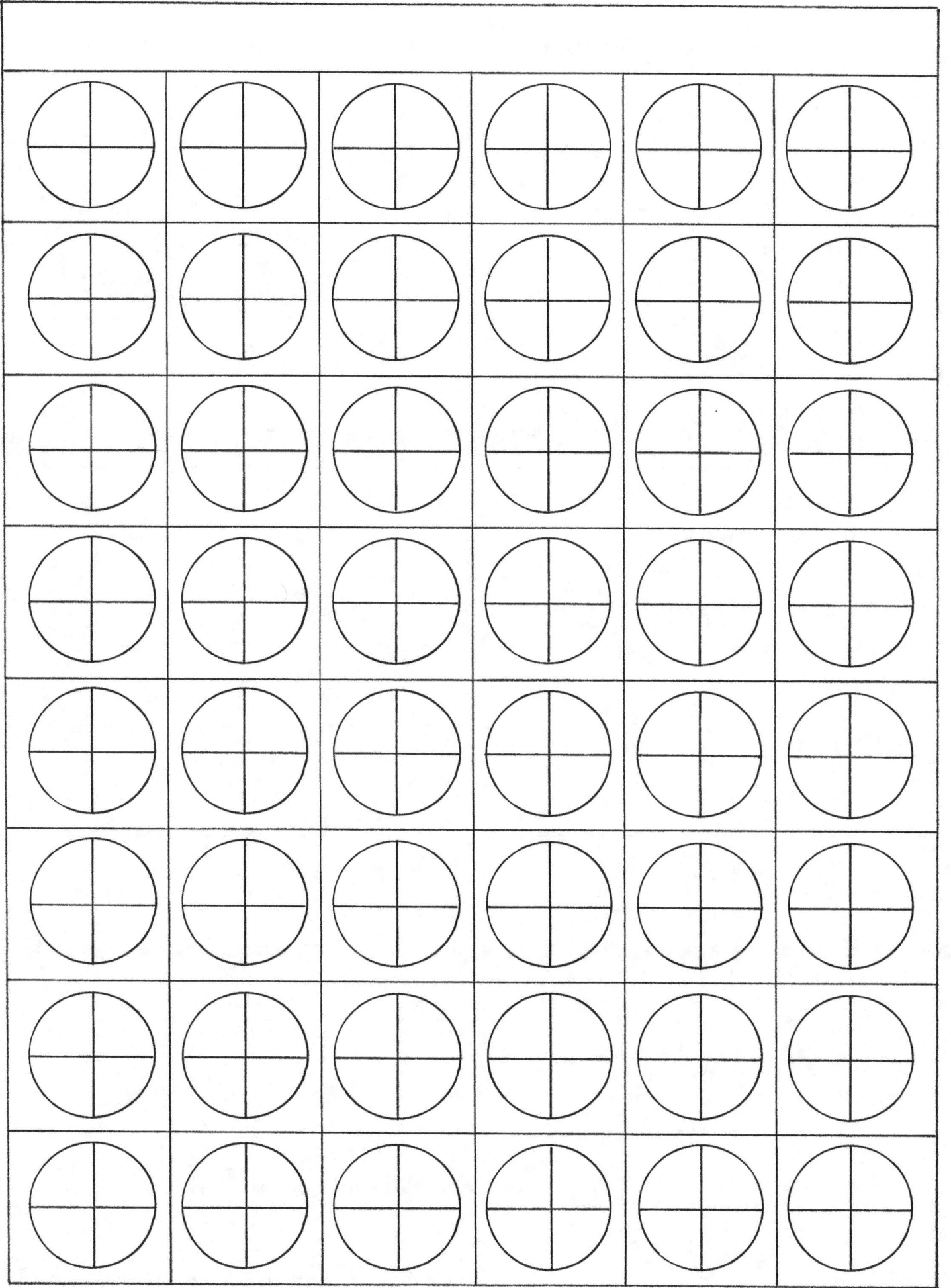

Template 2
2 Color Wheels with each 12 spaces = 24 spaces in total

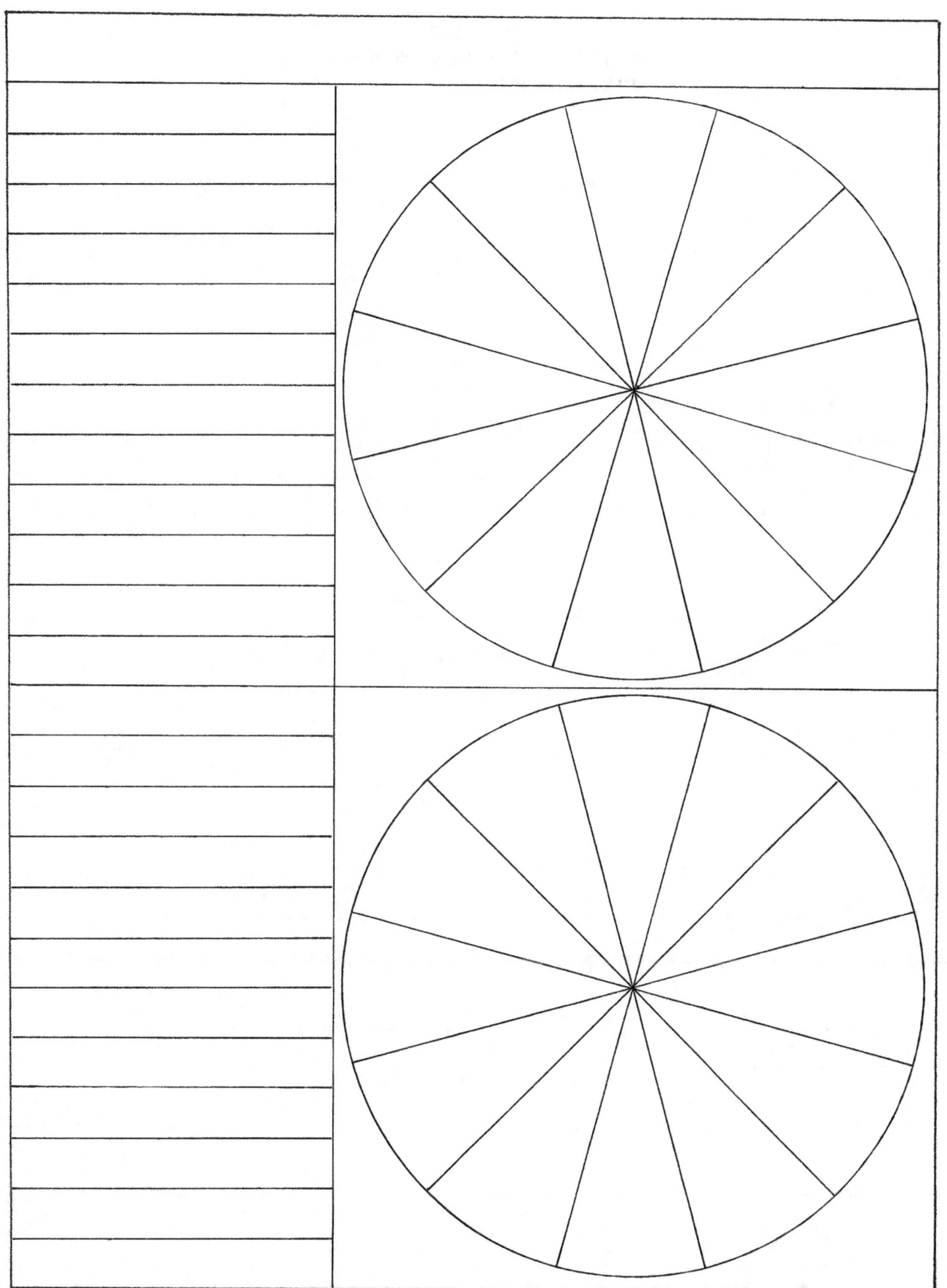

Template 3
Part 1 12 lines of 9 circles = 108 small circles
Part 2 24 lines of 9 squares = 216 squares

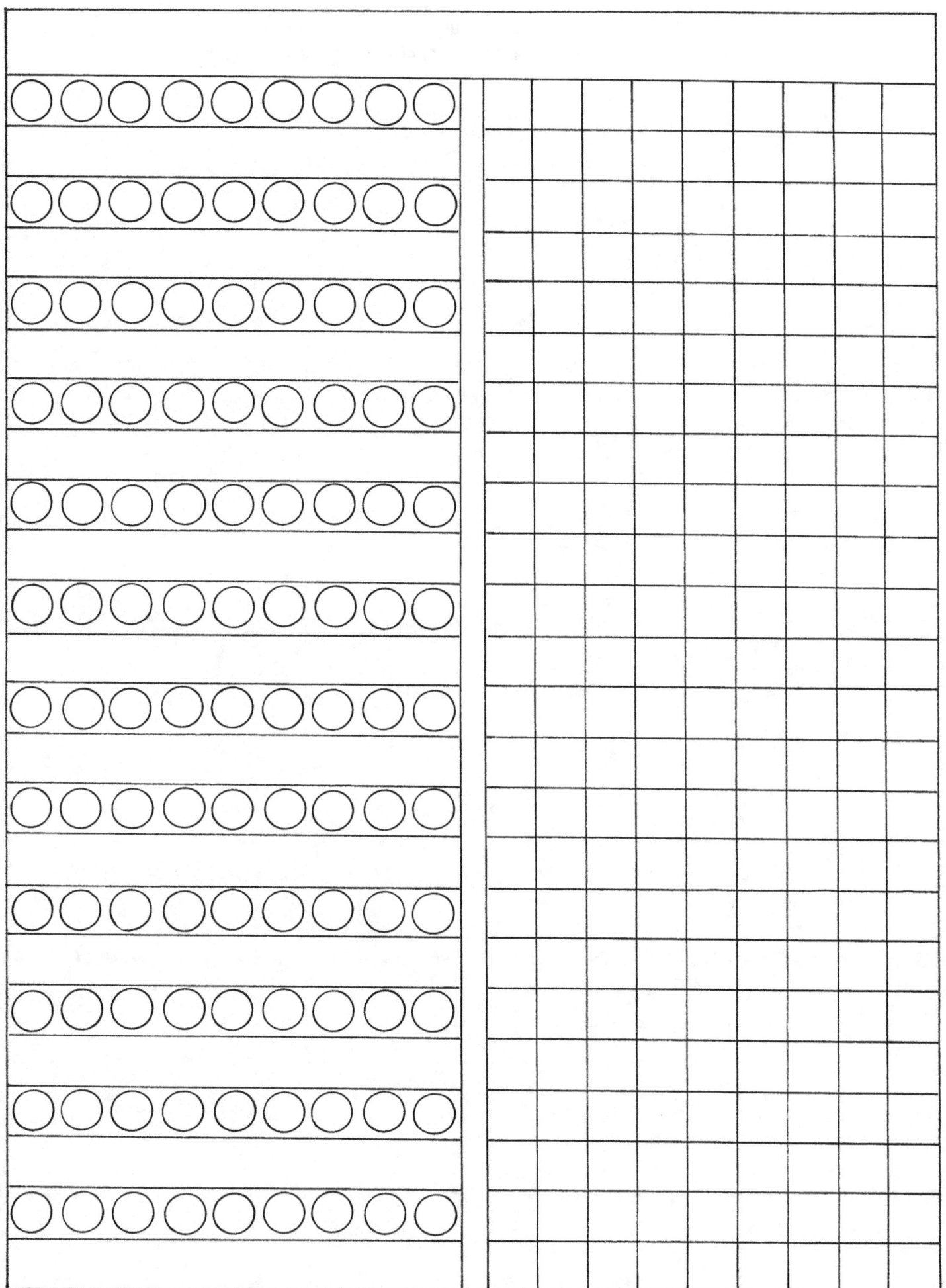

Template 4
8 lines of 37 spaces = total of 296 spaces

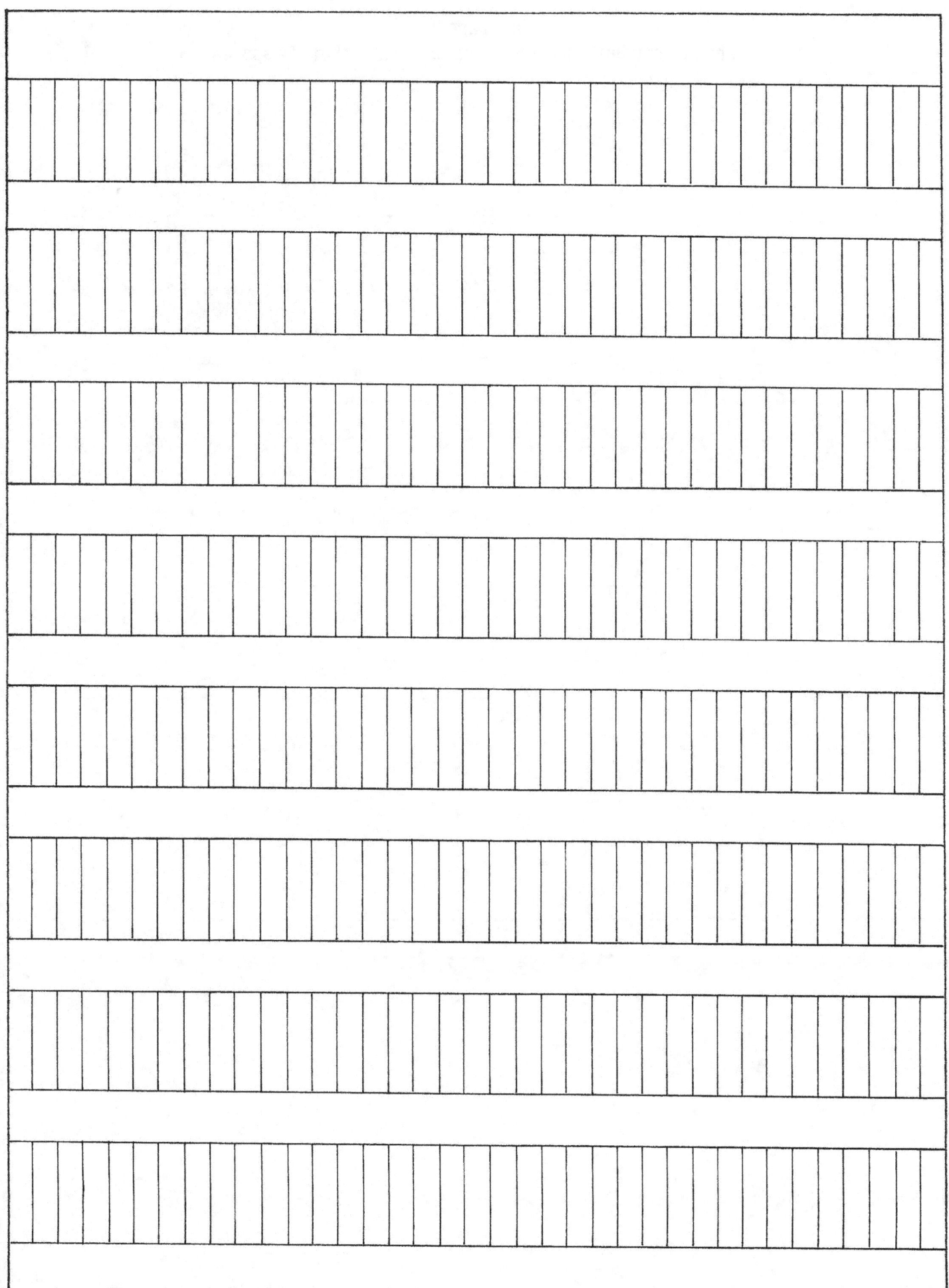

Template 5
8 half color wheel each with 18 spaces = a total of 144 spaces

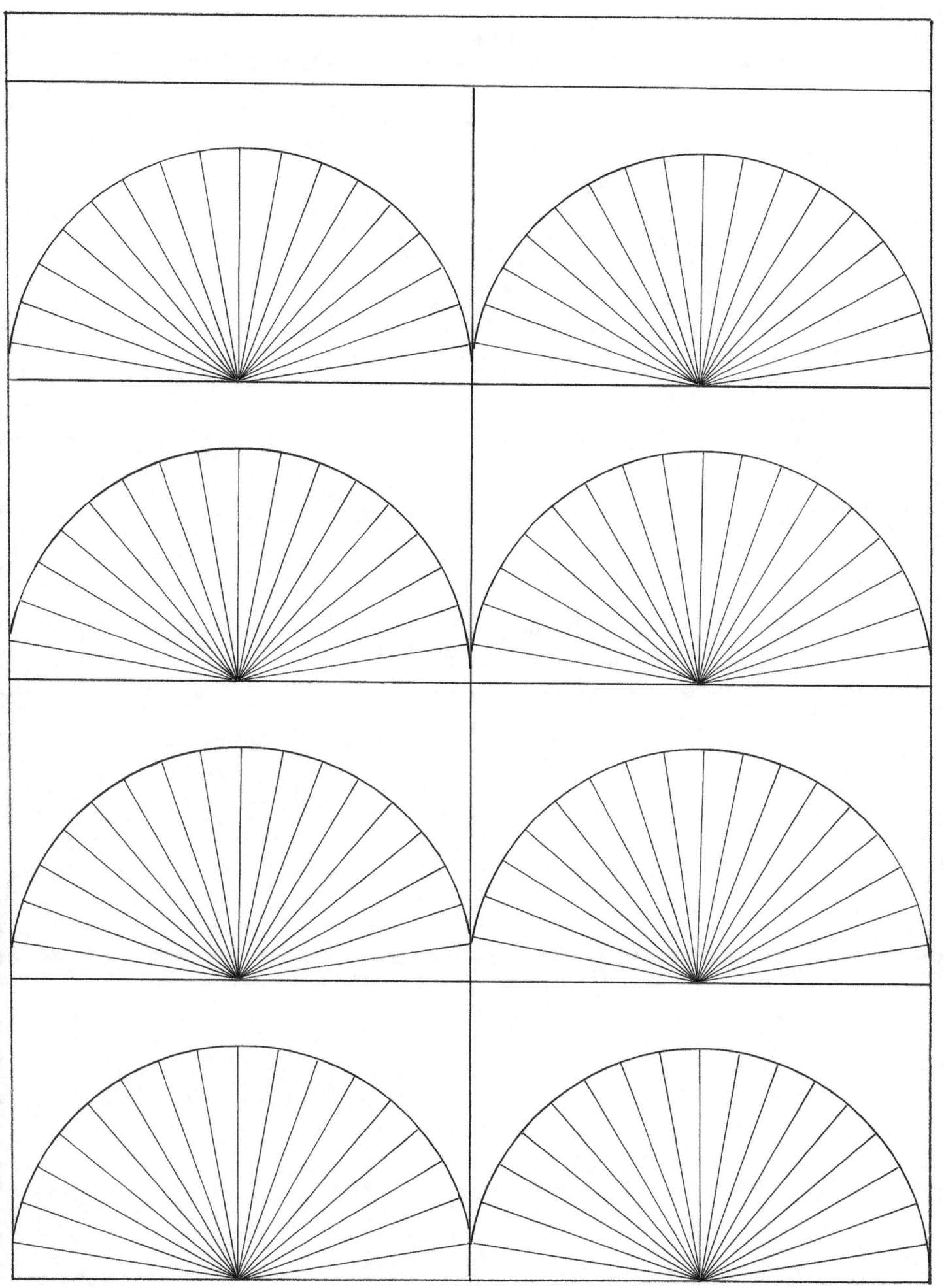

Template 6
6 rows of 8 circles = 48 circles x 8 spaces each = a total of 384 spaces

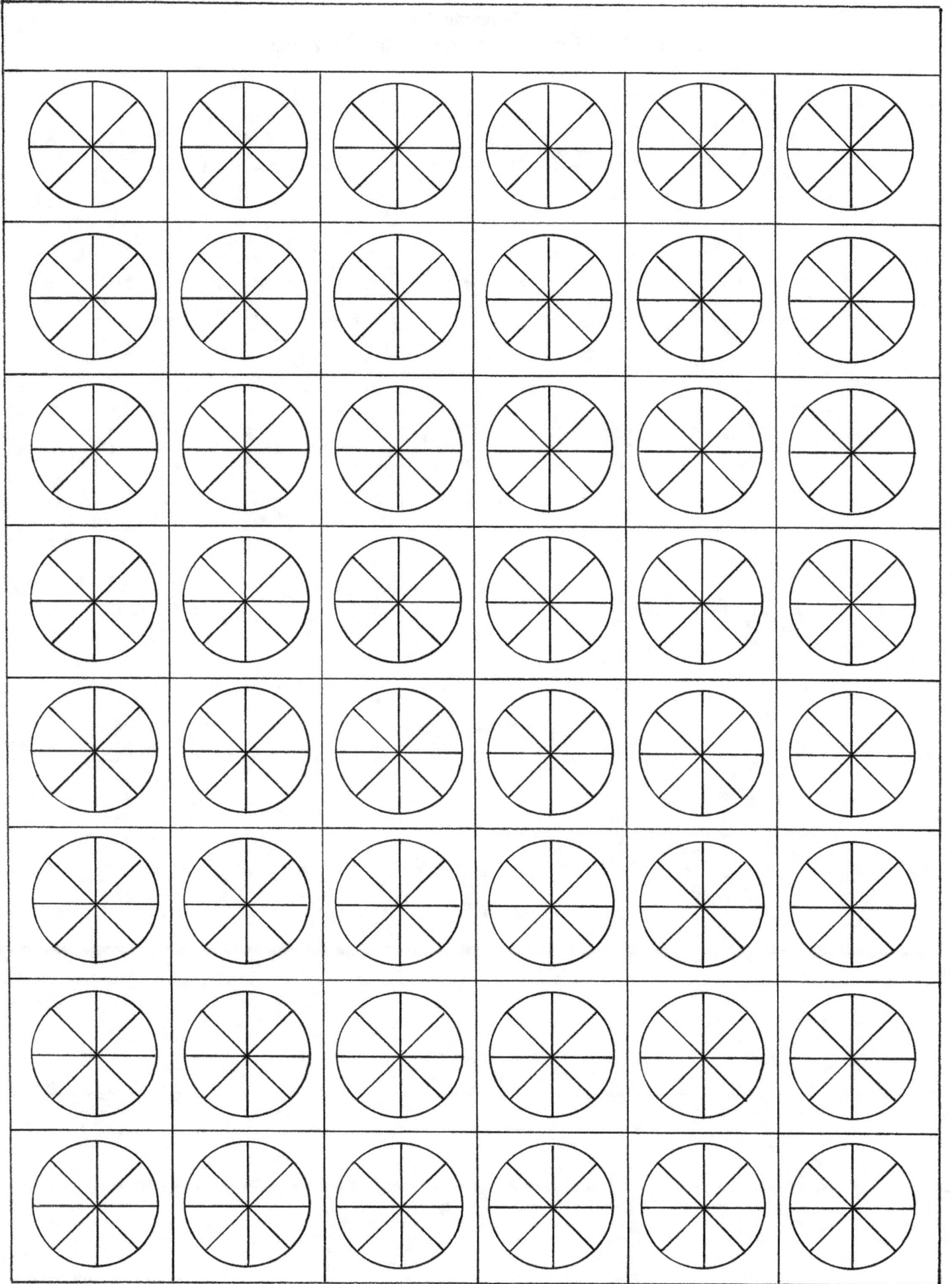

Template 7
8 lines of 24 triangular spaces = a total of 192 spaces

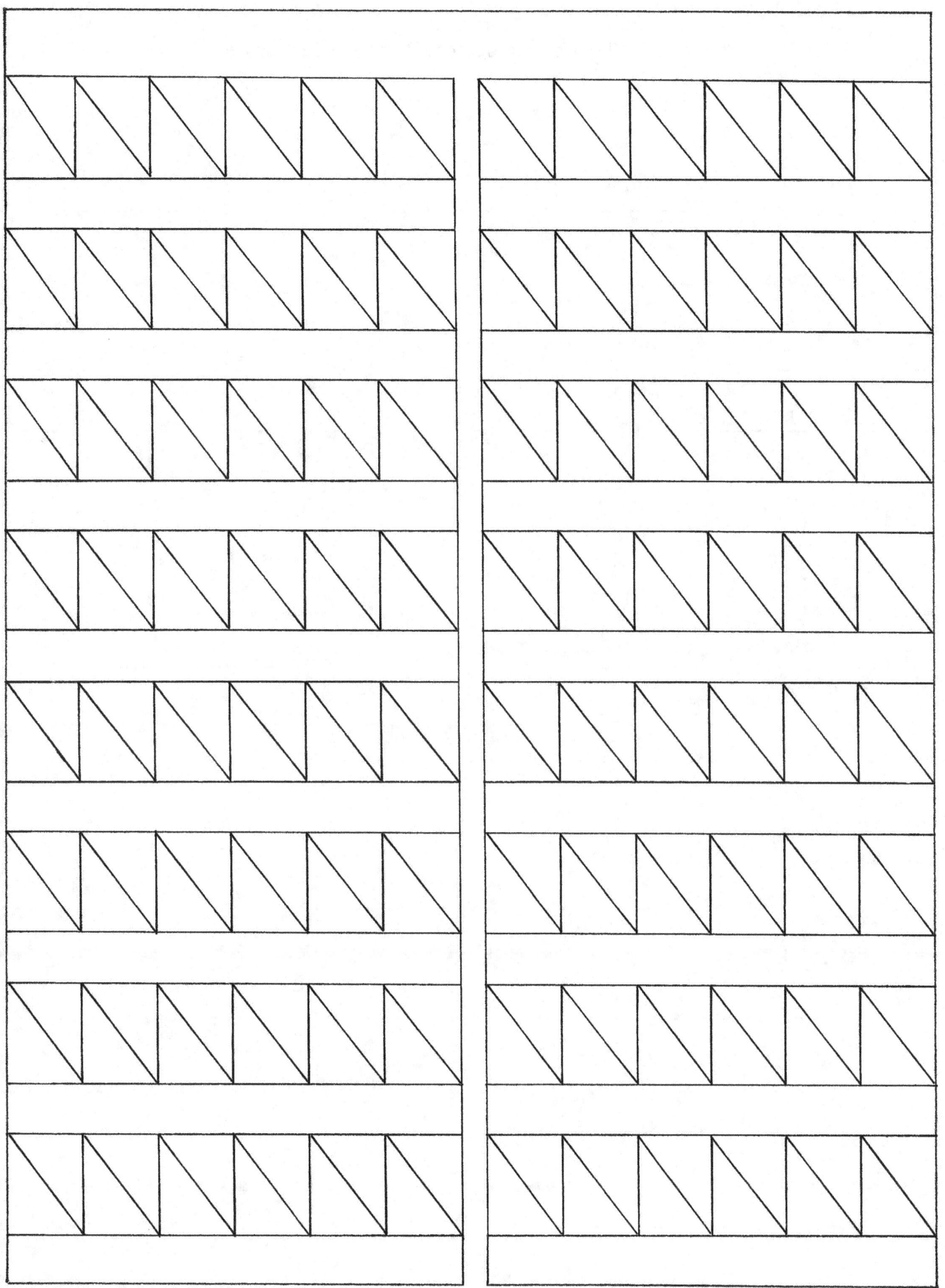

Template 8
3 rows of 2x48 spaces = 96 spaces x 3   a total of 288 spaces

Template 9
Big Color wheel 4 sections of 36 spaces = a total of 144 spaces

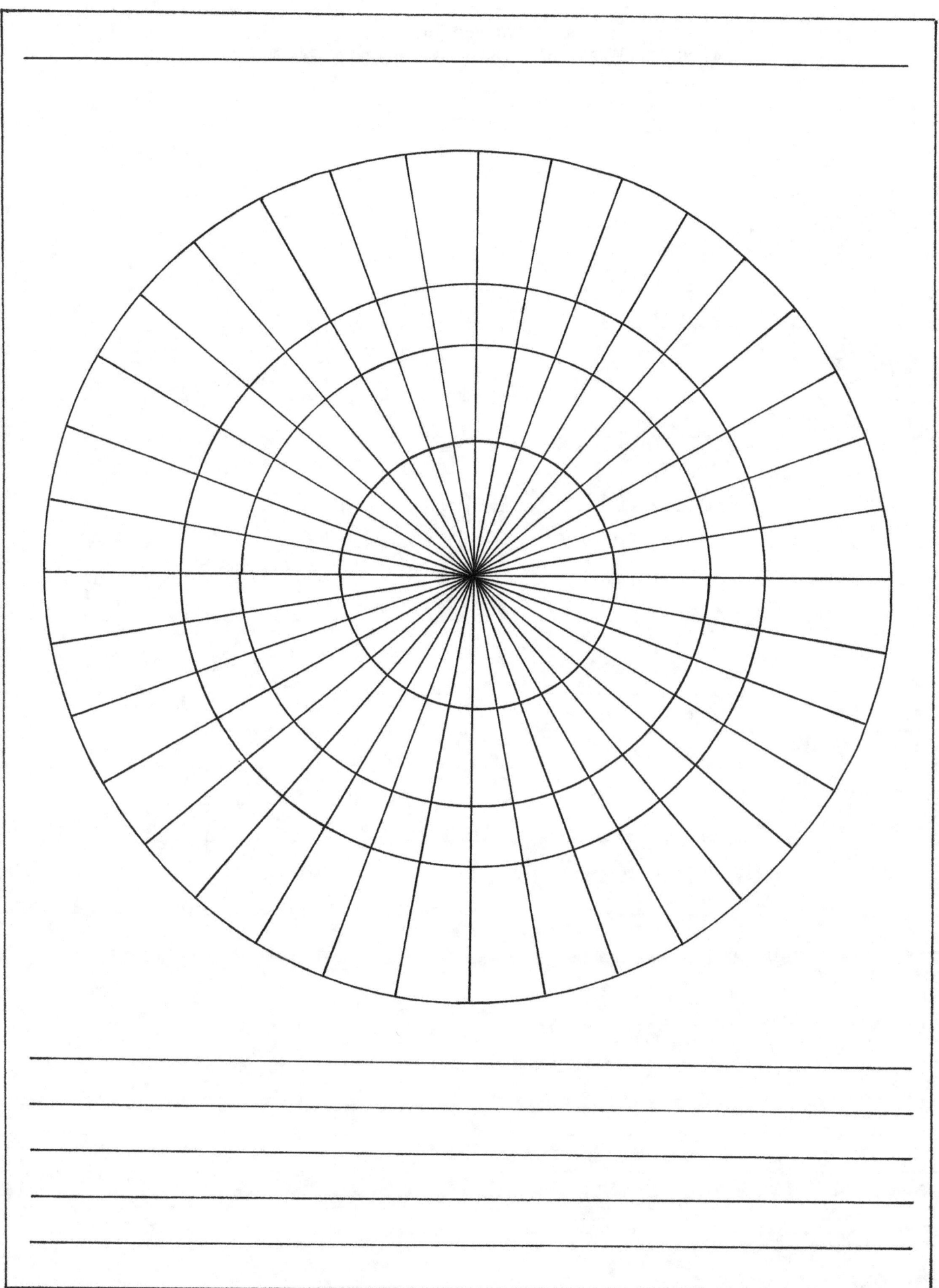

Template 10
4 half Color Wheels of 2x 18 spaces = a total of 144 spaces

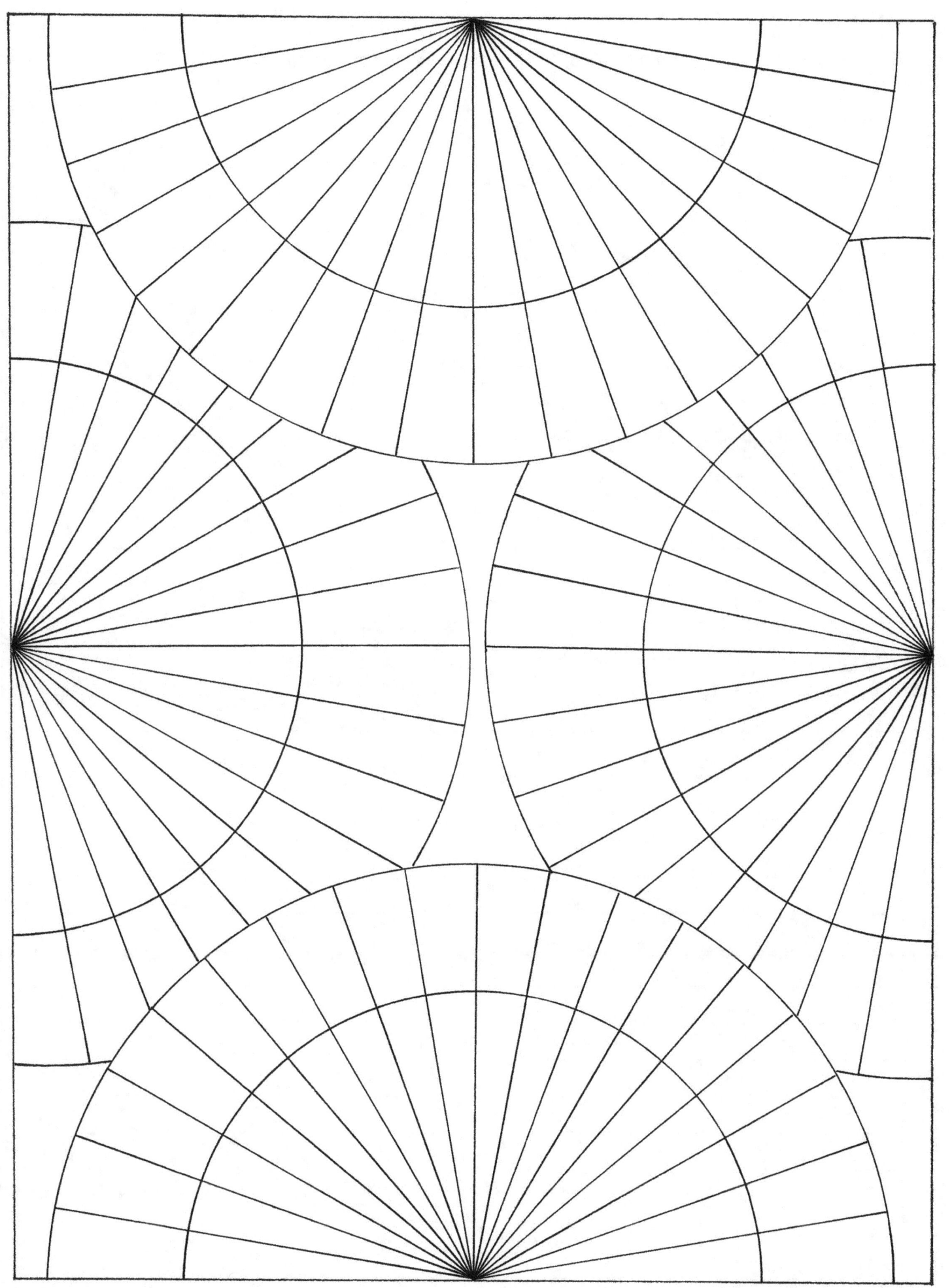

Template 11
Color Wheels of 4x 12 spaces = a total of 48 spaces

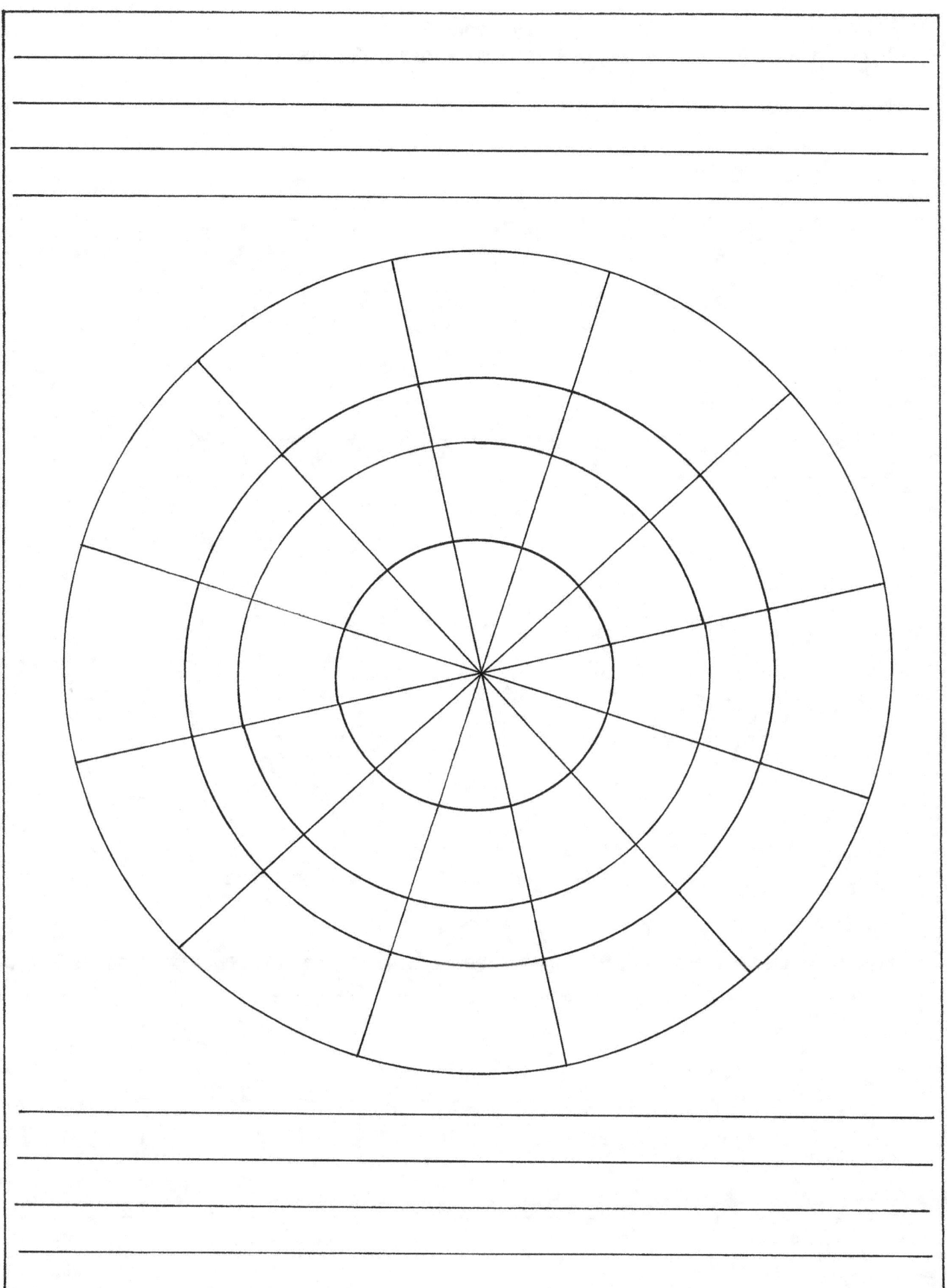

Template 12
24 circles of 3 spaces = a total of 72 spaces

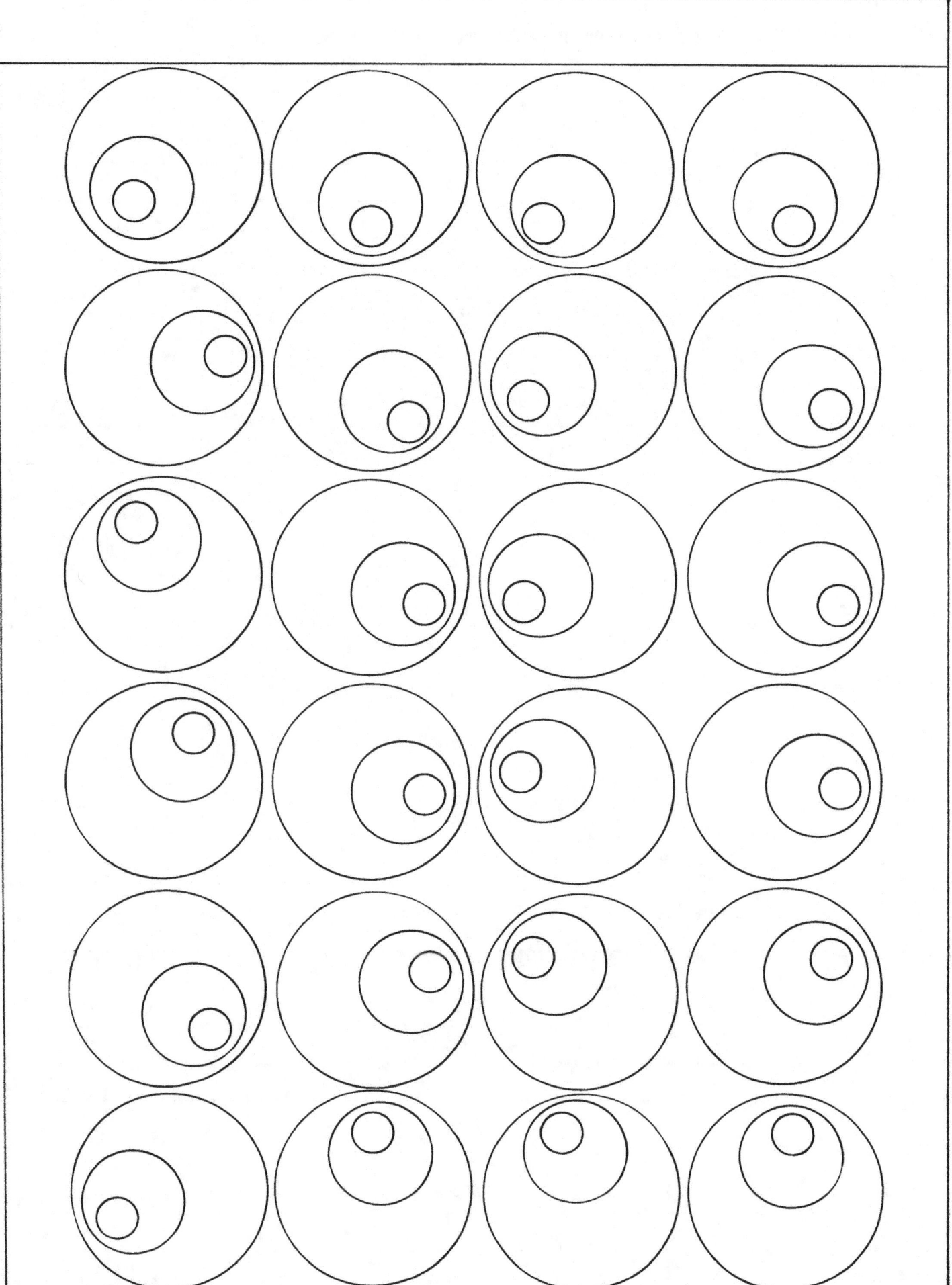

Template 13
2 Color Wheels of 4x12 spaces = a total of 96 spaces

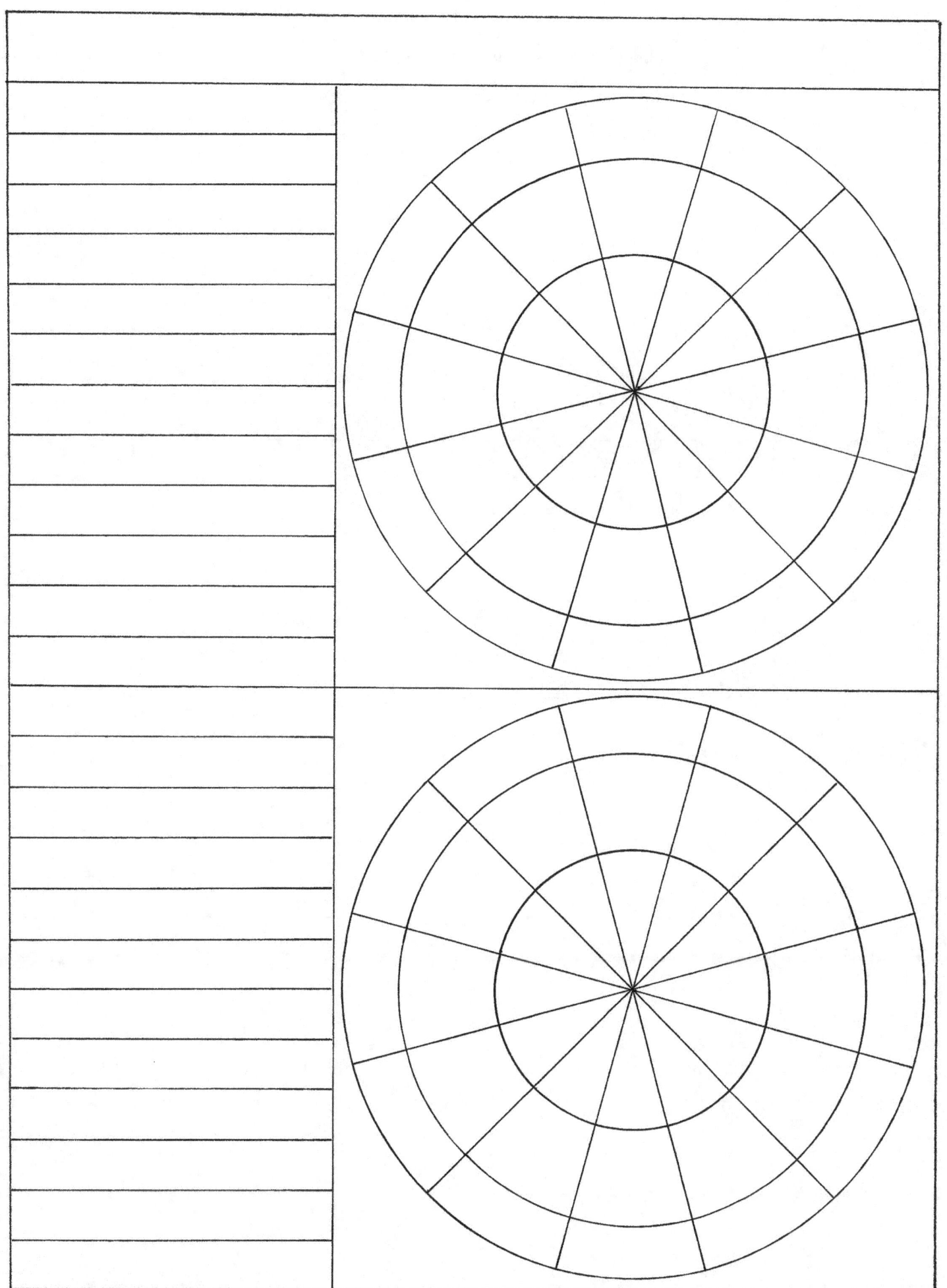

Template 14
8 lines of 2x37 spaces = a total of 592 spaces

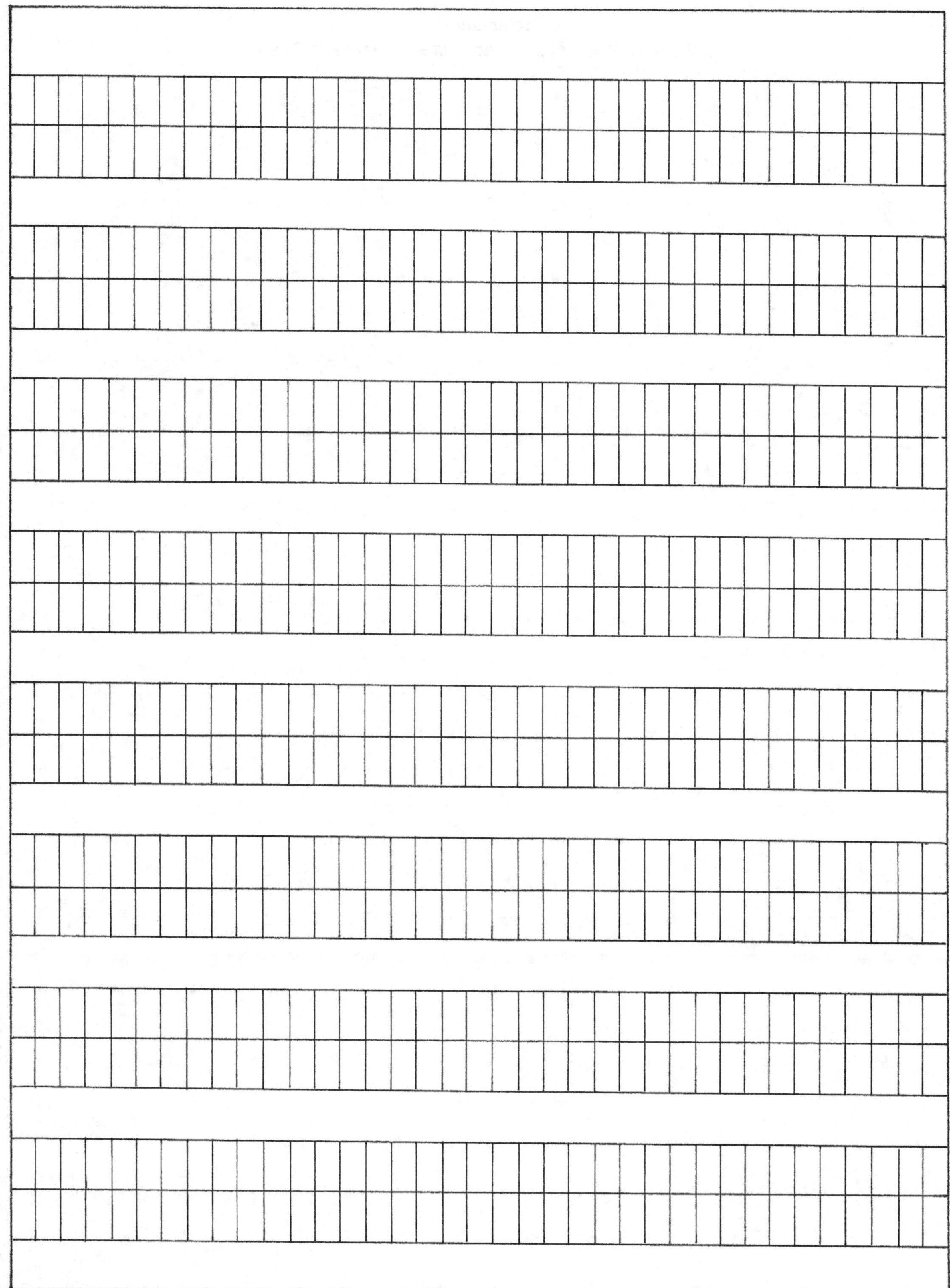

Template 15
8 half Color Wheels of 2x 18 spaces = a total of 288 spaces

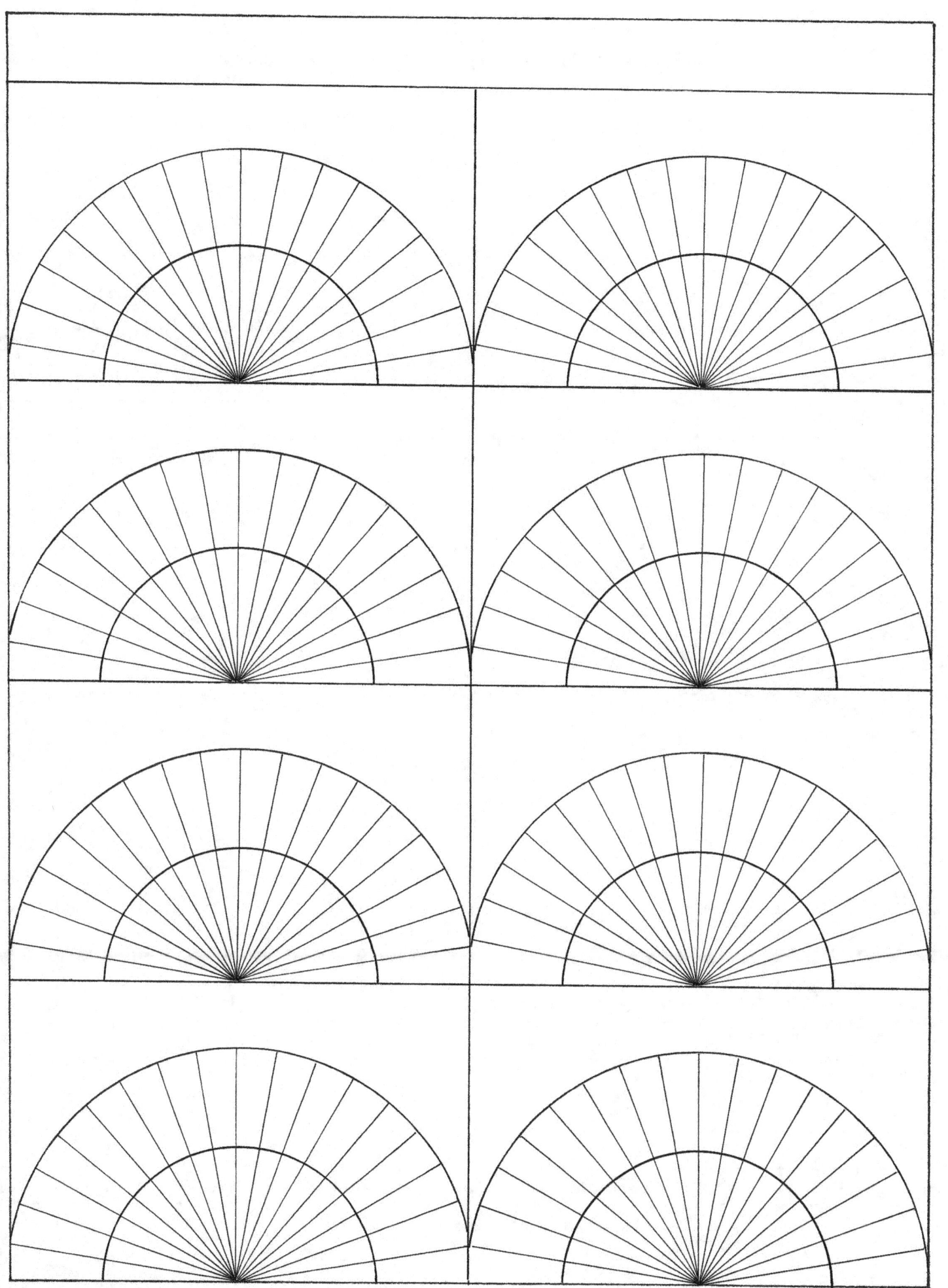

Template 16
4 half Color Wheels of 3x 18 spaces = a total of 216 spaces

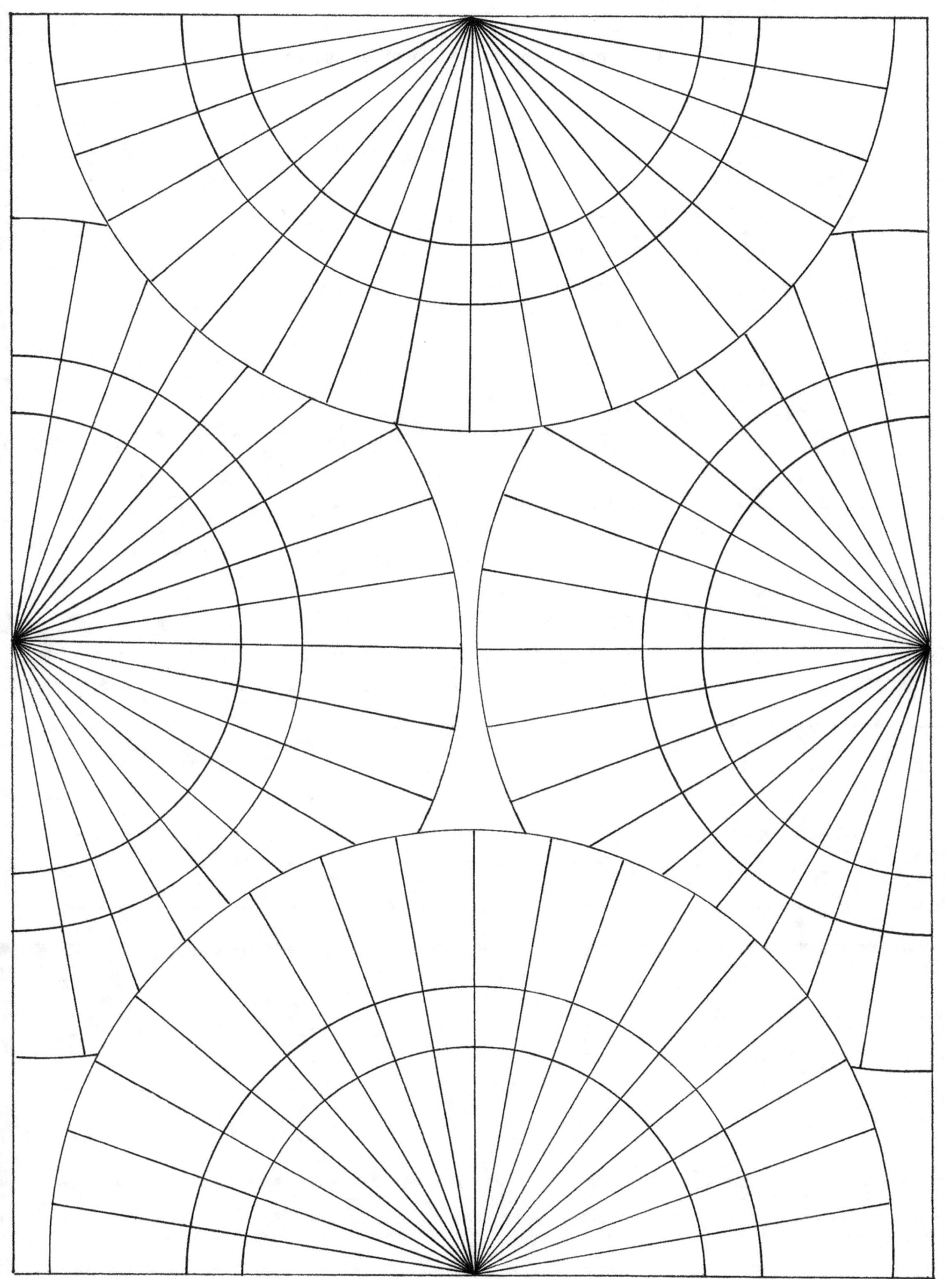

Template 17
3 rows of 4x48 spaces = a total of 576 spaces

Template 18
8 lines of 4x37 spaces = a total of 1184 spaces

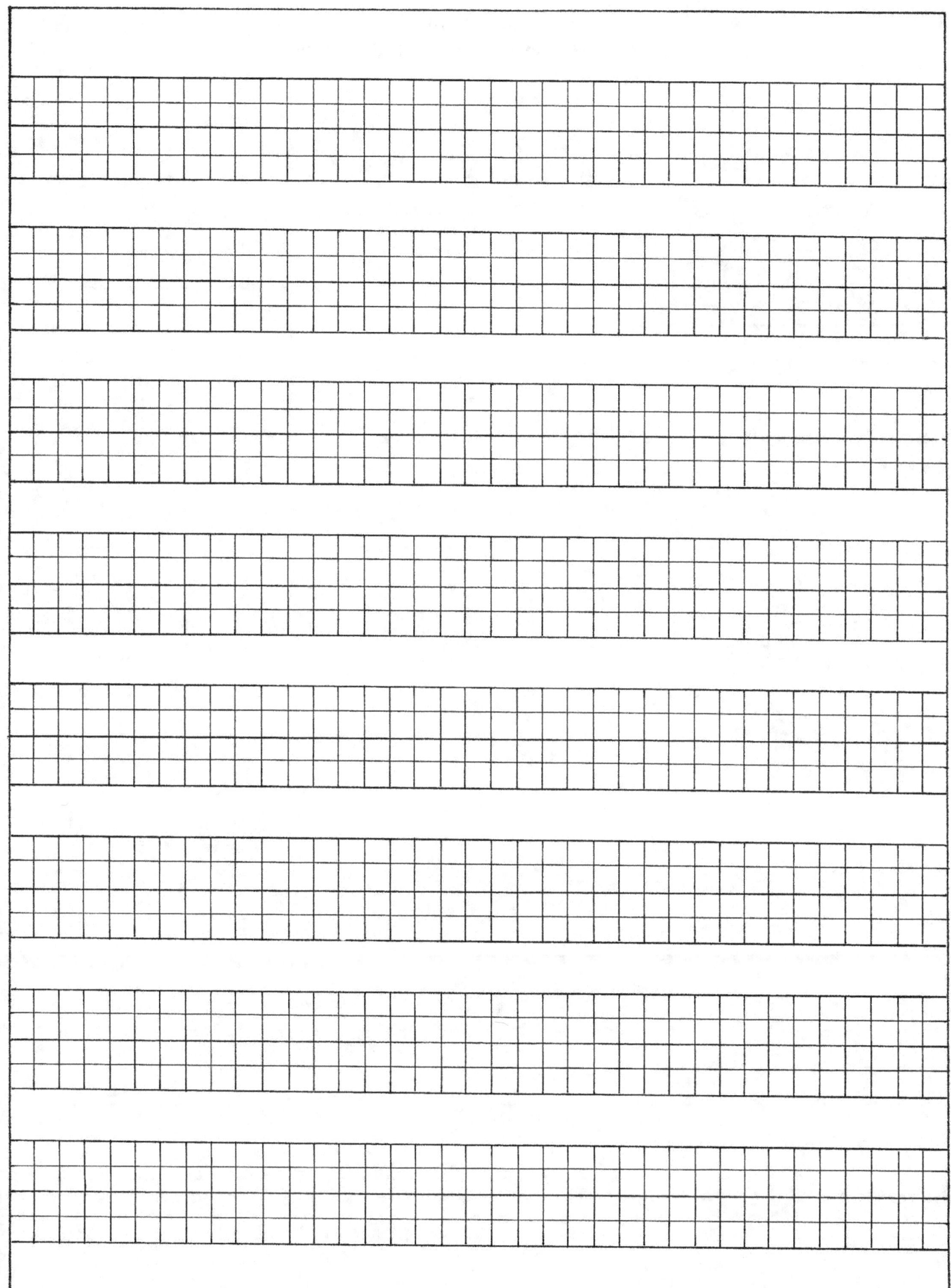

Template 19
8 lines of 12x4 spaces = a total of 384 spaces

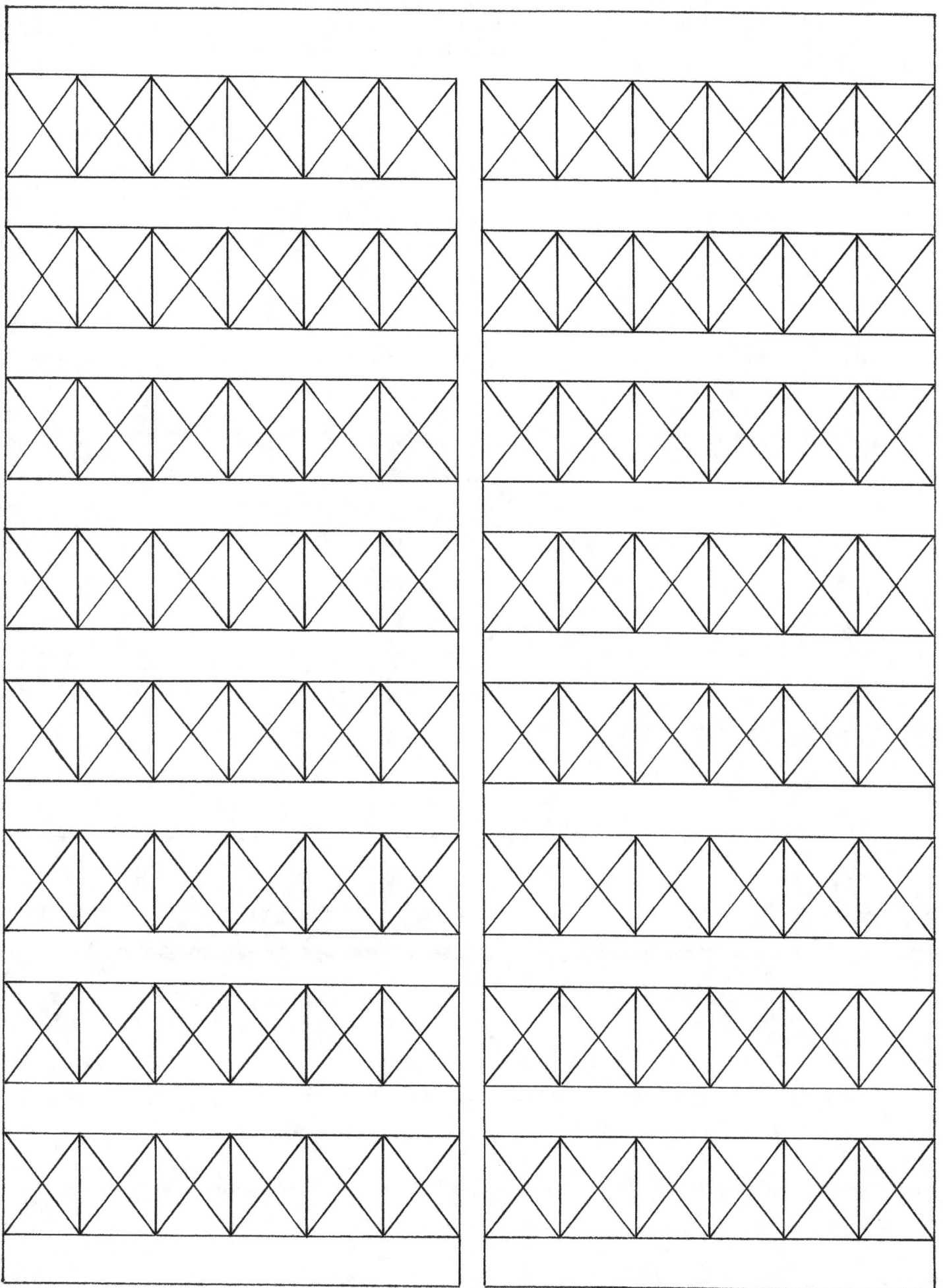

Template 20
Color Wheel with 36 spaces

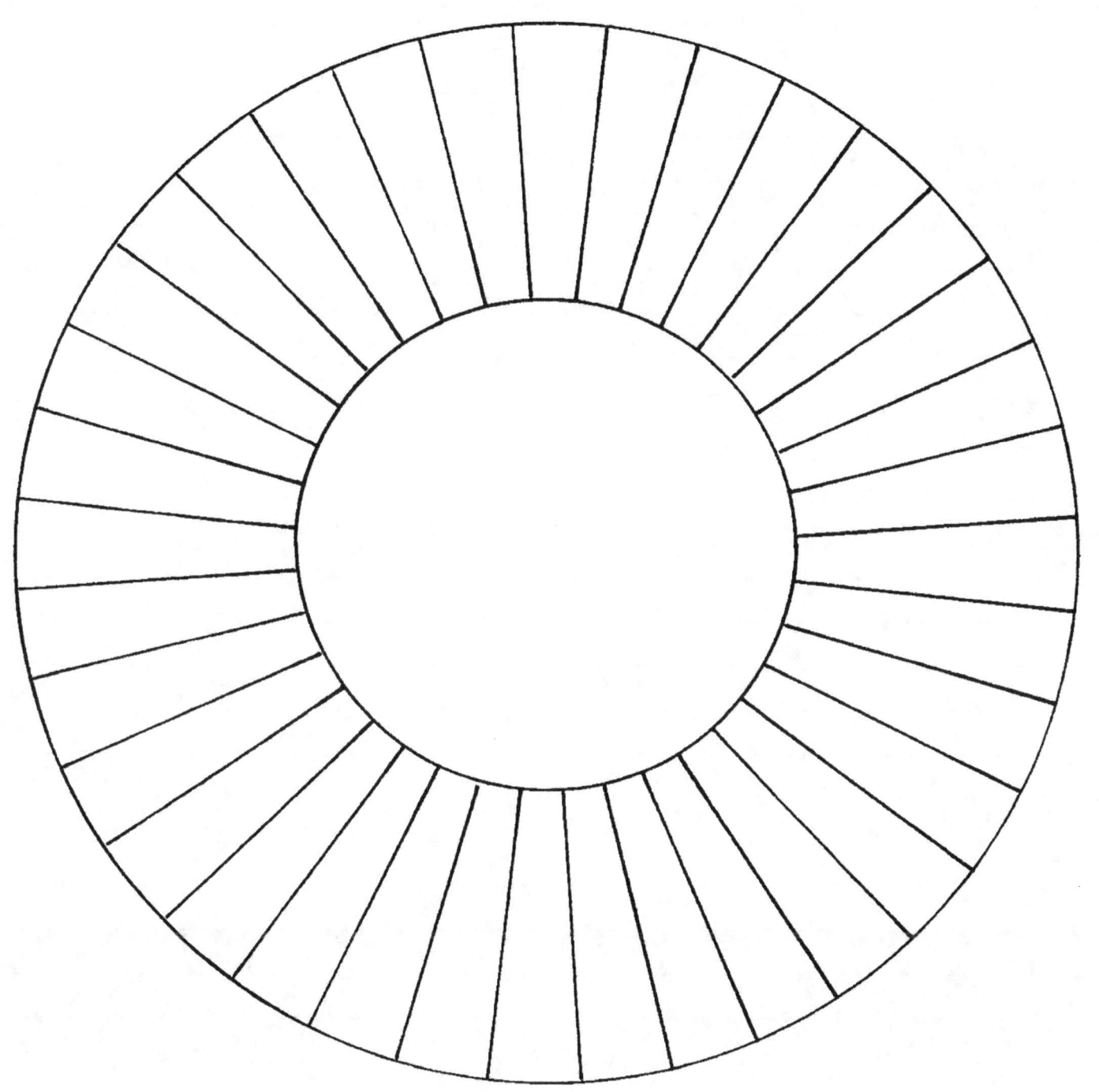

Template 21
Circle explosion of 16x 7 circles = 112 circles

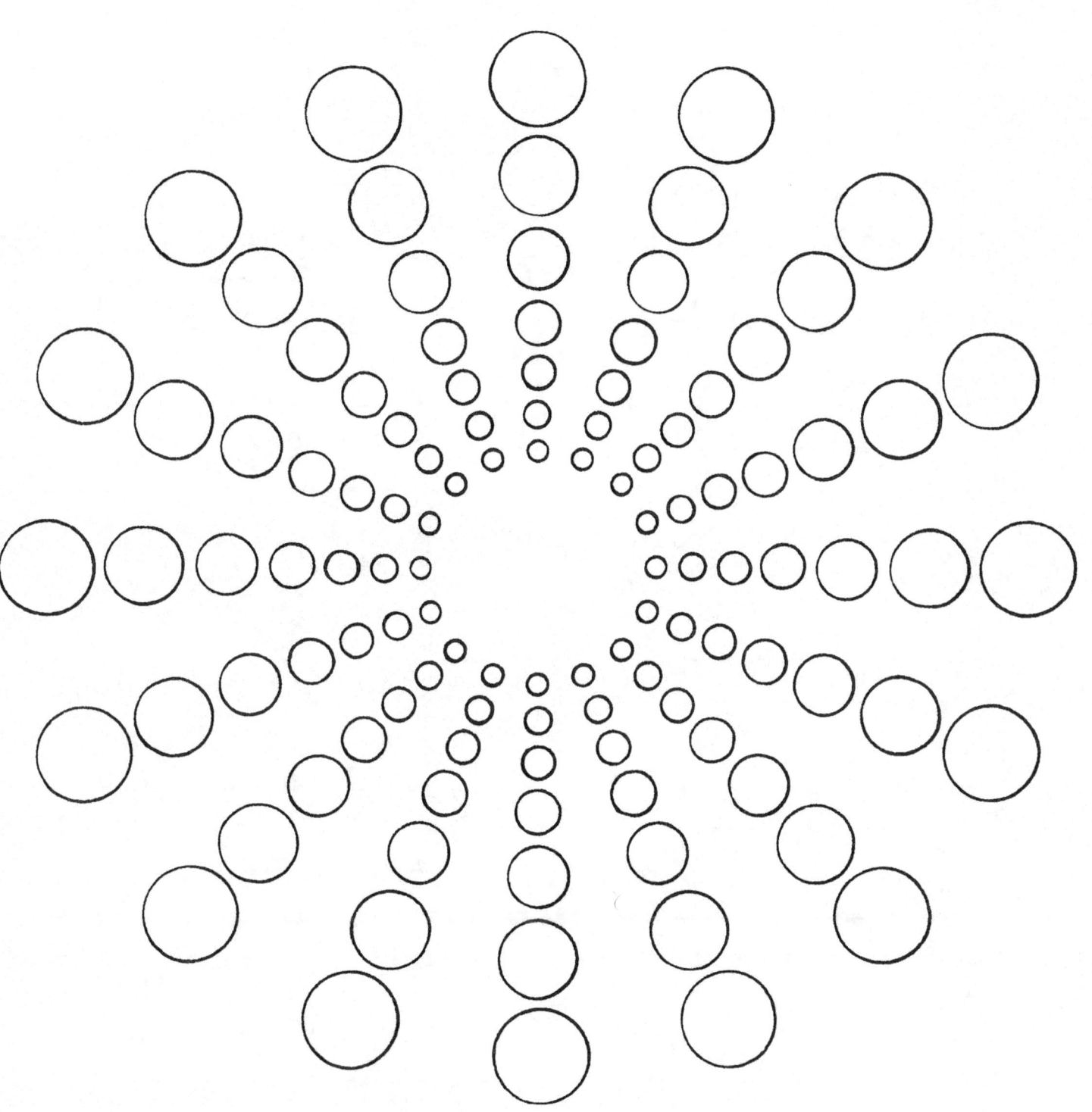

Template 22
Color flowe 16x9 spaces = a total of 144 spaces

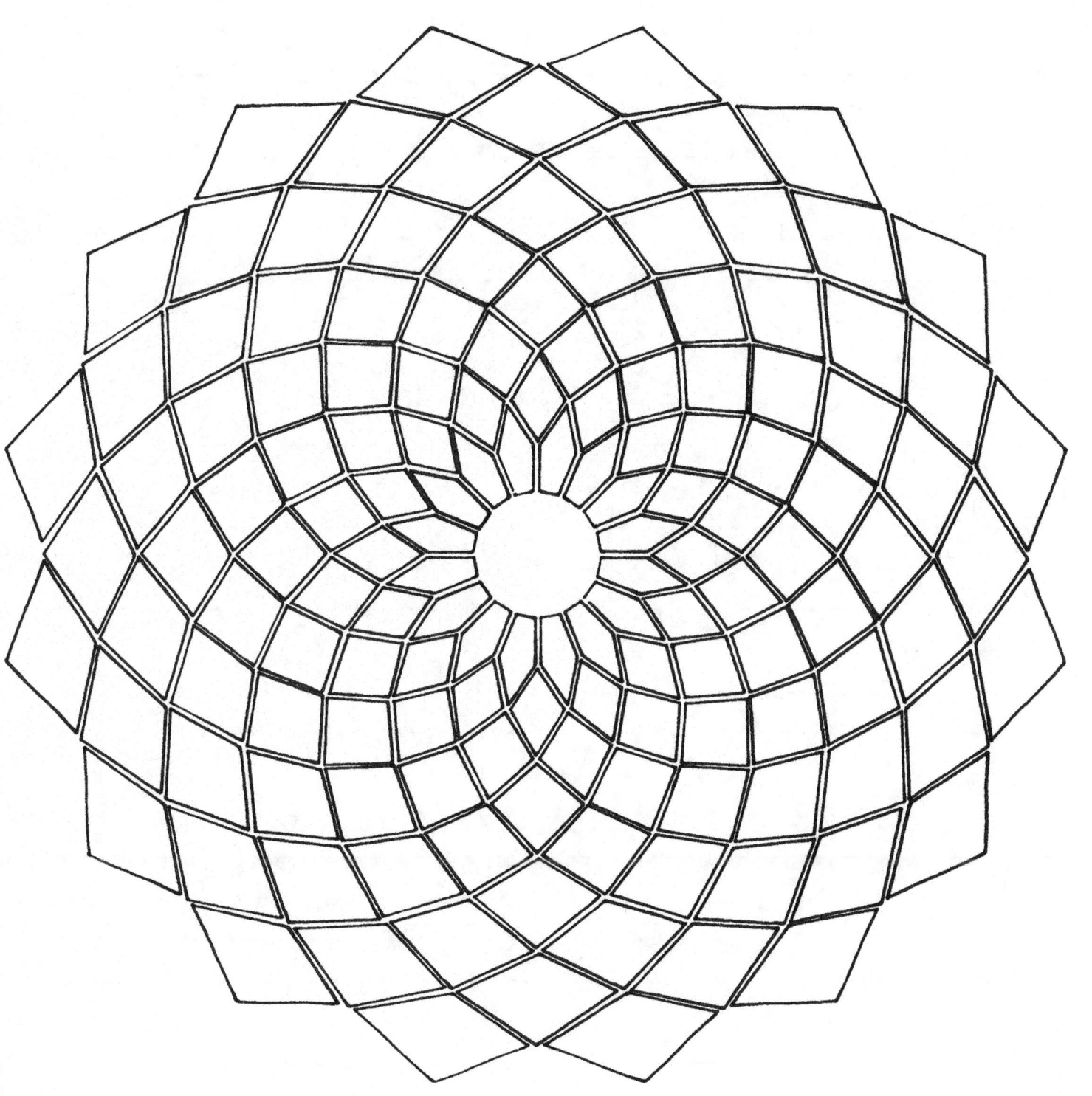

Template 23
1 color wheel of 6x 36 spaces = 216 spaces
4 quarter color wheels of 6 x 9 spaces = 216 spaces
A grand total of 432 spaces

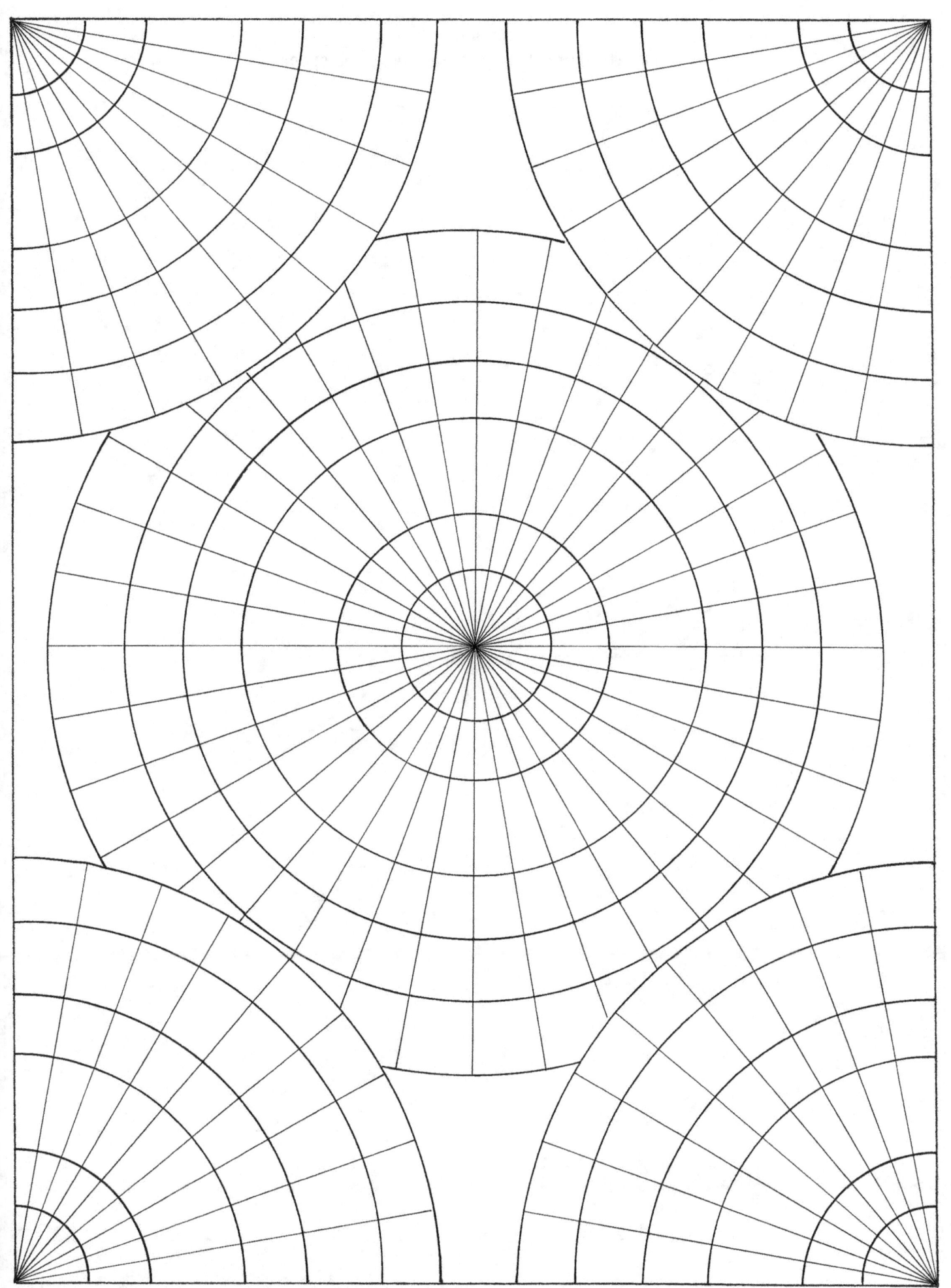

Template 24
Great wheel of colors 5x 32 spaces = 160 spaces

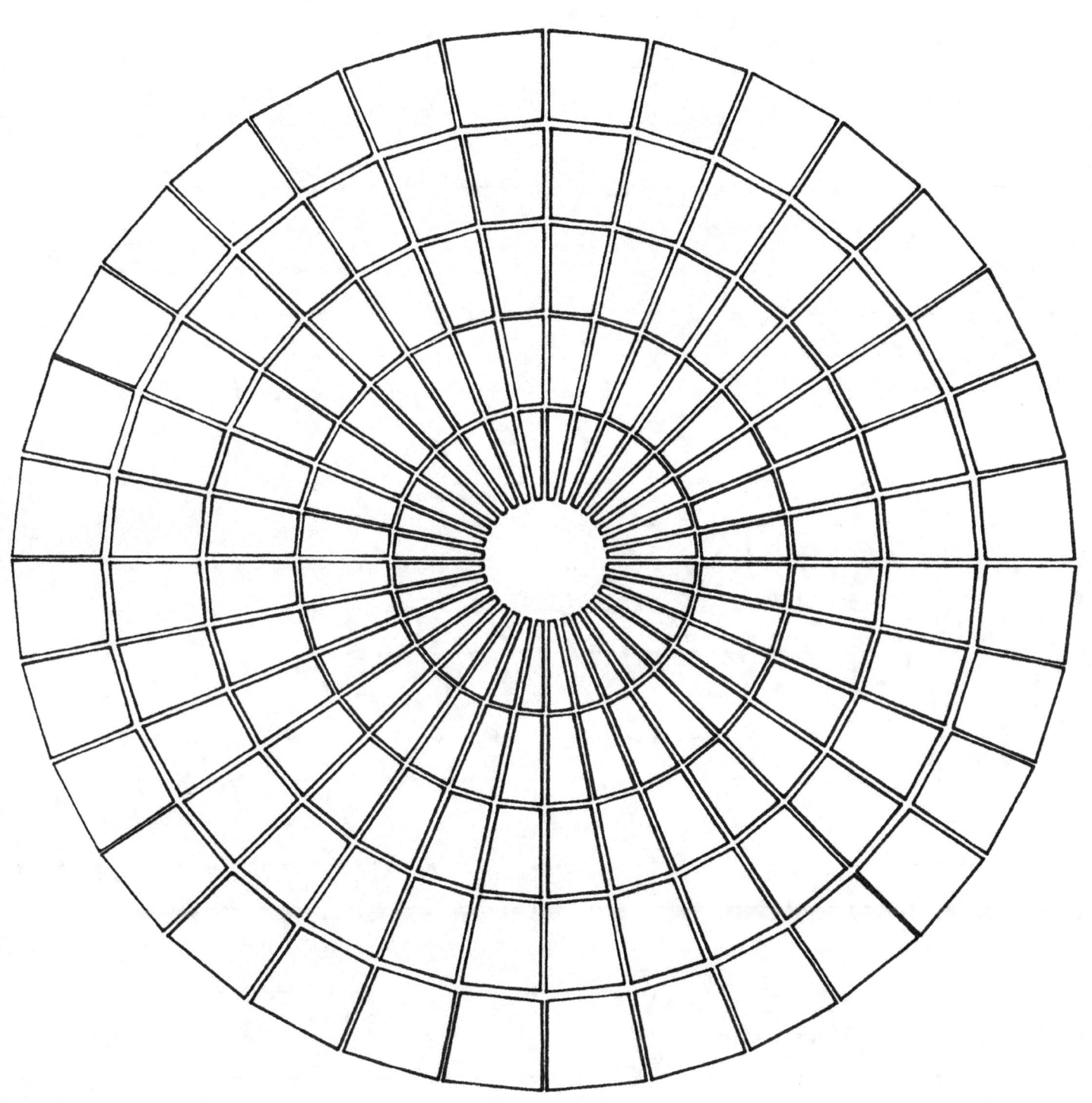

Template 25
8 lines of 12 spaces = a total of 96 spaces

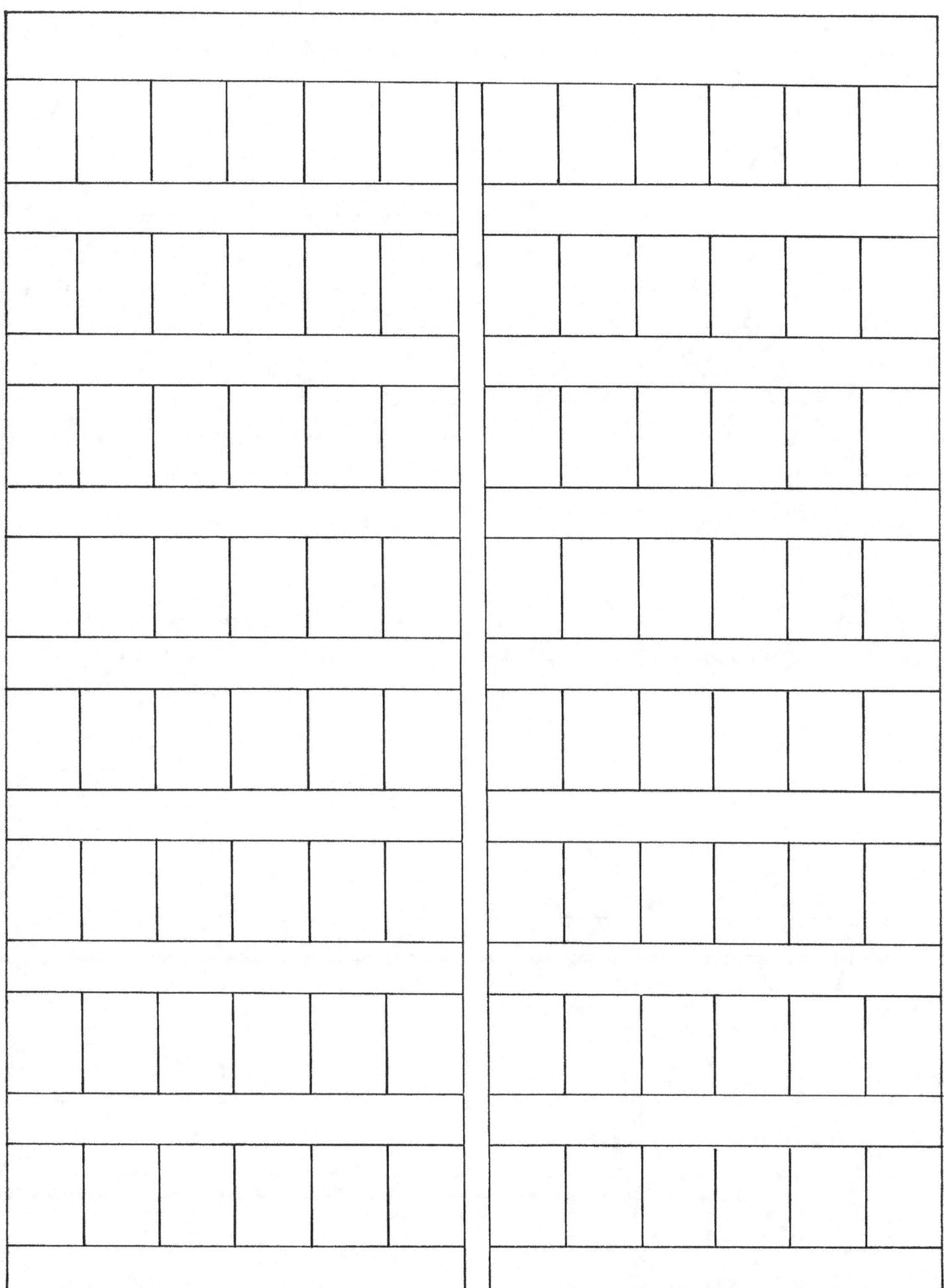

Template 26
3 rows of 48 spaces = a total of 144 spaces

Template 27
Big Color wheel of 36 spaces

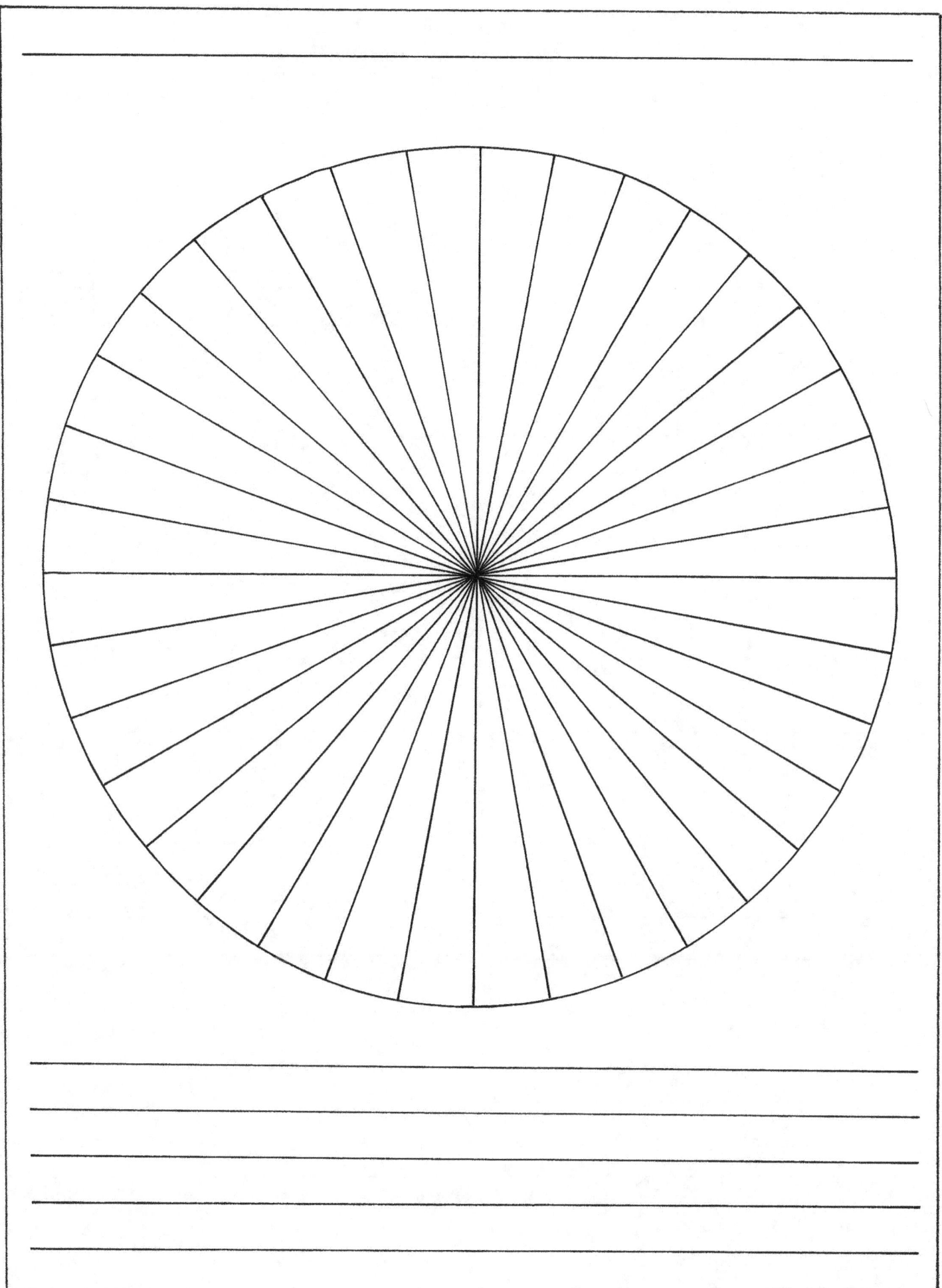

Template 28
4 half color wheels of 18 spaces = a total of 72 spaces

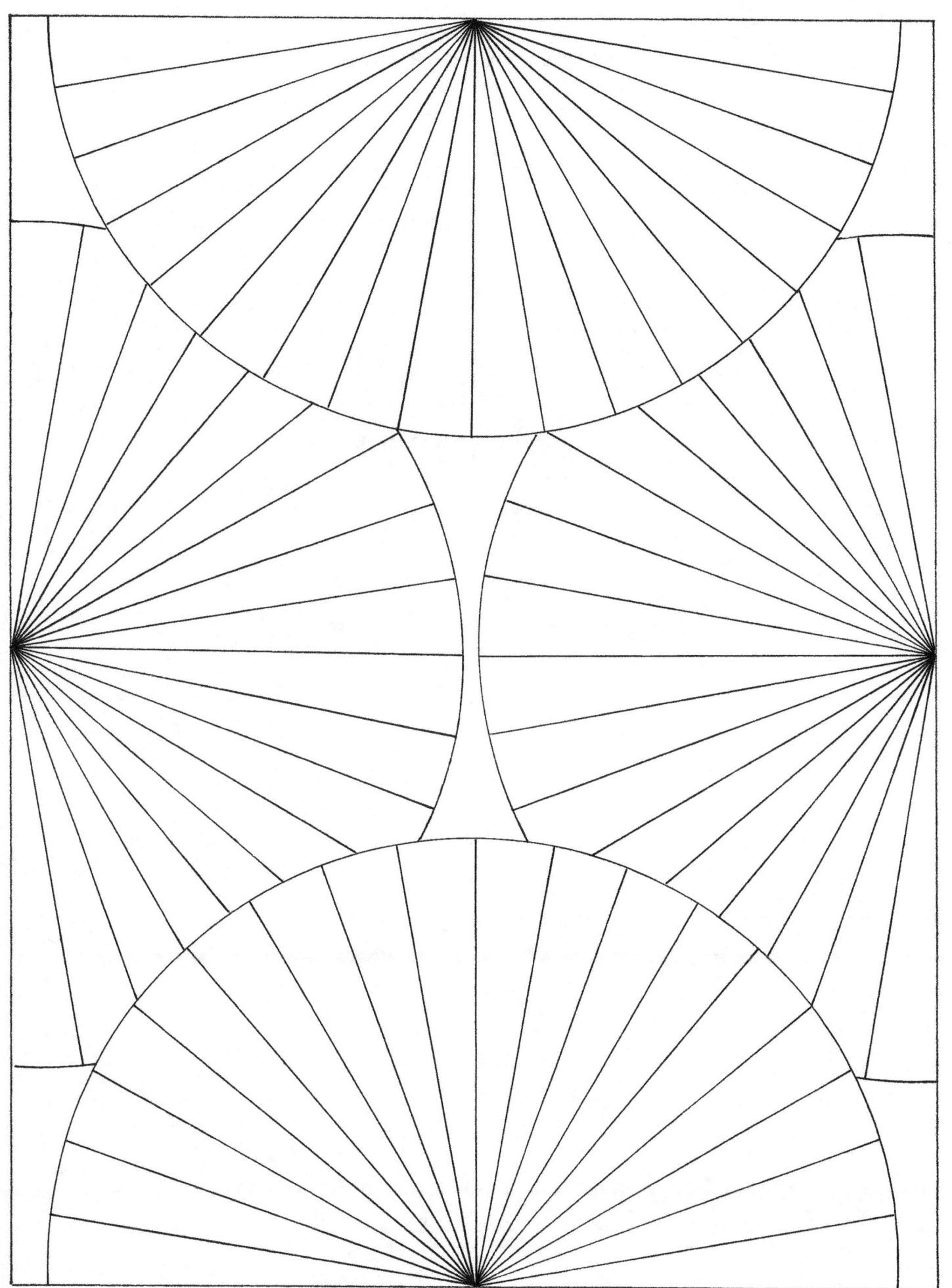

Template 29
10 lines of 9 circles = 90 circles

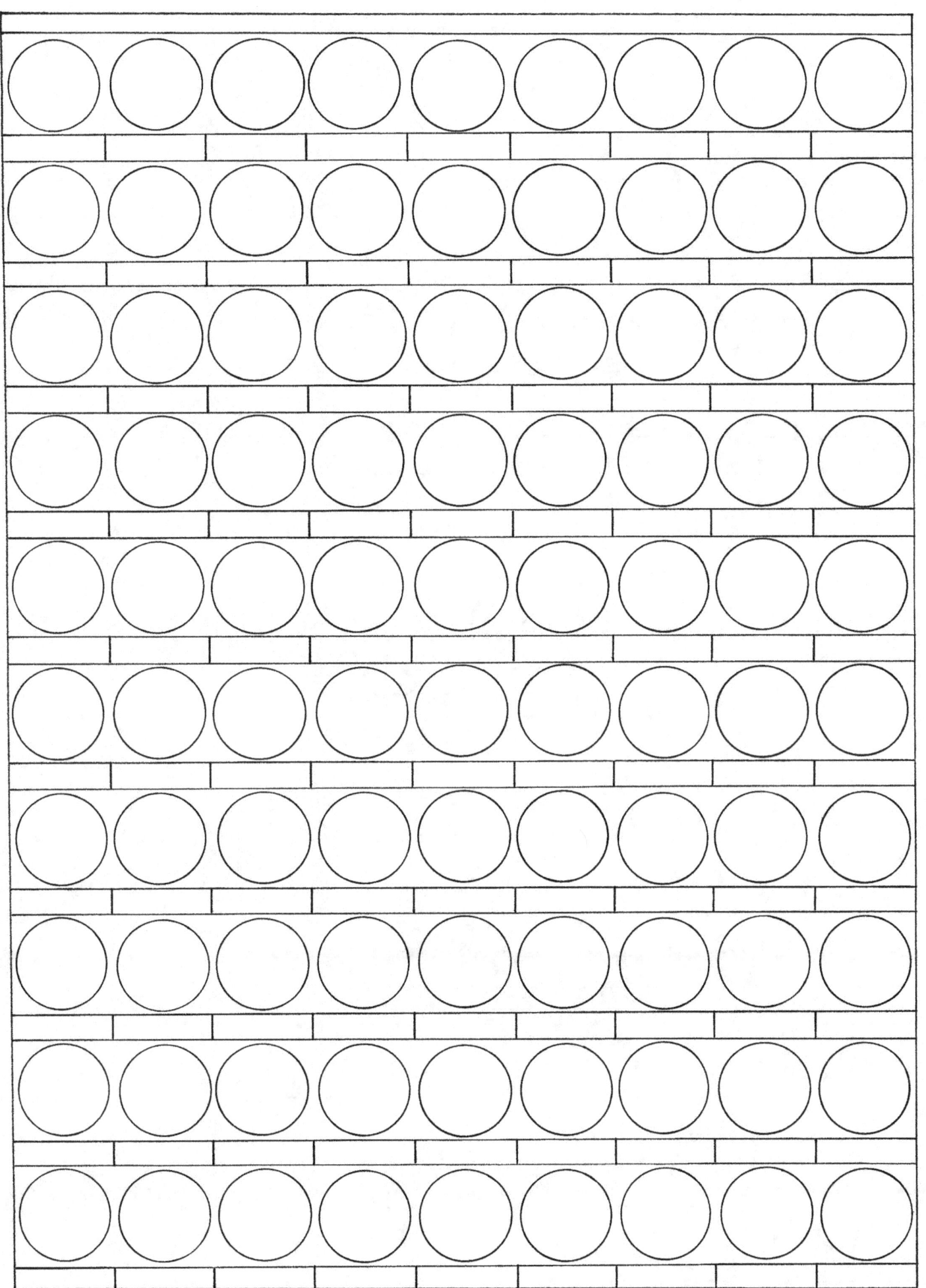

Template 30
Big Color Wheel of 12 spaces

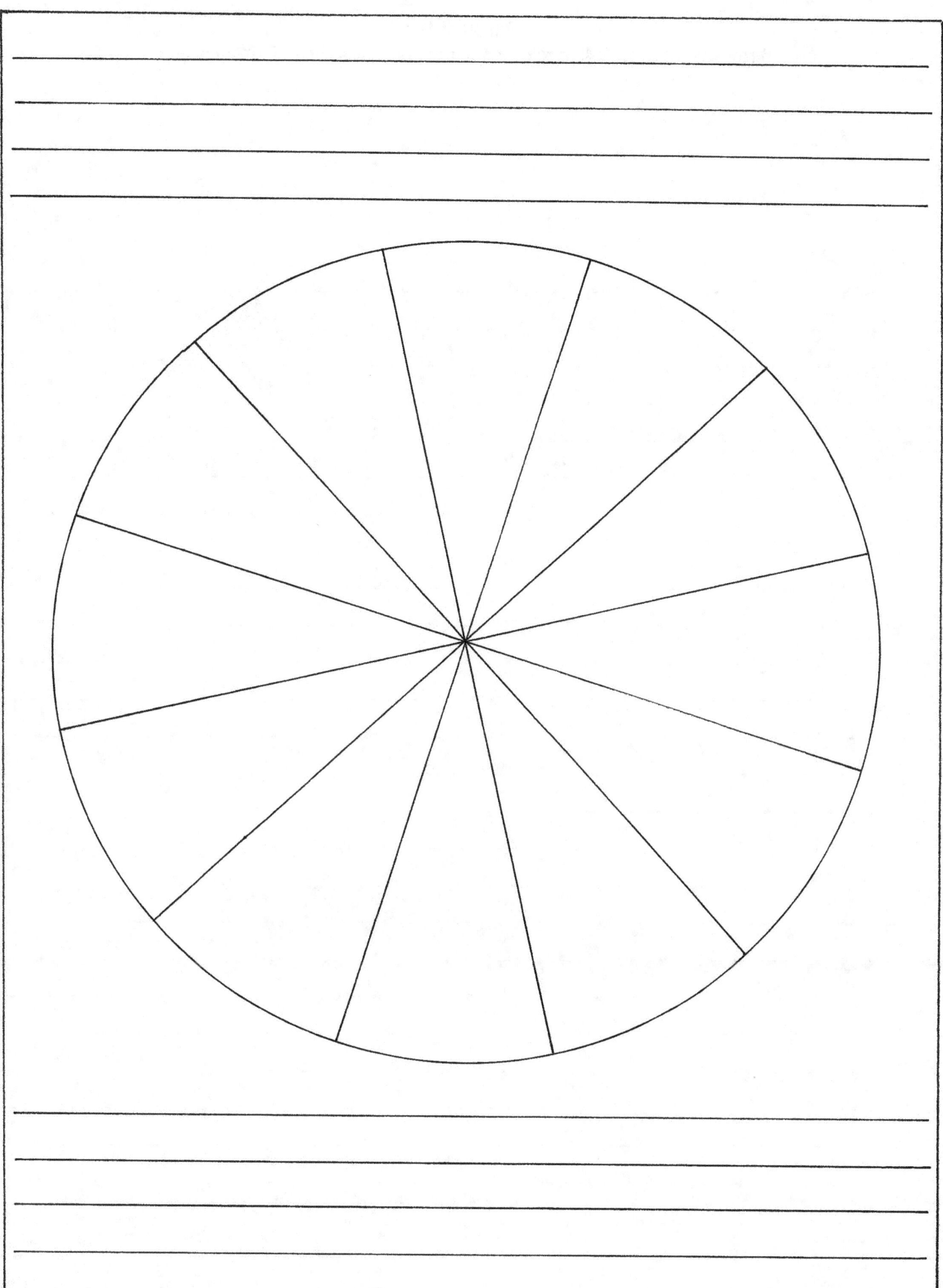

Template 1
6 rows of 8 circles = 48 circles x 4 spaces each = a total of 192 spaces

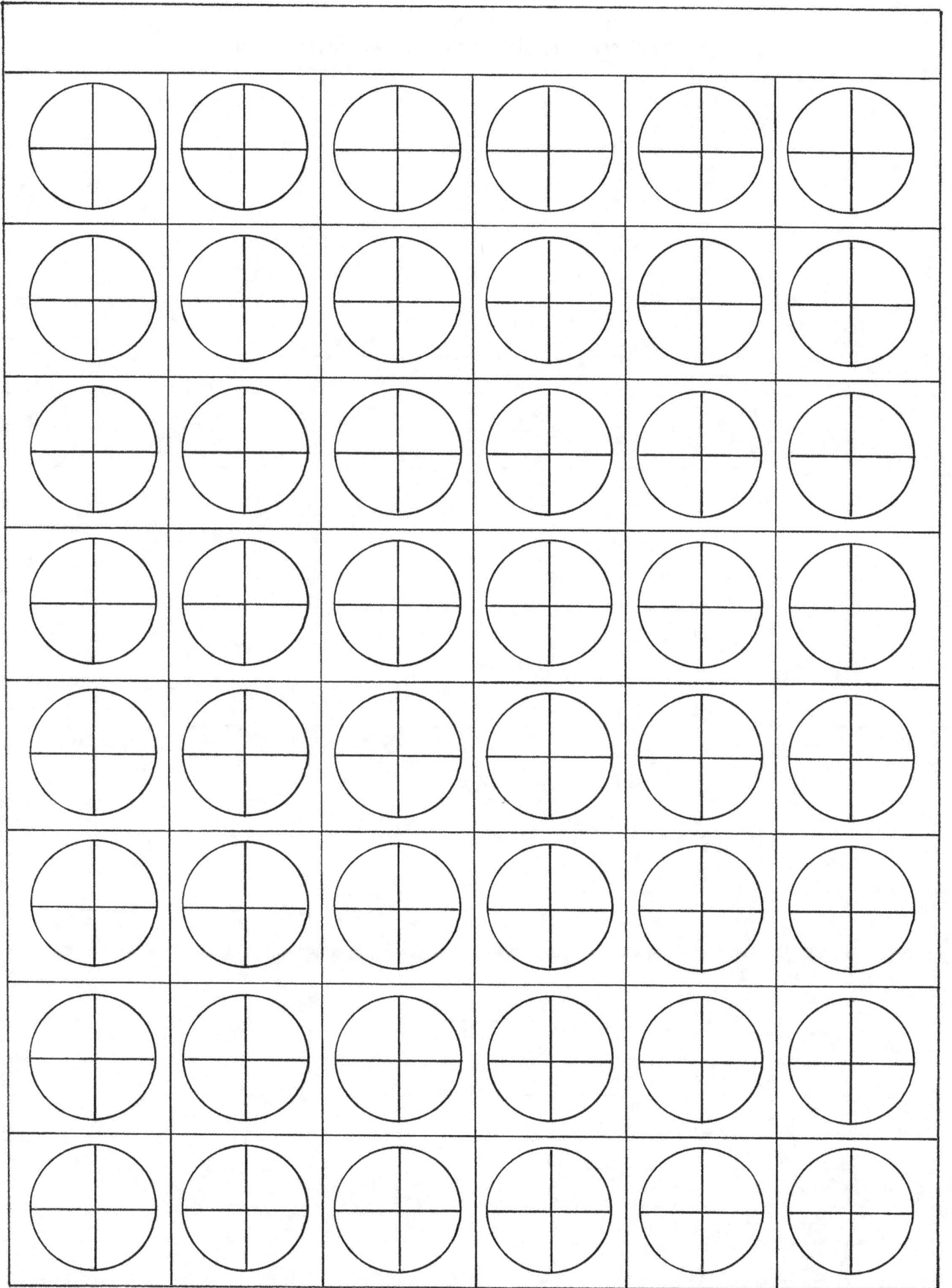

Template 2
2 Color Wheels with each 12 spaces = 24 spaces in total

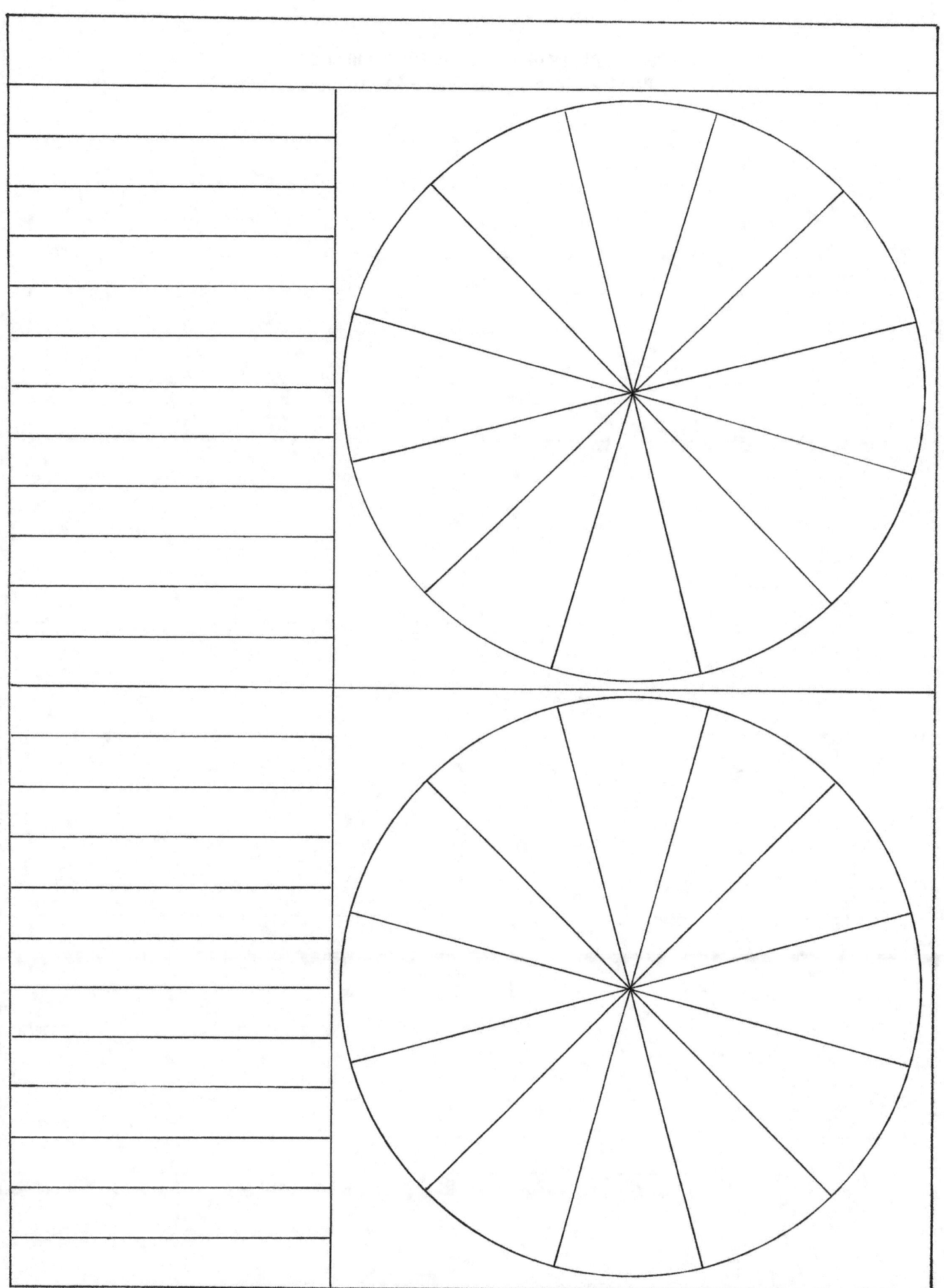

Template 3
Part 1 12 lines of 9 circles = 108 small circles
Part 2 24 lines of 9 squares = 216 squares

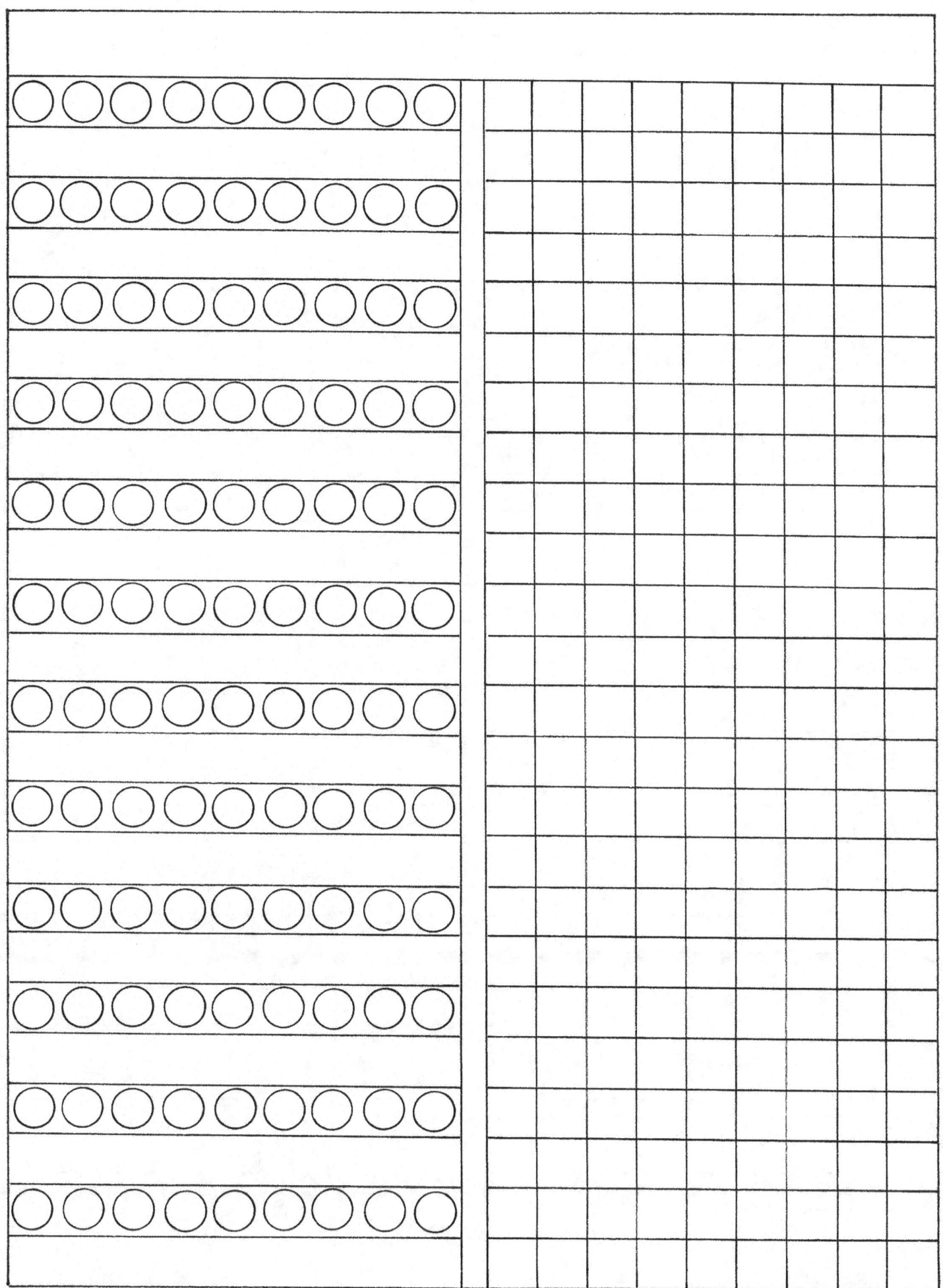

Template 4
8 lines of 37 spaces = total of 296 spaces

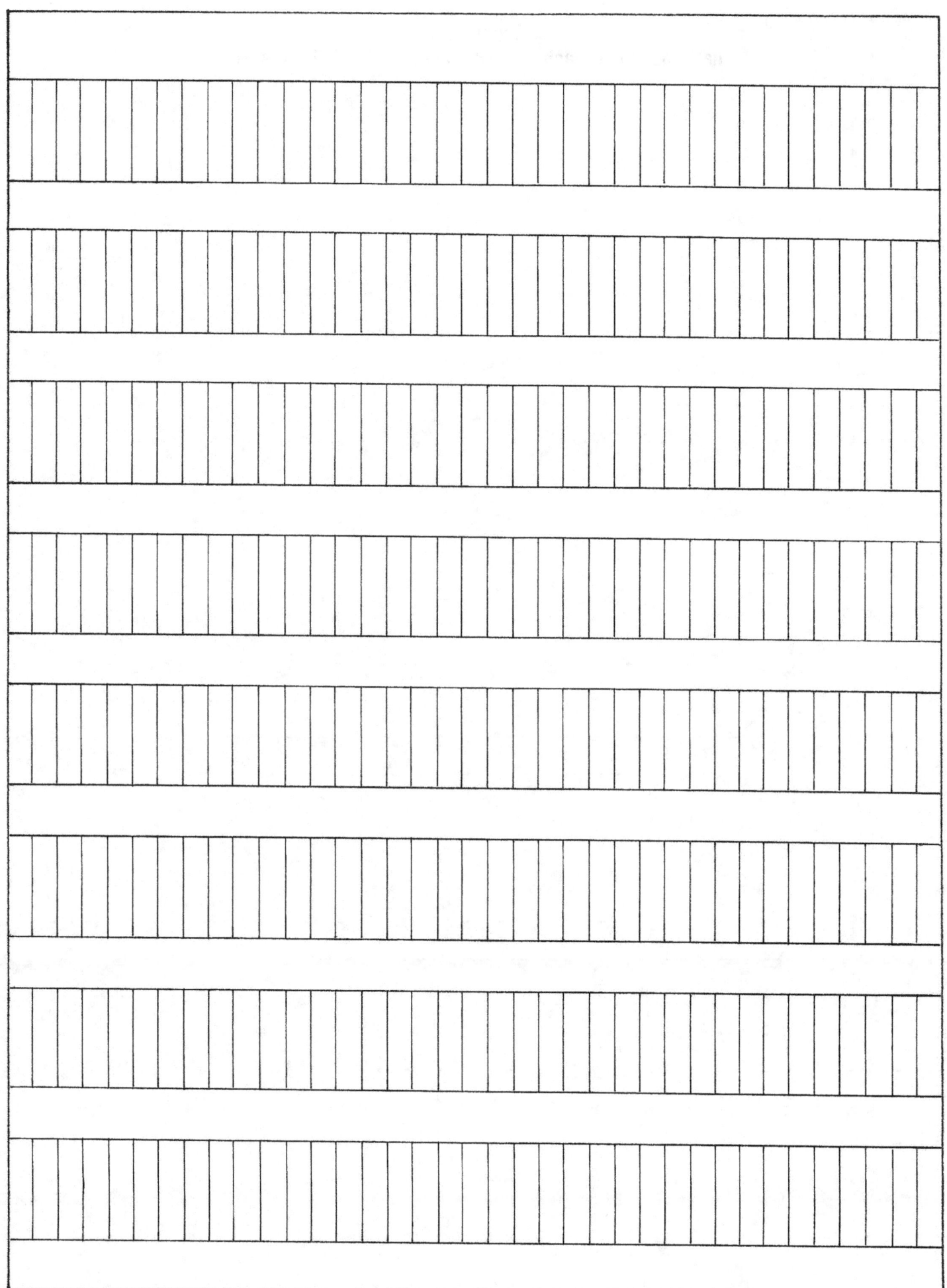

Template 5
8 half color wheel each with 18 spaces = a total of 144 spaces

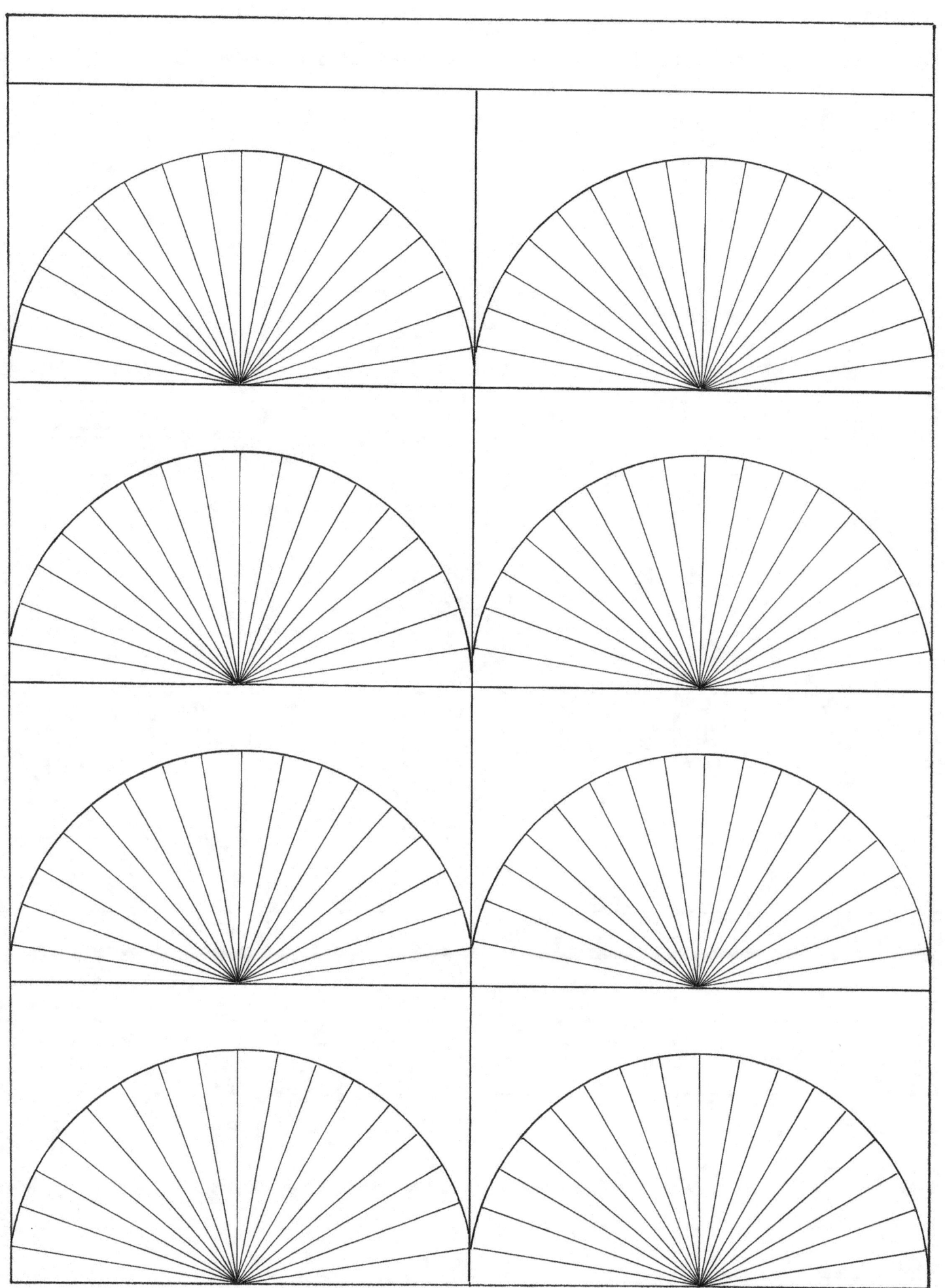

Template 6
6 rows of 8 circles = 48 circles x 8 spaces each = a total of 384 spaces

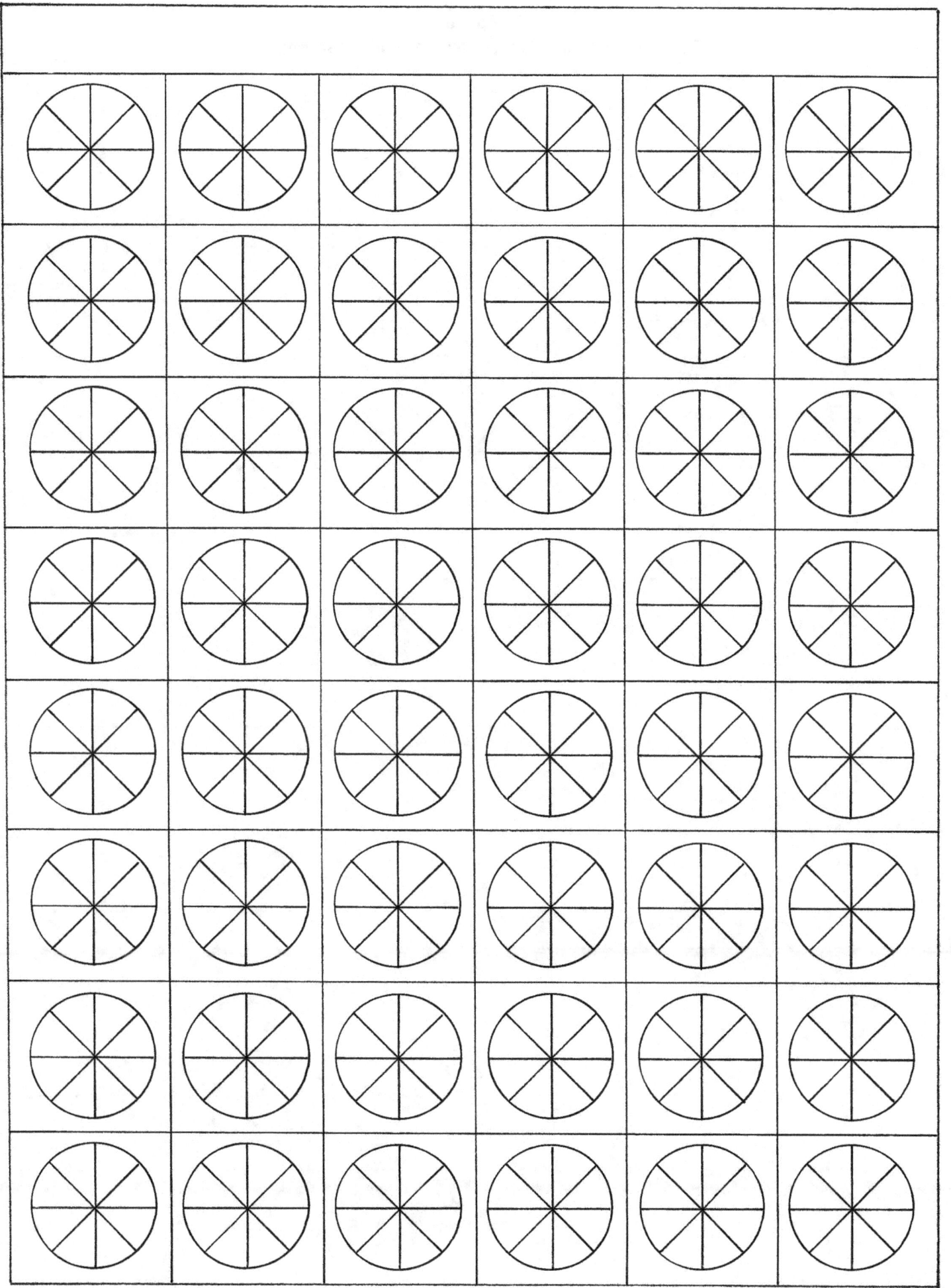

Template 7
8 lines of 24 triangular spaces = a total of 192 spaces

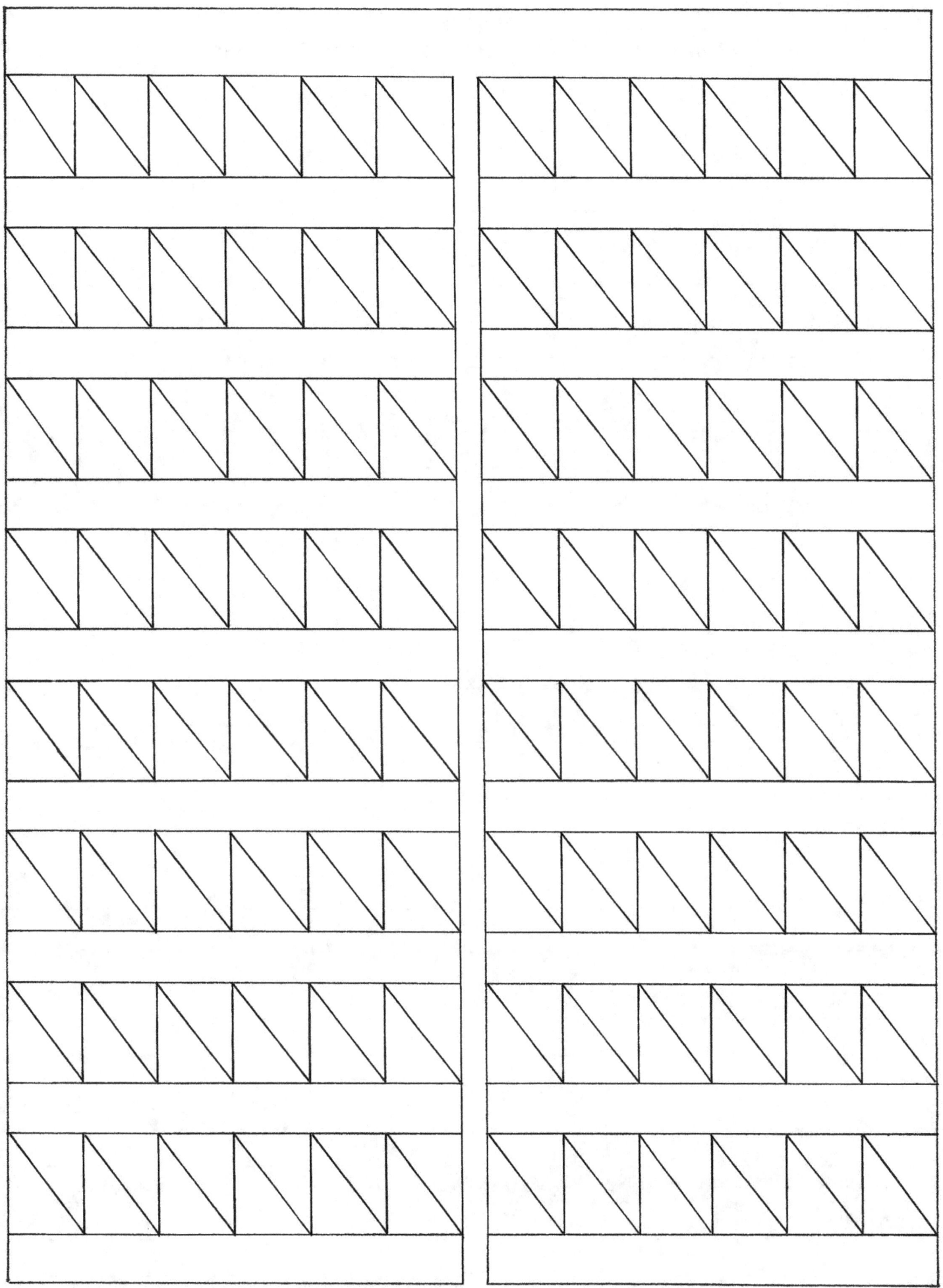

Template 8
3 rows of 2x48 spaces = 96 spaces x 3   a total of 288 spaces

Template 9
Big Color wheel 4 sections of 36 spaces = a total of 144 spaces

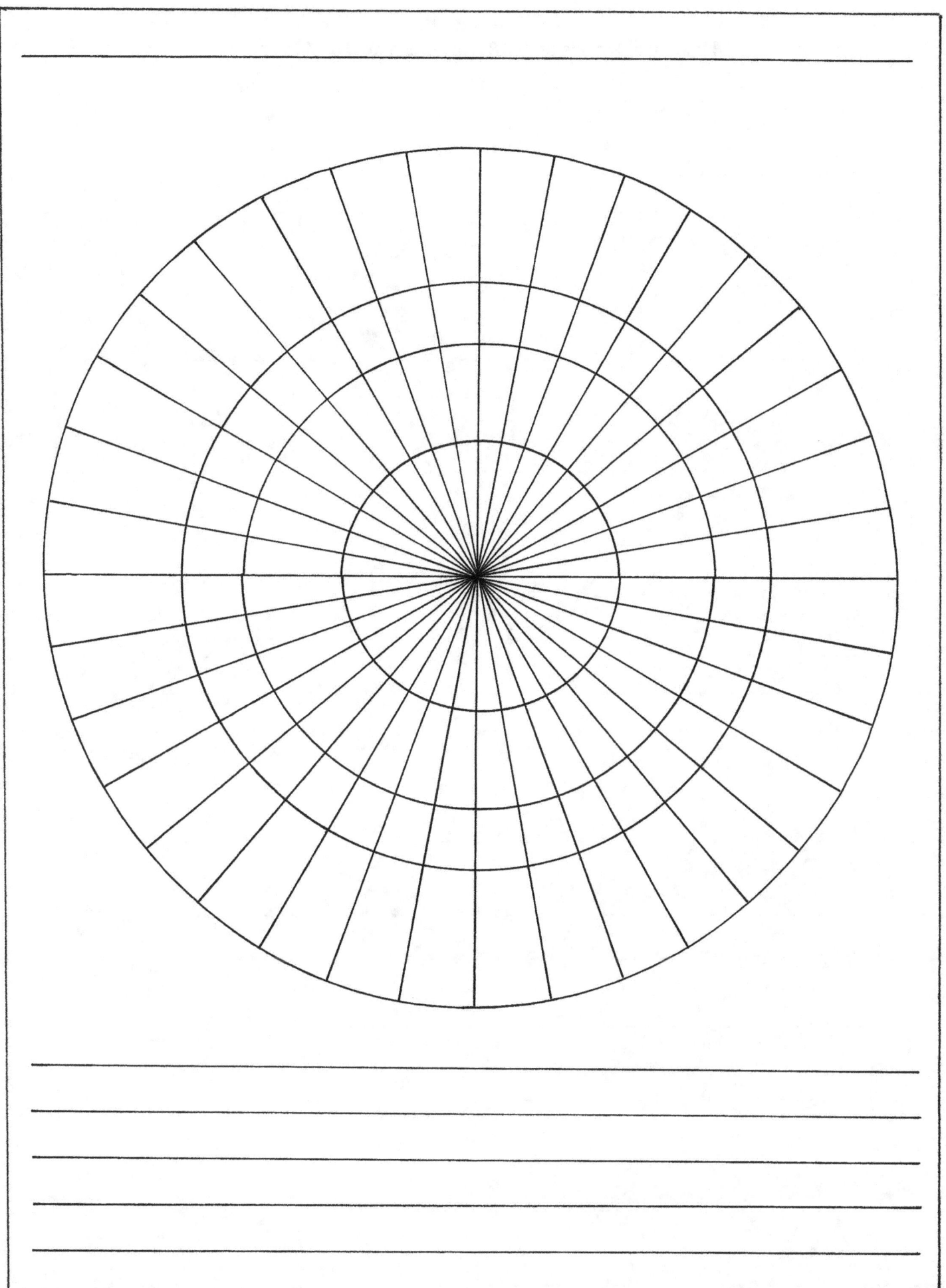

Template 10
4 half Color Wheels of 2x 18 spaces = a total of 144 spaces

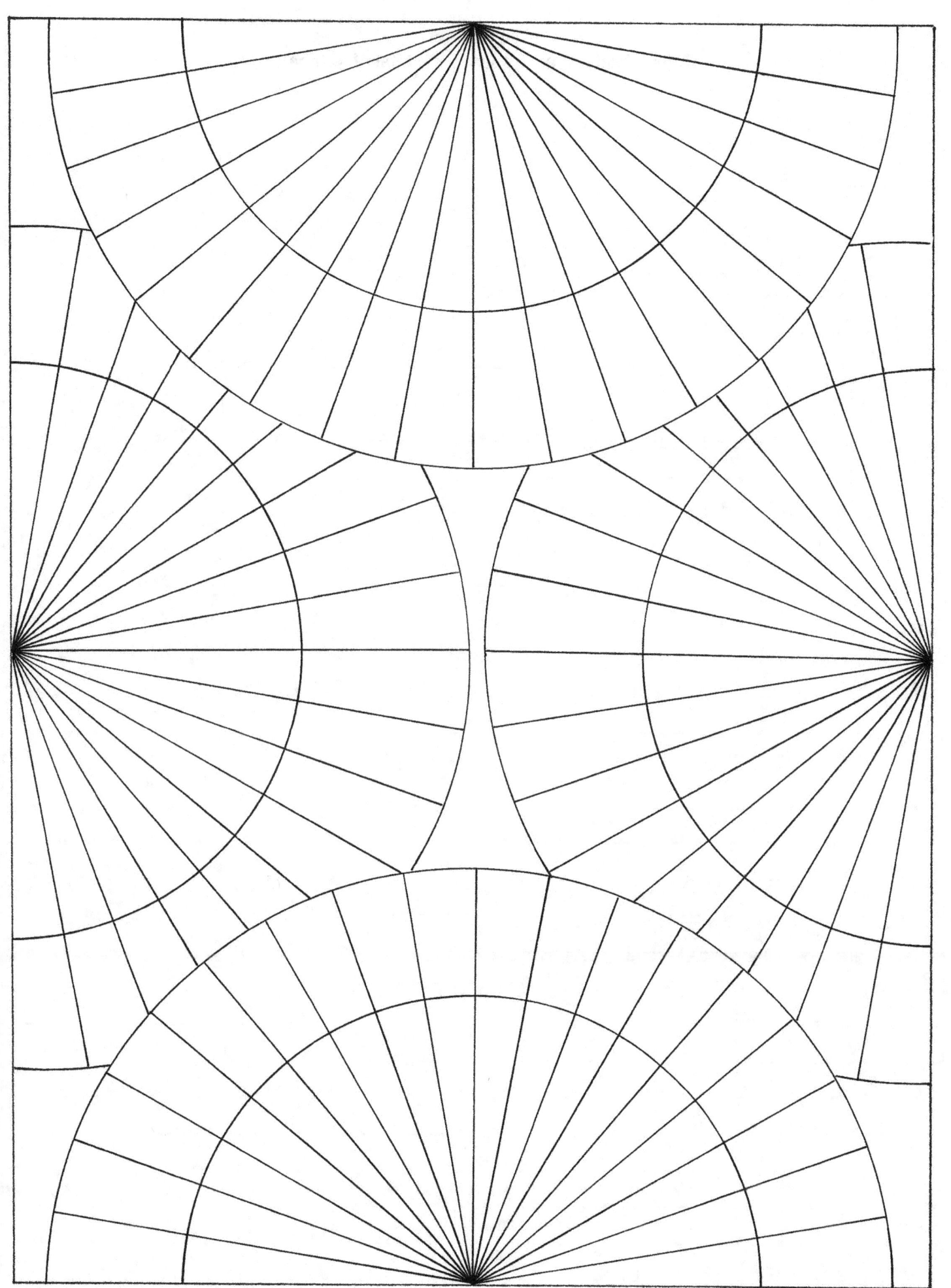

Template 11
Color Wheels of 4x 12 spaces = a total of 48 spaces

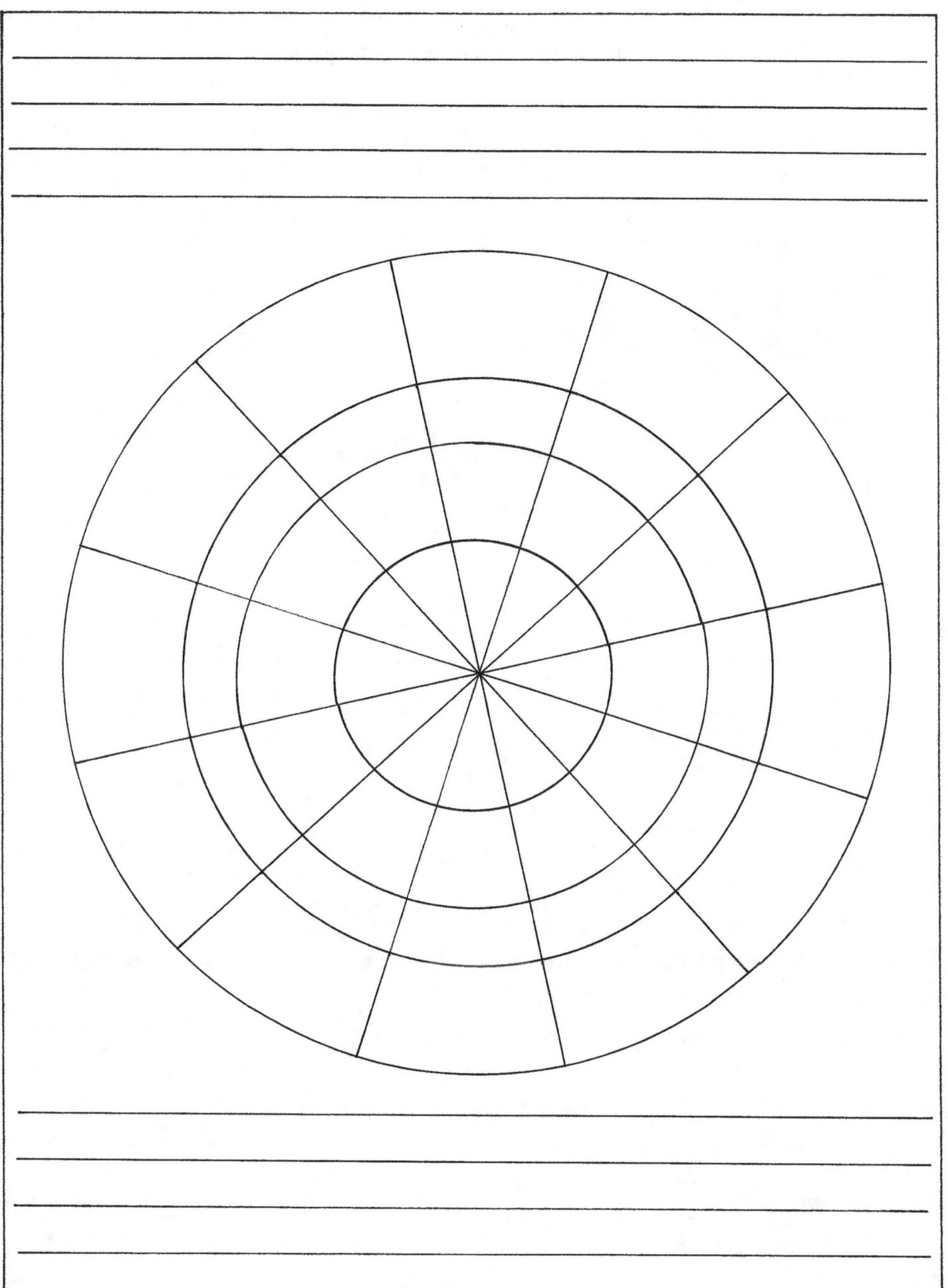

Template 12
24 circles of 3 spaces = a total of 72 spaces

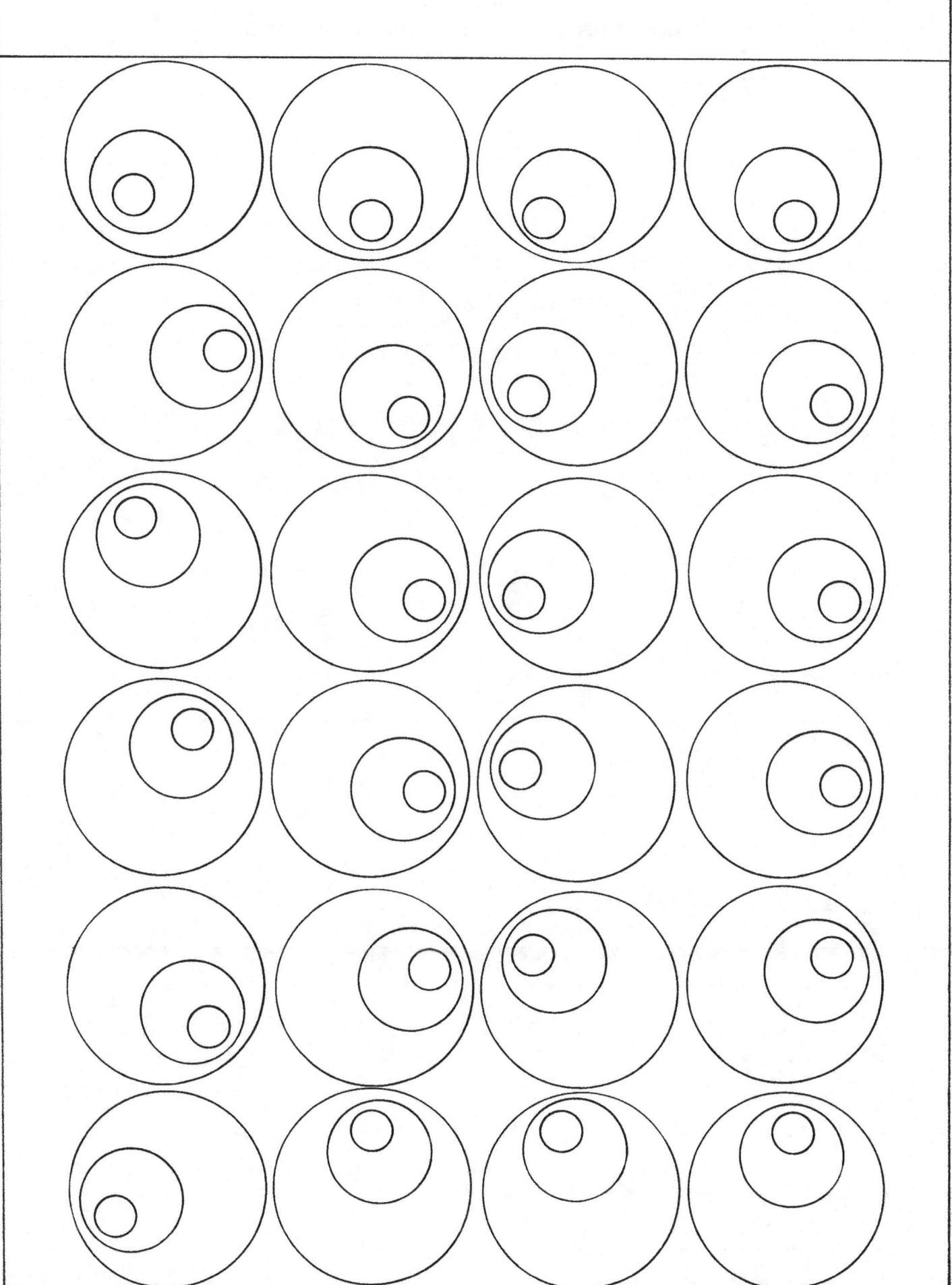

Template 13
2 Color Wheels of 4x12 spaces = a total of 96 spaces

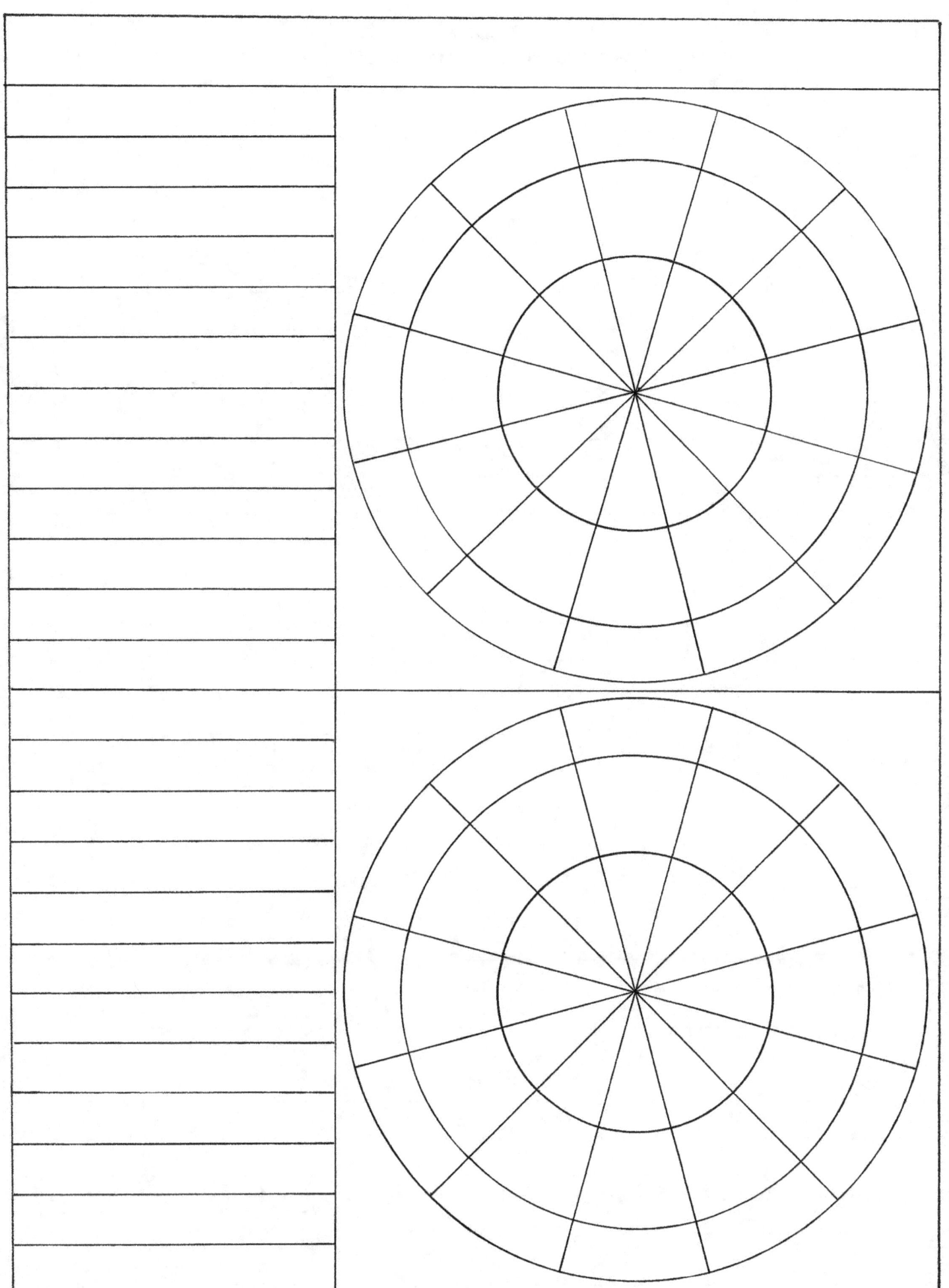

Template 14
8 lines of 2x37 spaces = a total of 592 spaces

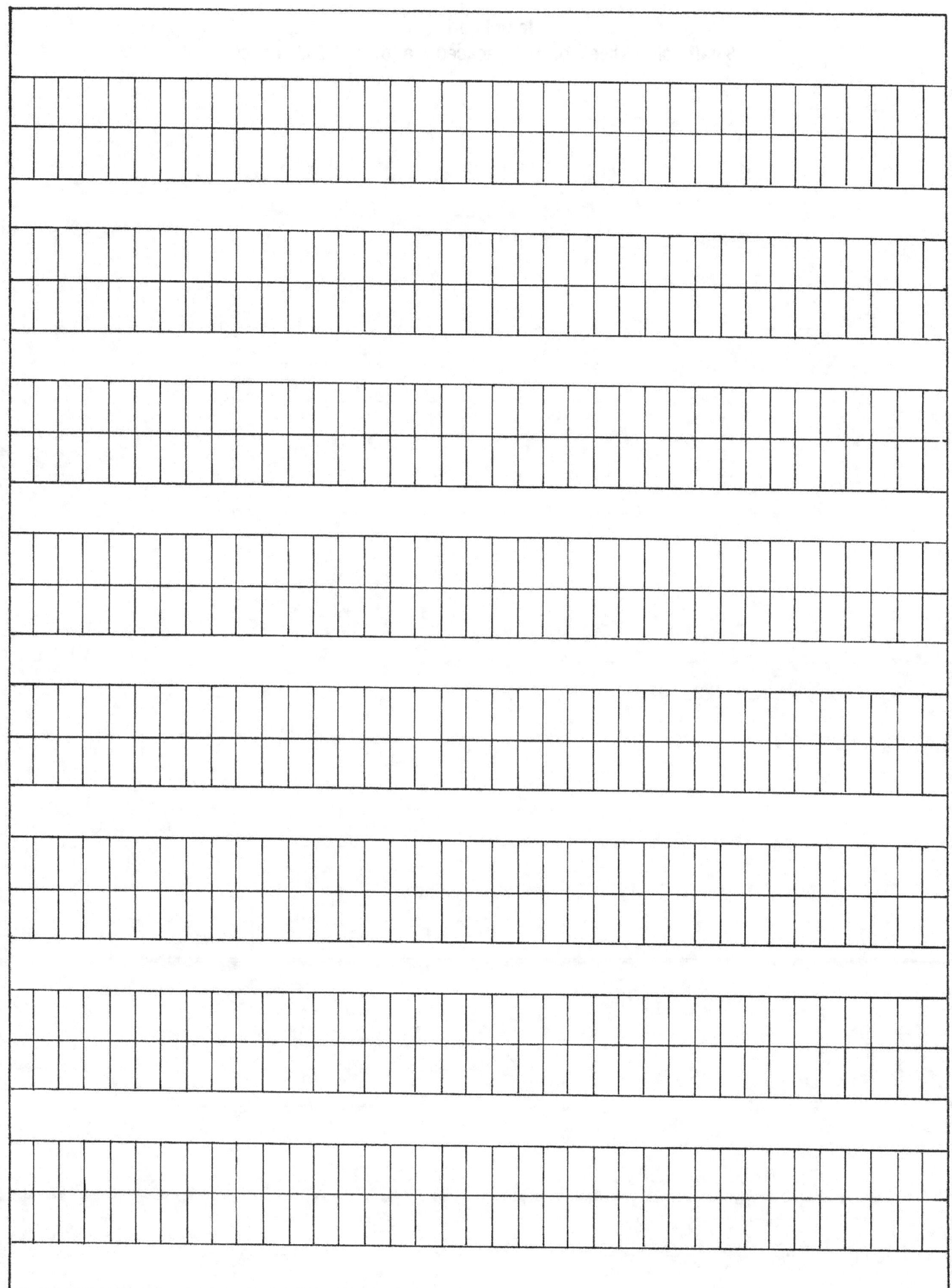

Template 15
8 half Color Wheels of 2x 18 spaces = a total of 288 spaces

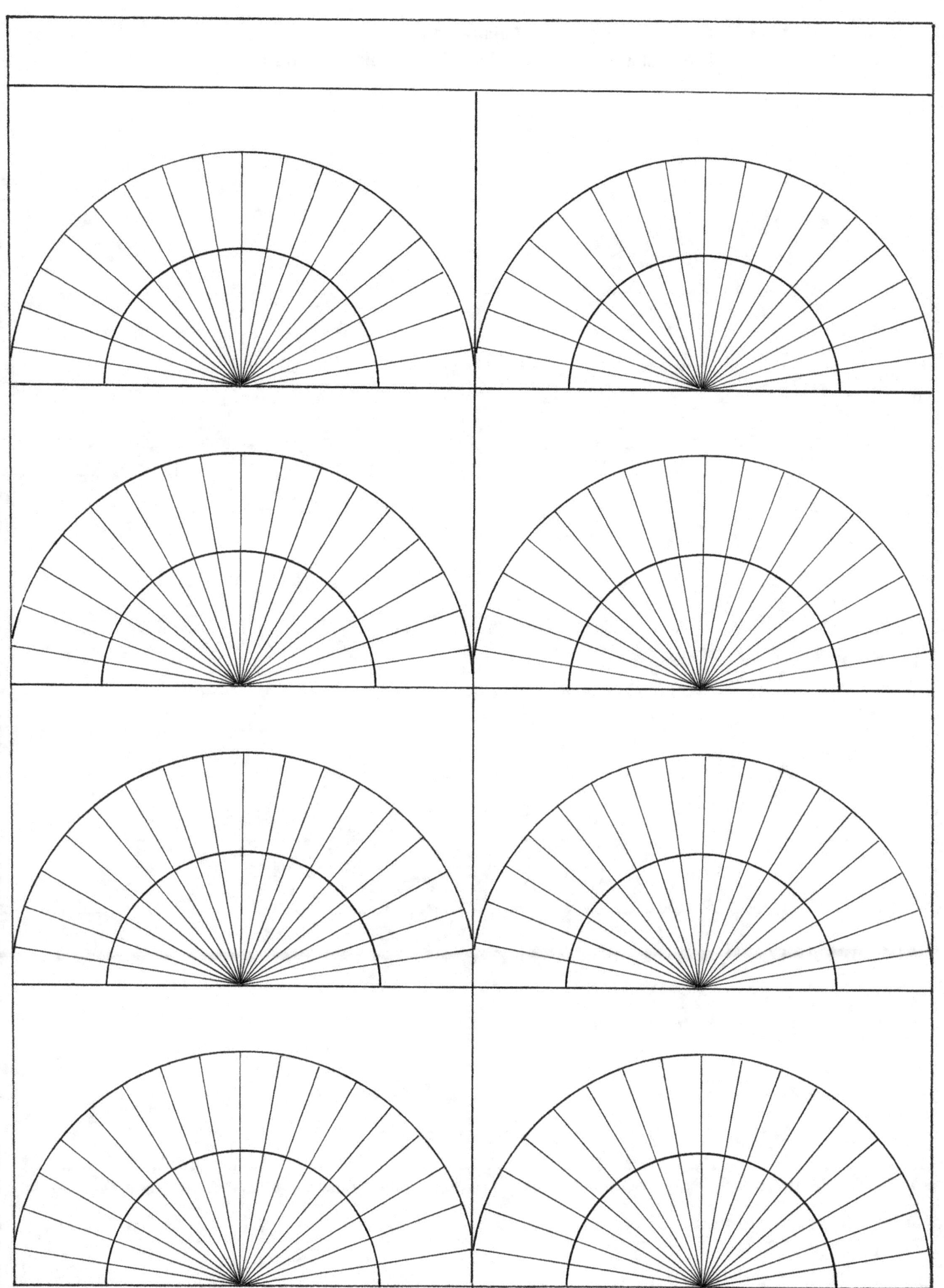

Template 16
4 half Color Wheels of 3x 18 spaces = a total of 216 spaces

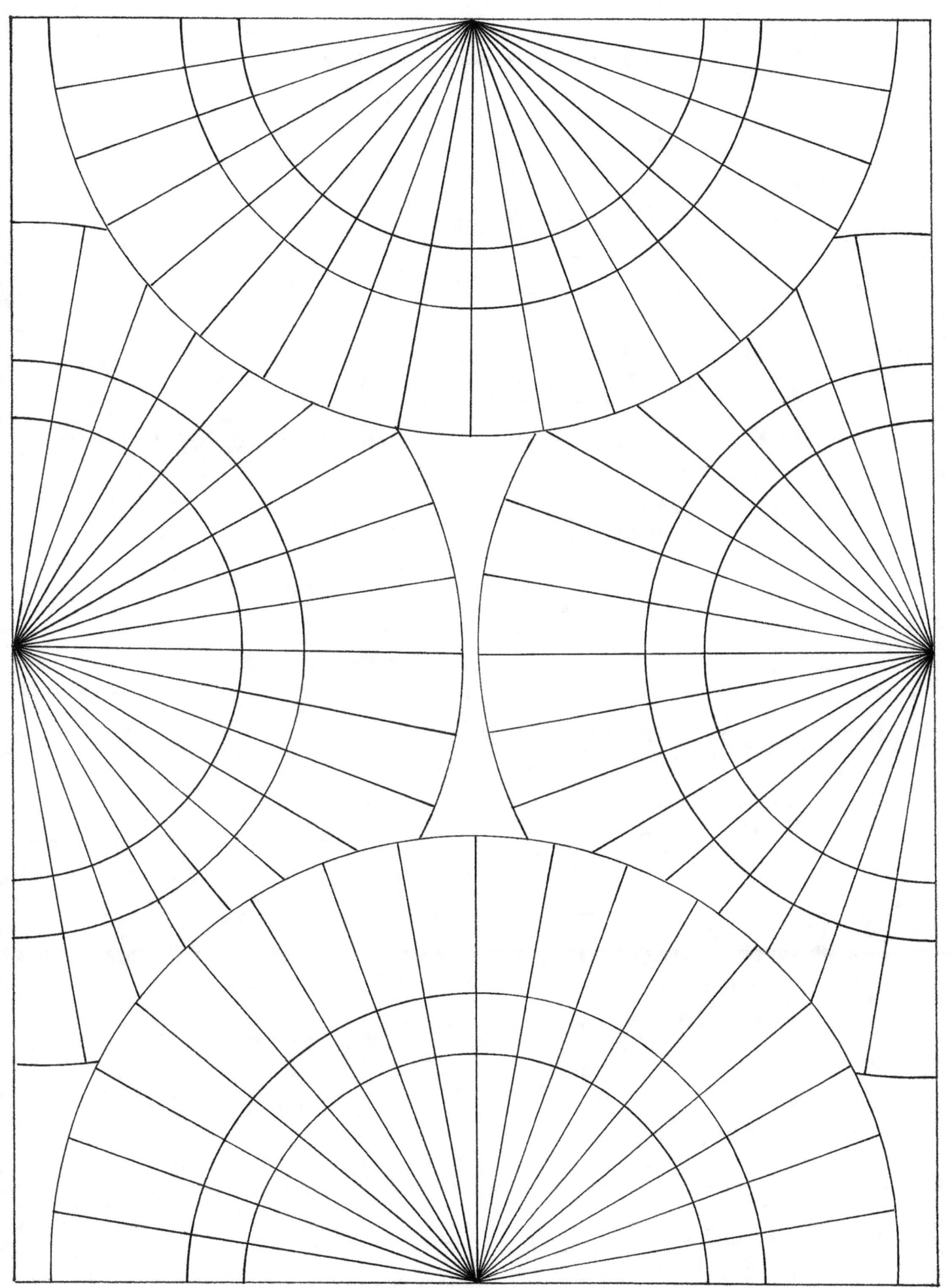

Template 17
3 rows of 4x48 spaces = a total of 576 spaces

Template 18
8 lines of 4x37 spaces = a total of 1184 spaces

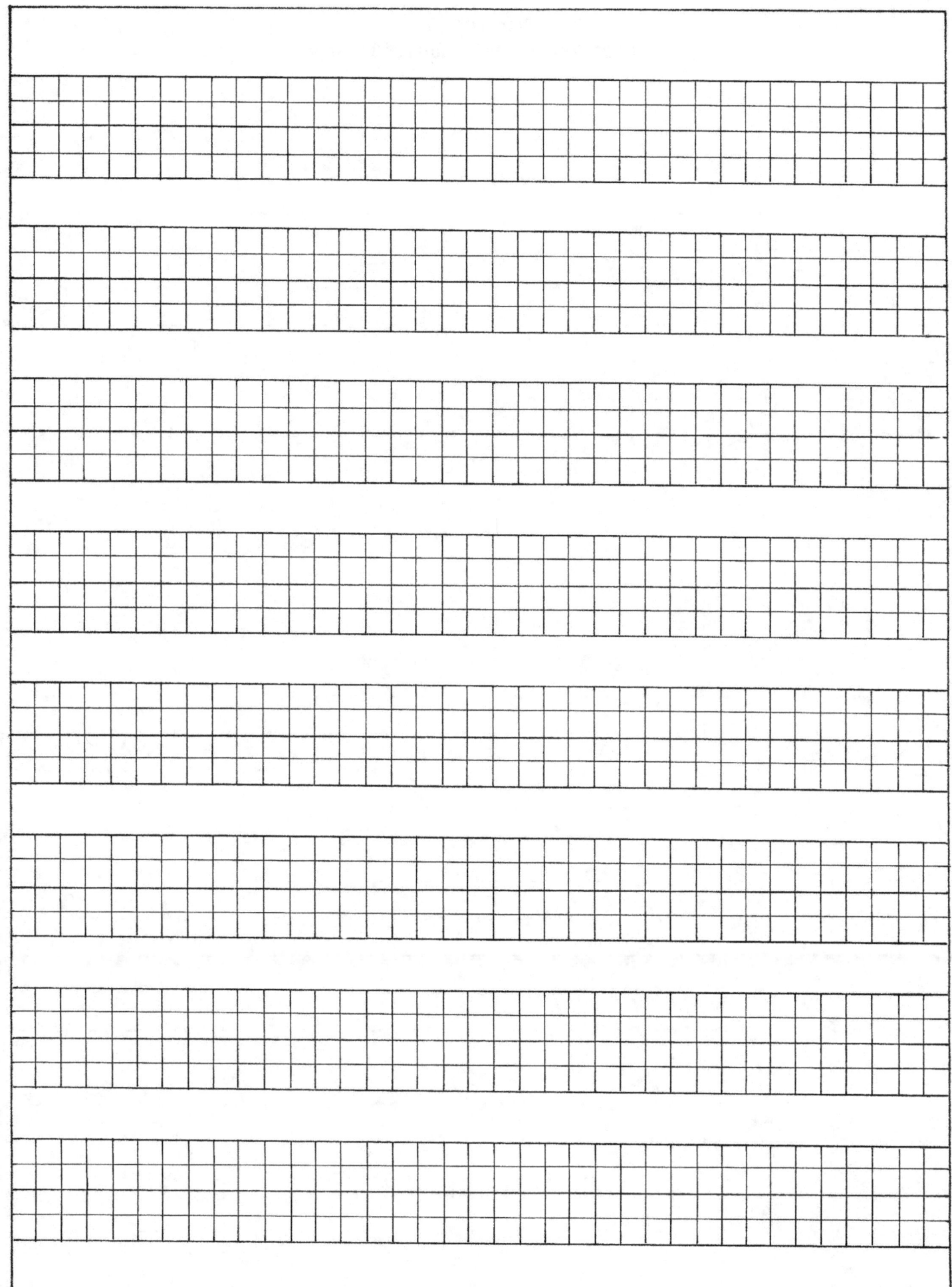

Template 19
8 lines of 12x4 spaces = a total of 384 spaces

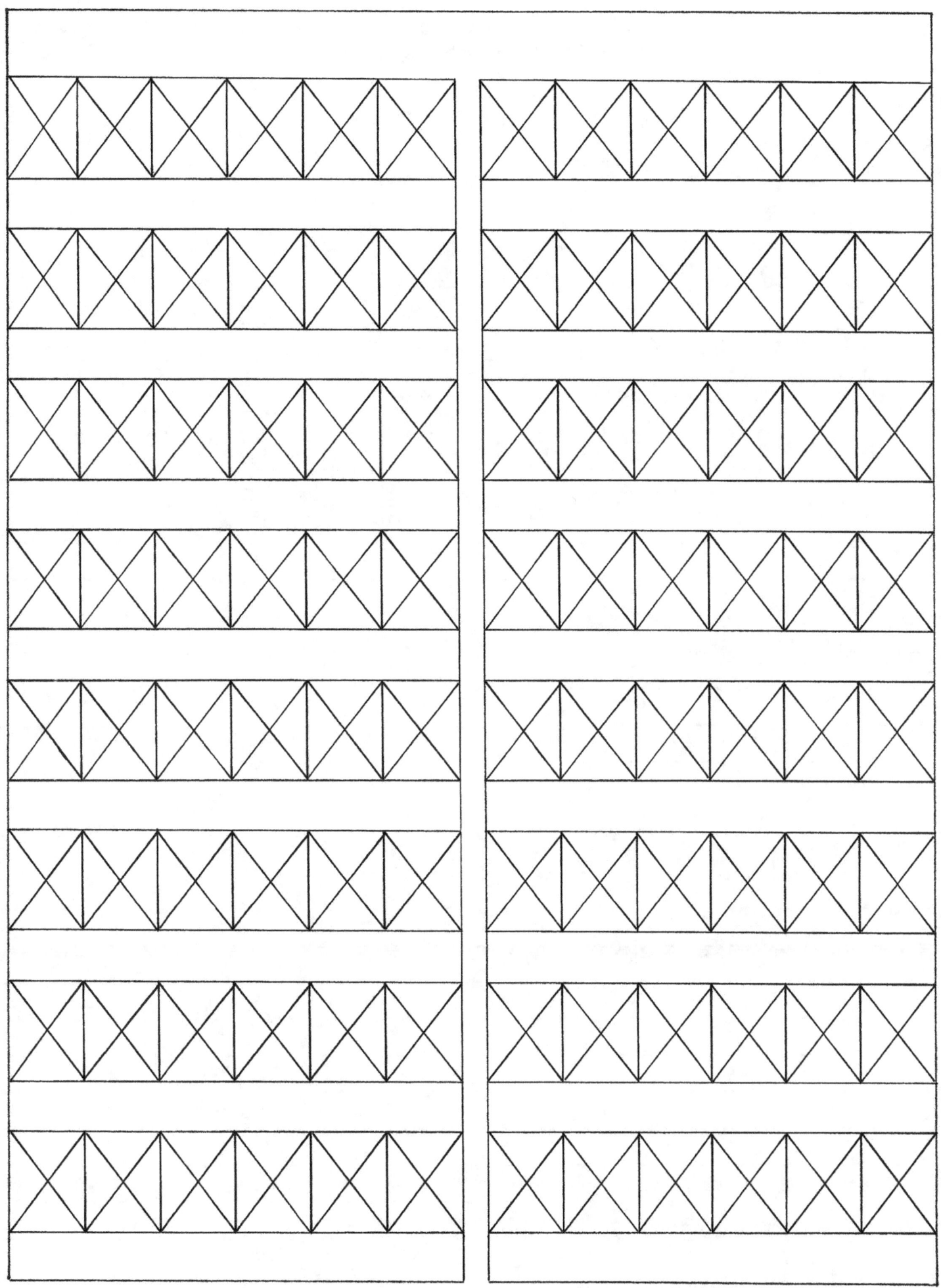

Template 20
Color Wheel with 36 spaces

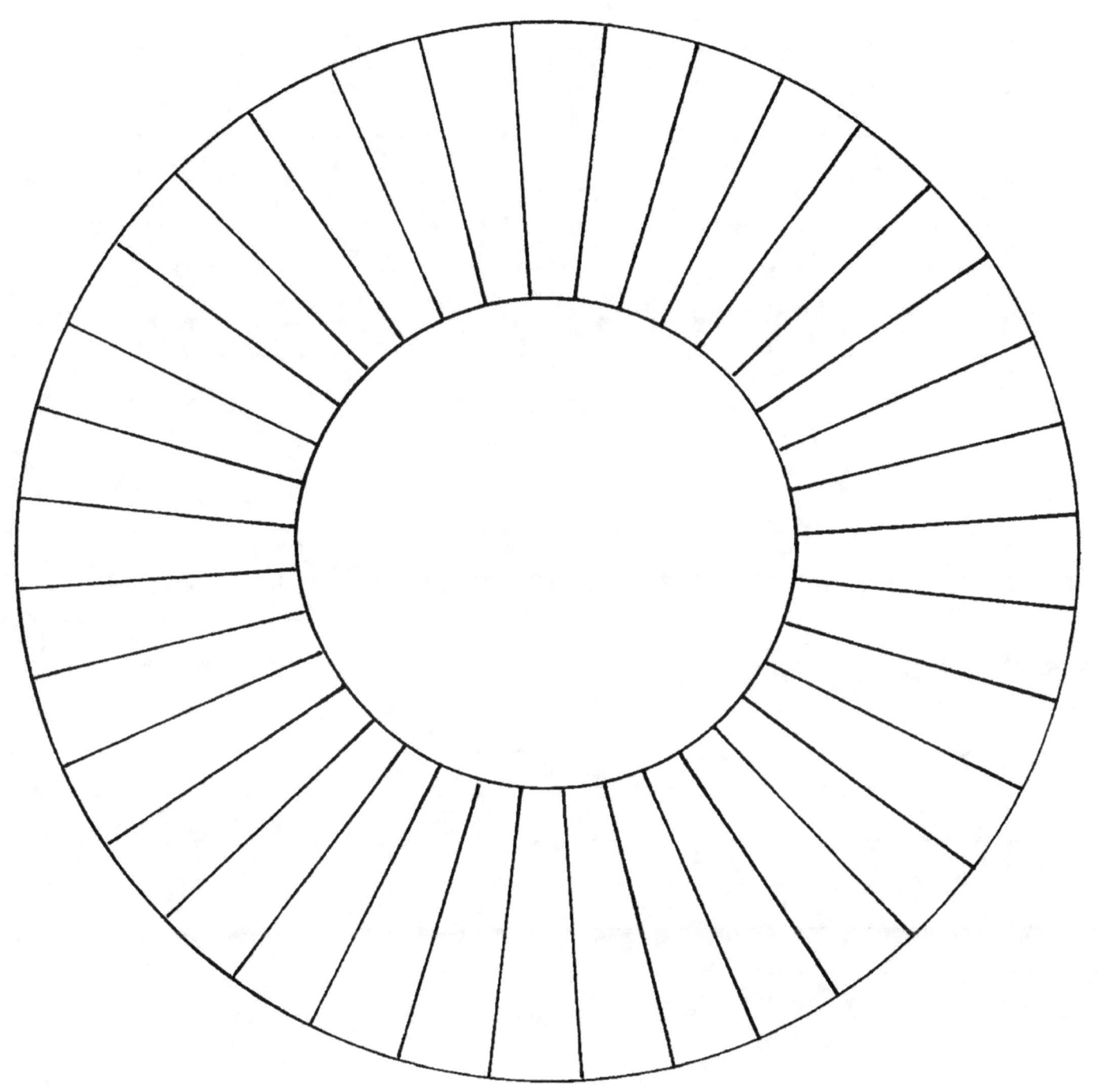

Template 21
Circle explosion of 16x 7 circles = 112 circles

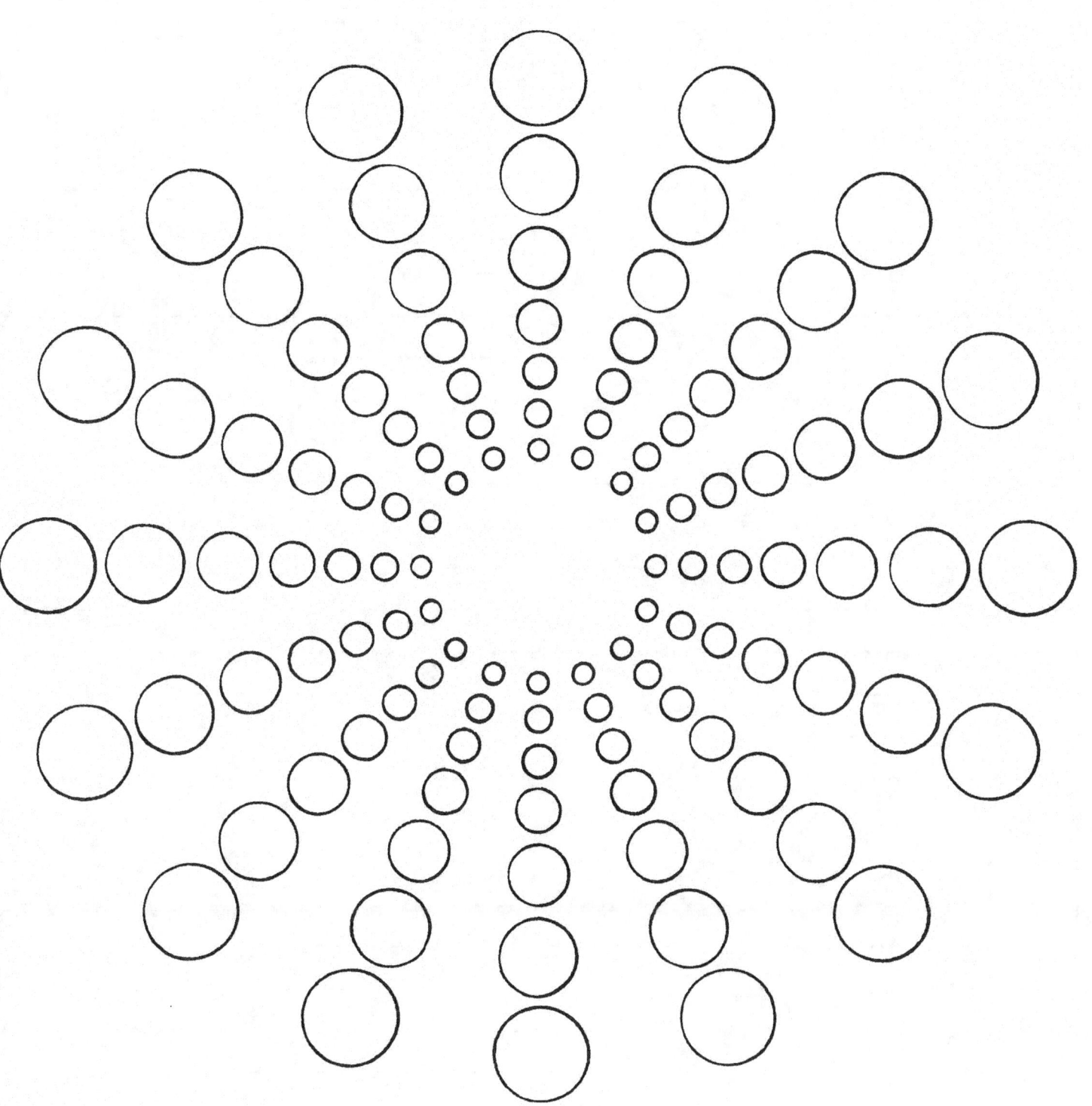

Template 22
Color flowe 16x9 spaces = a total of 144 spaces

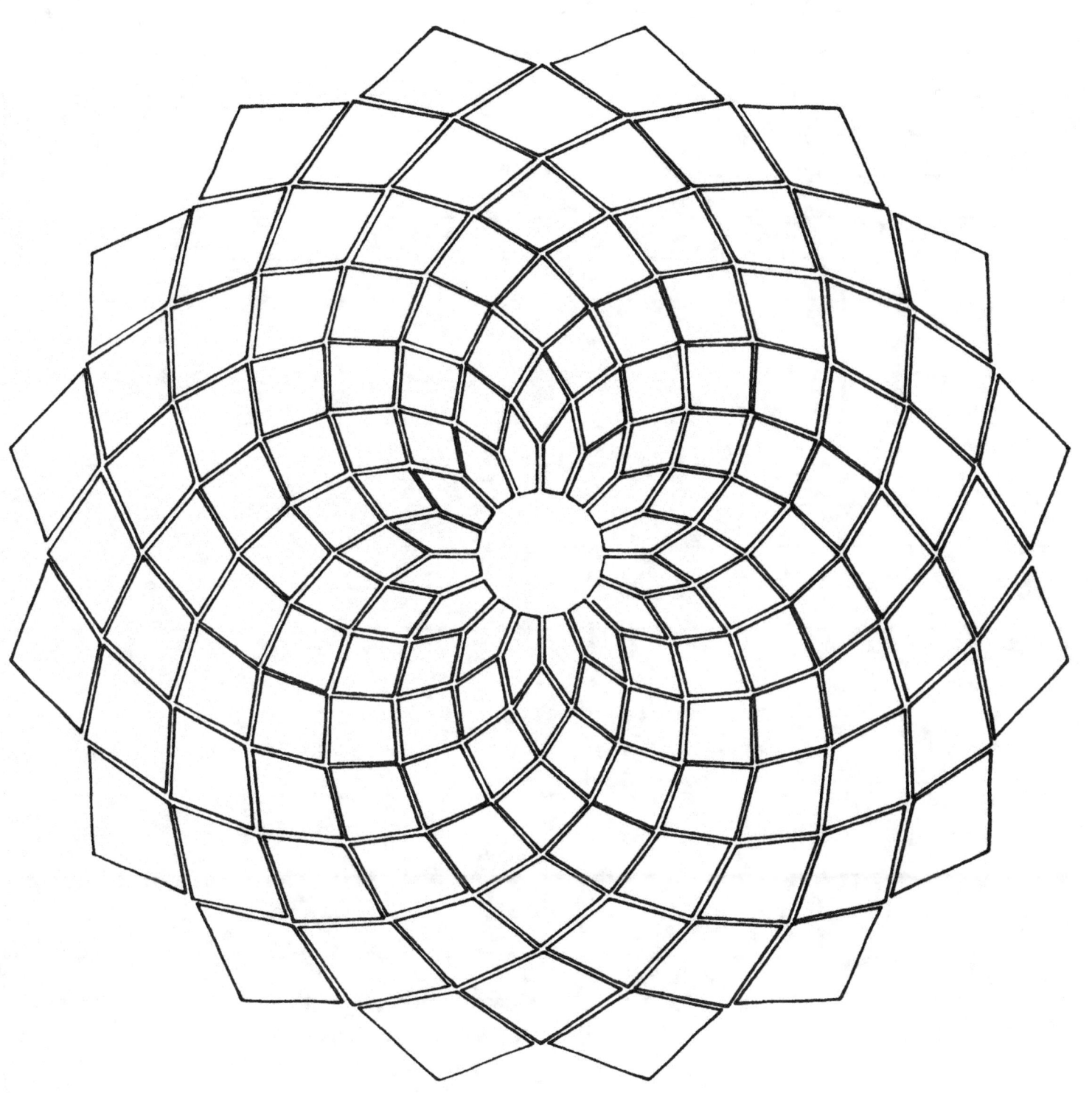

Template 23
1 color wheel of 6x 36 spaces = 216 spaces
4 quarter color wheels of 6 x 9 spaces = 216 spaces
A grand total of 432 spaces

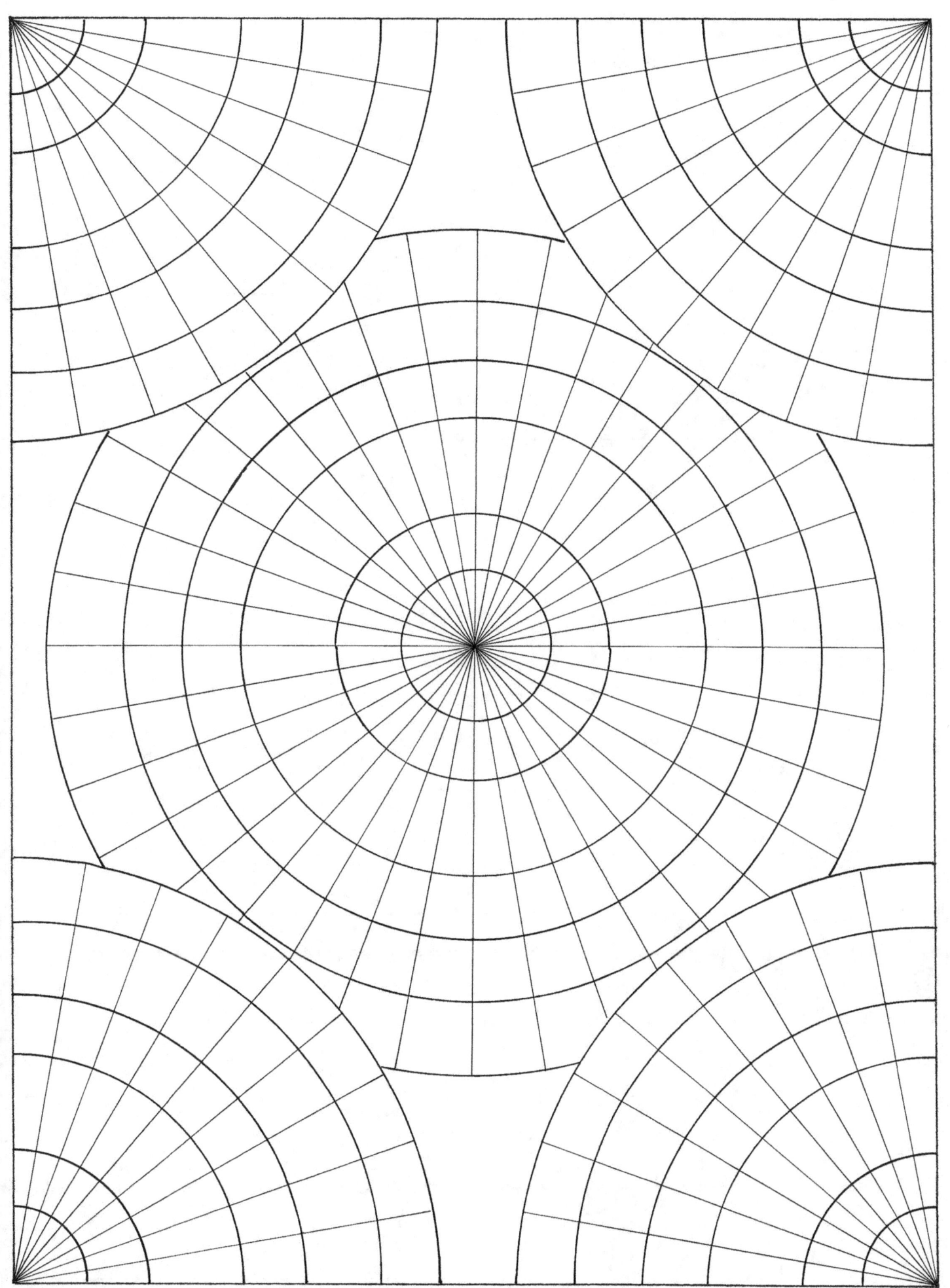

Template 24
Great wheel of colors 5x 32 spaces = 160 spaces

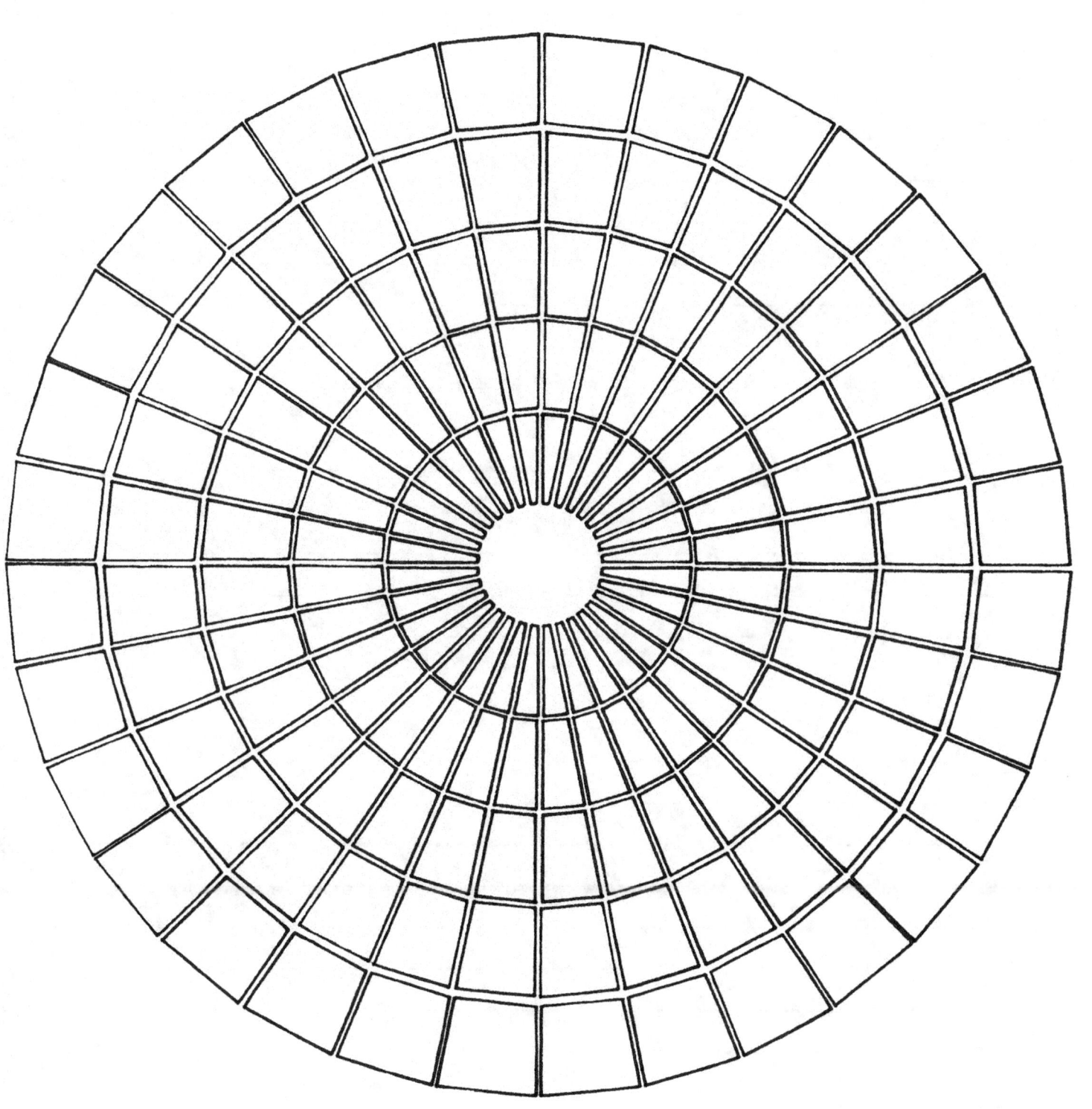

Template 25
8 lines of 12 spaces = a total of 96 spaces

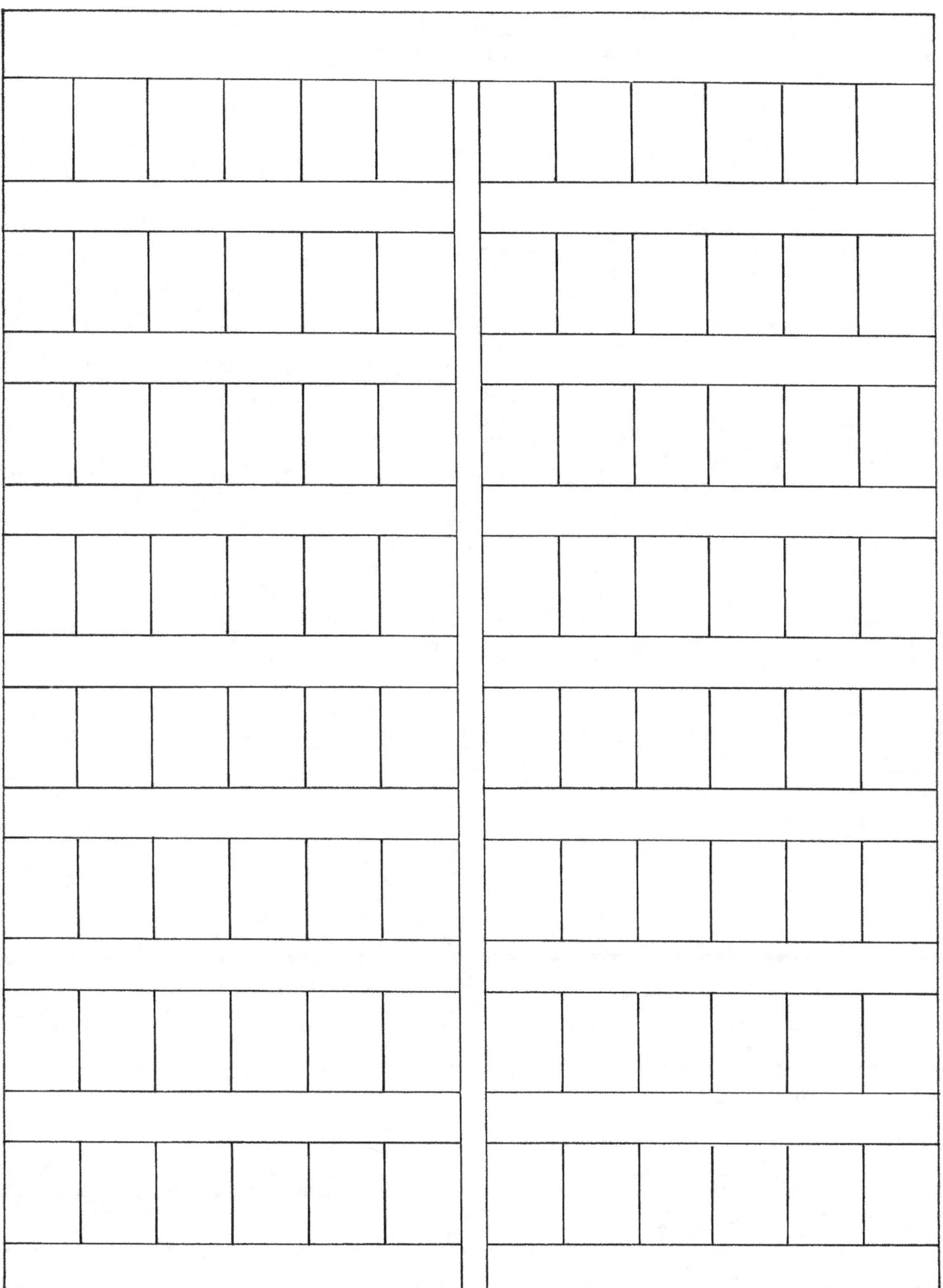

Template 26
3 rows of 48 spaces = a total of 144 spaces

Template 27
Big Color wheel of 36 spaces

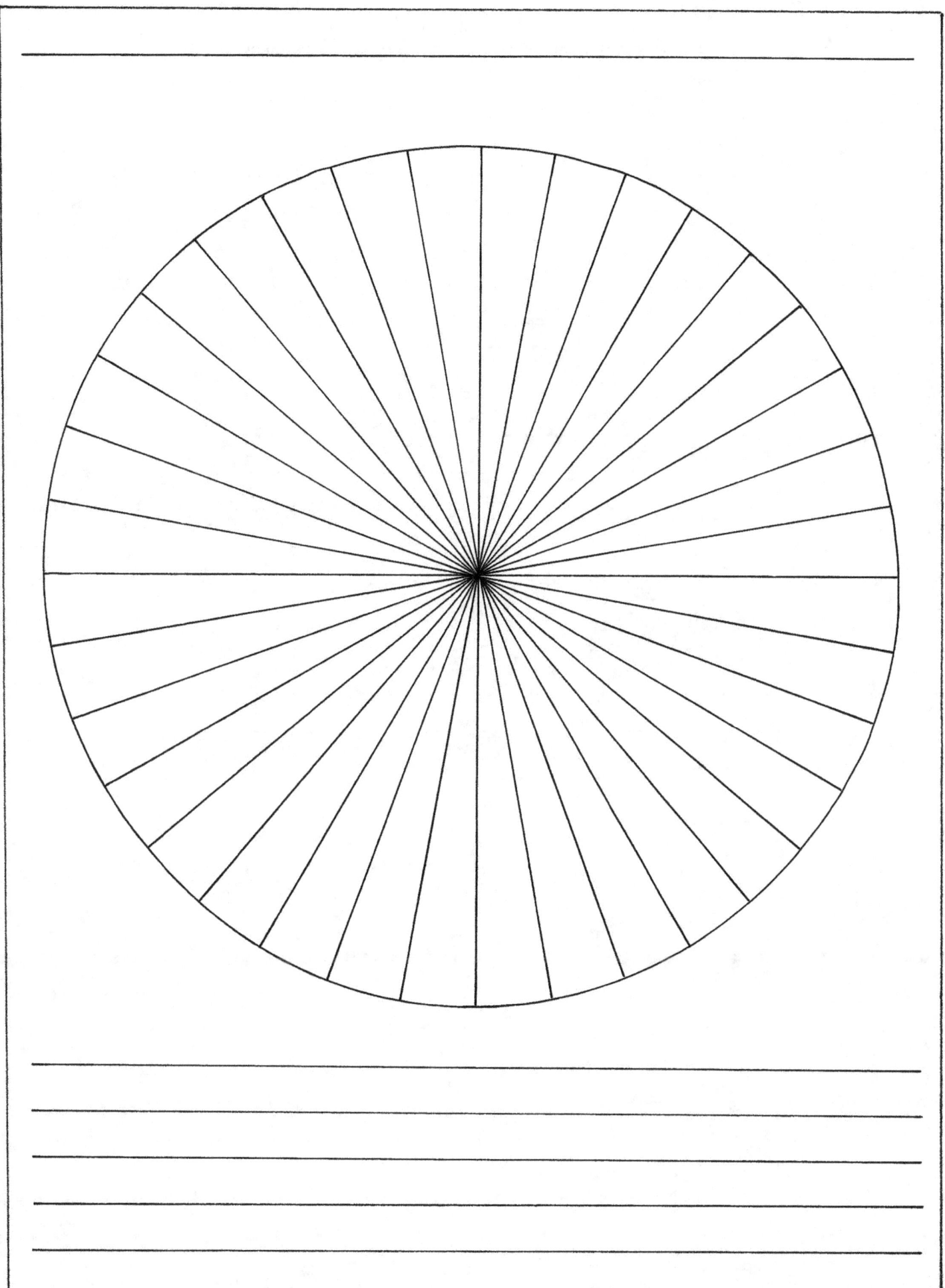

Template 28
4 half color wheels of 18 spaces = a total of 72 spaces

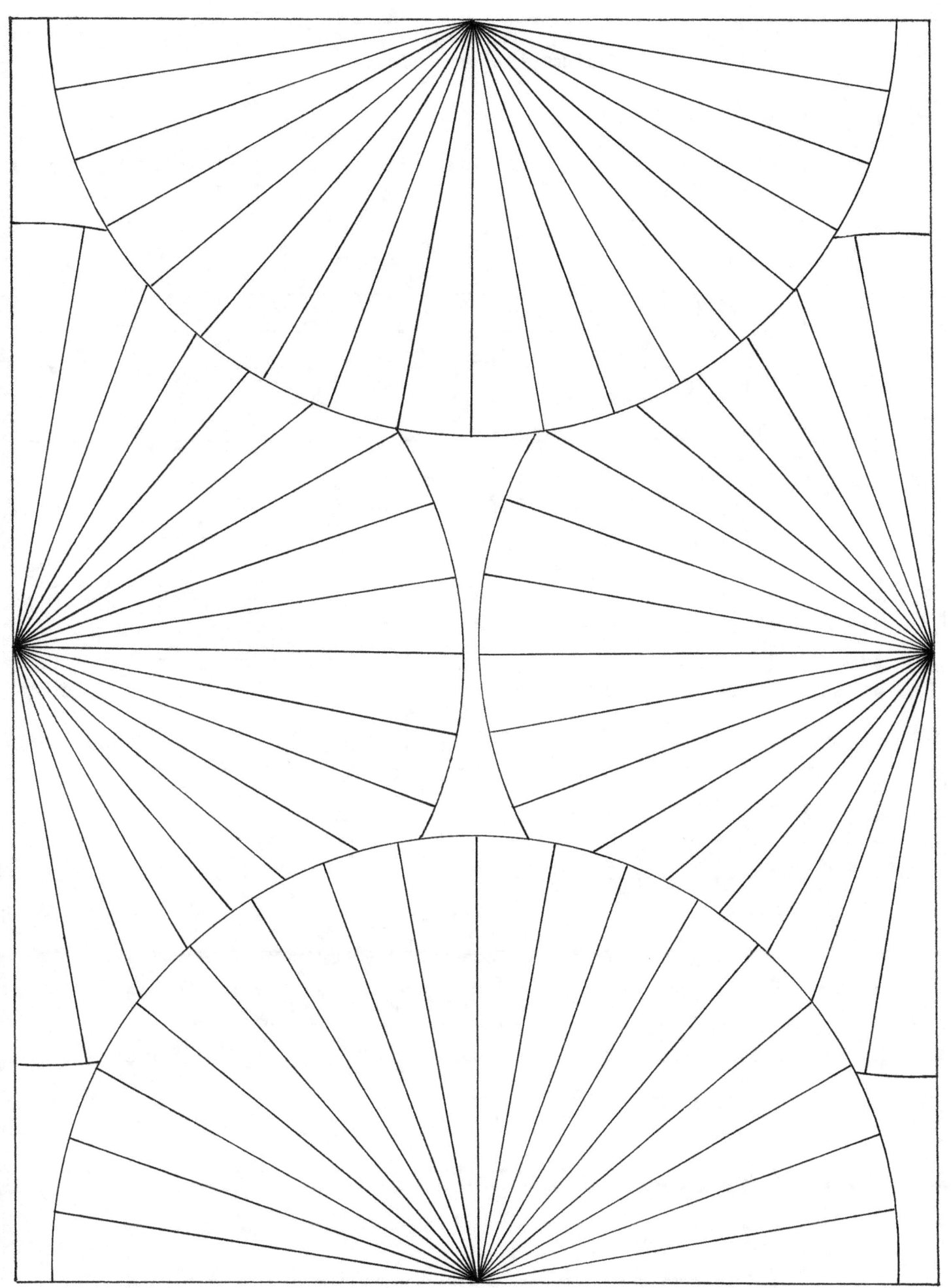

Template 29
10 lines of 9 circles = 90 circles

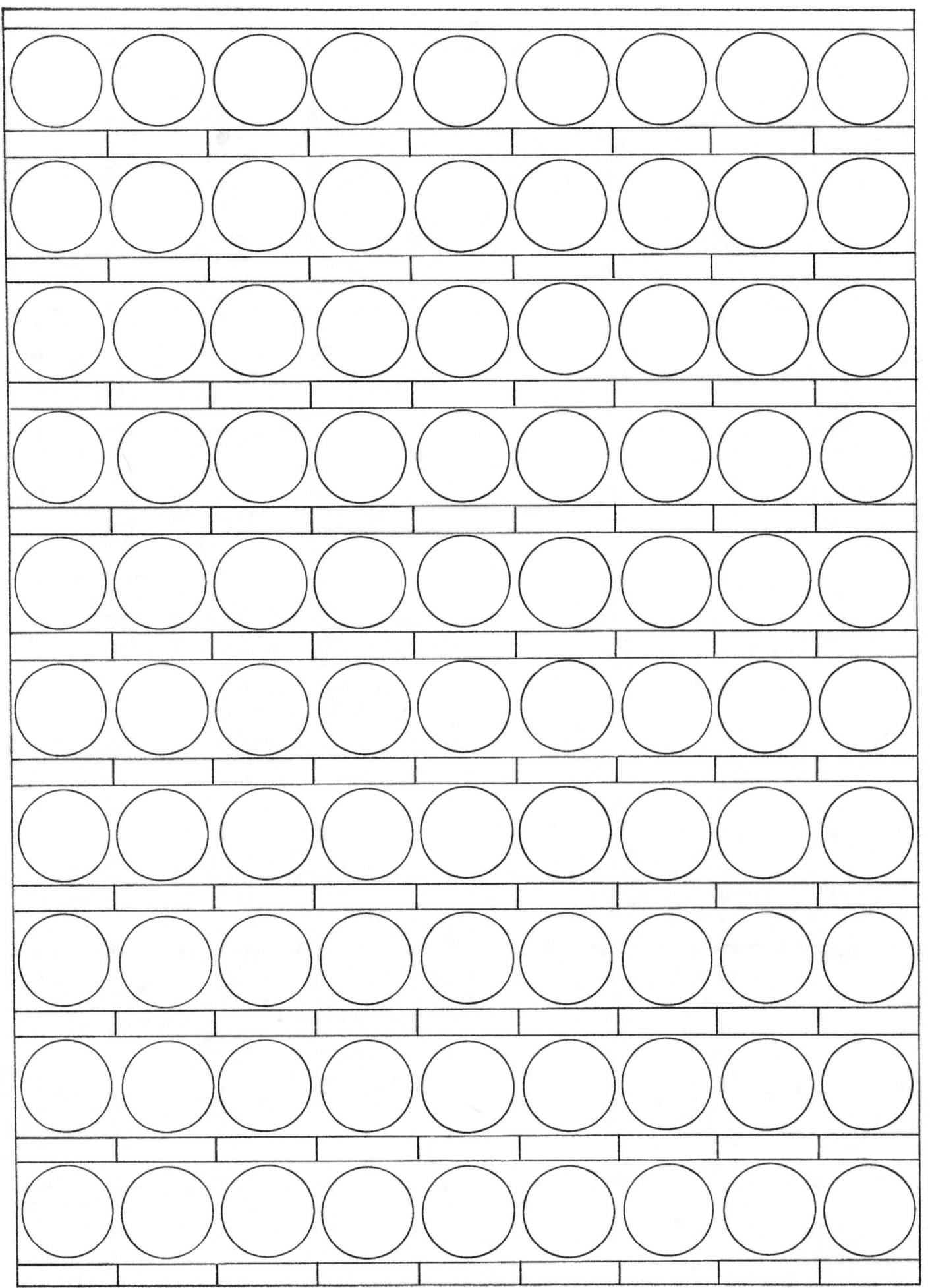

Template 30
Big Color Wheel of 12 spaces

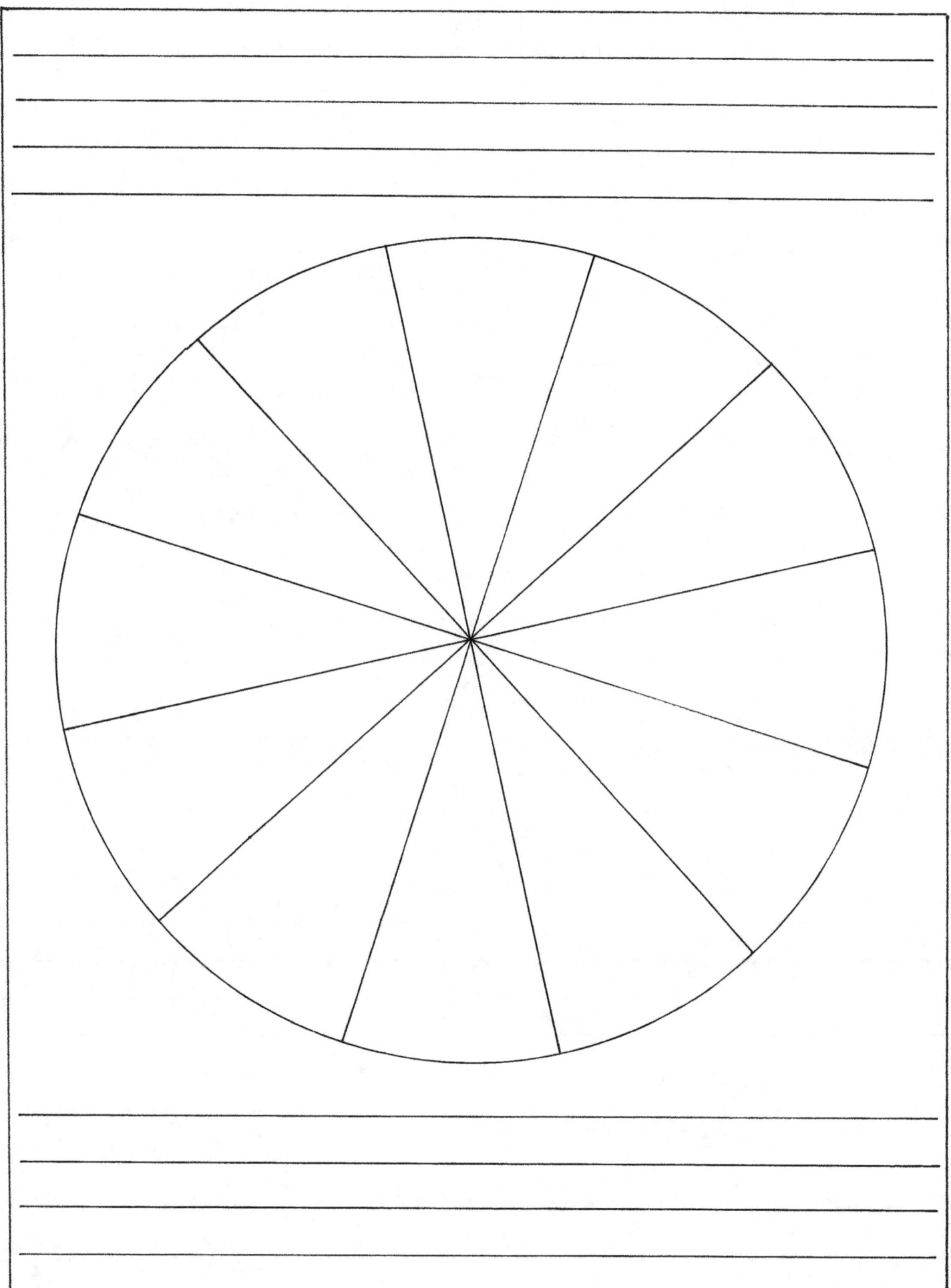

Template 1
6 rows of 8 circles = 48 circles x 4 spaces each = a total of 192 spaces

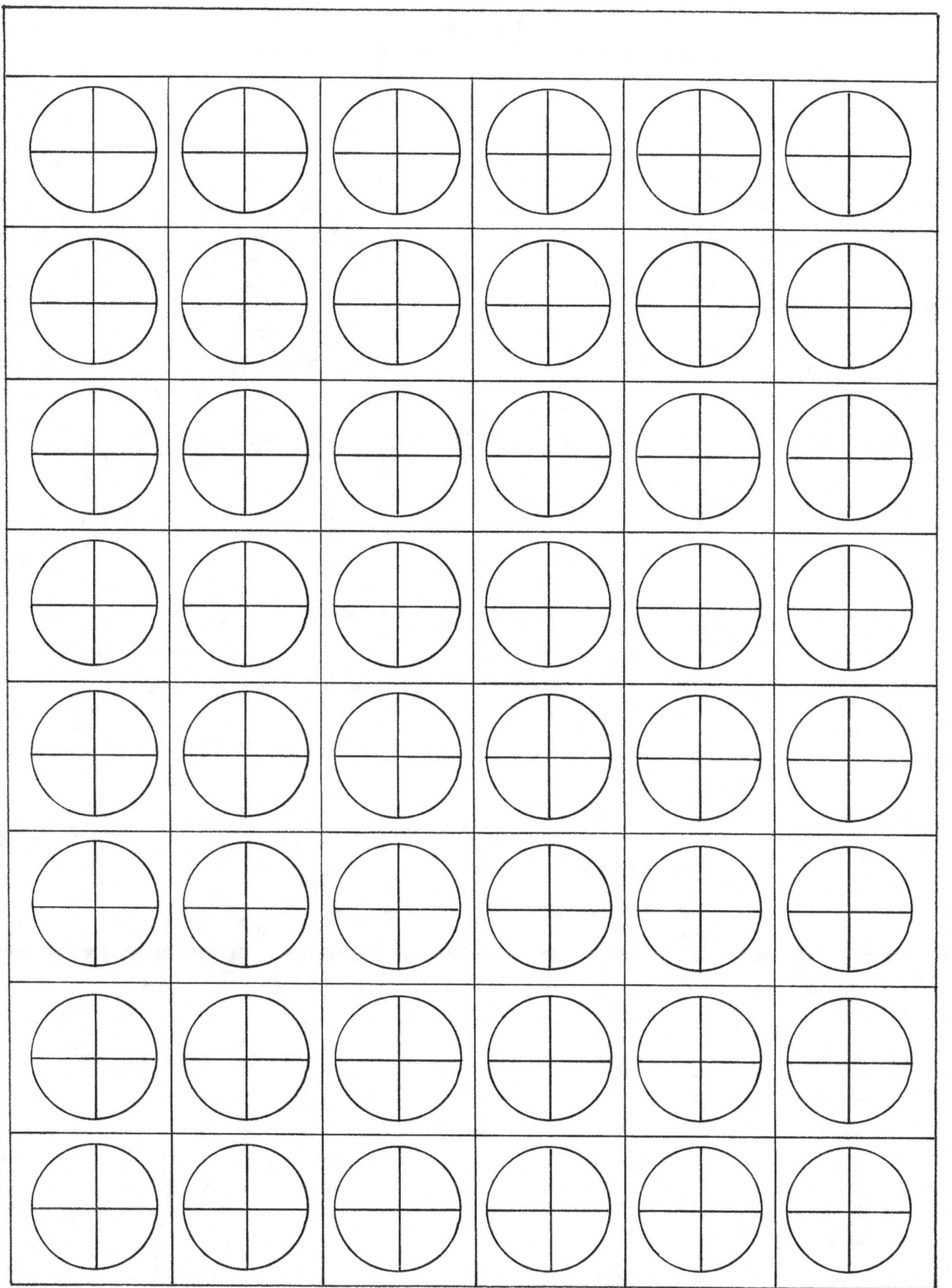

Template 2
2 Color Wheels with each 12 spaces = 24 spaces in total

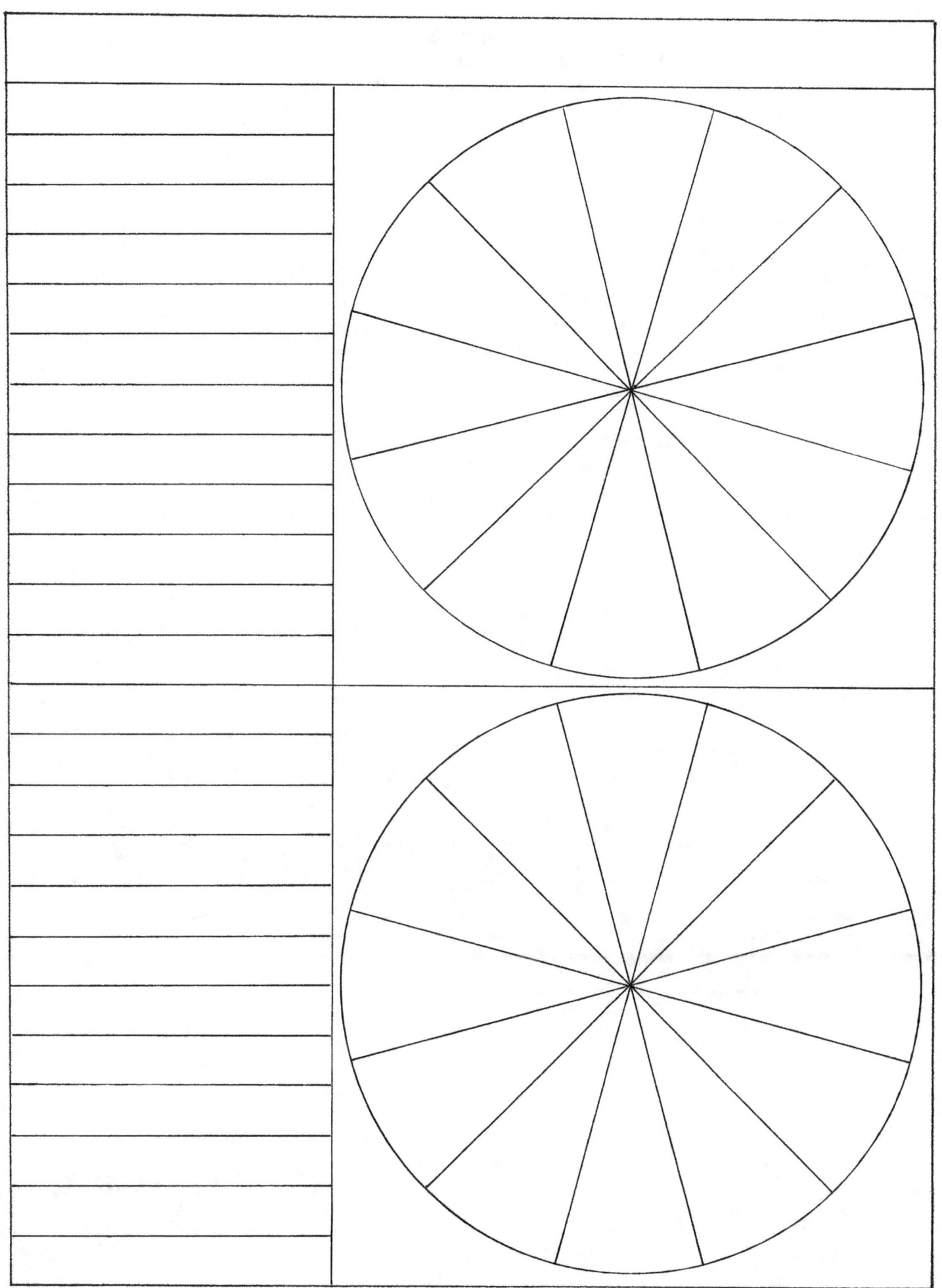

Template 3
Part 1 12 lines of 9 circles = 108 small circles
Part 2 24 lines of 9 squares = 216 squares

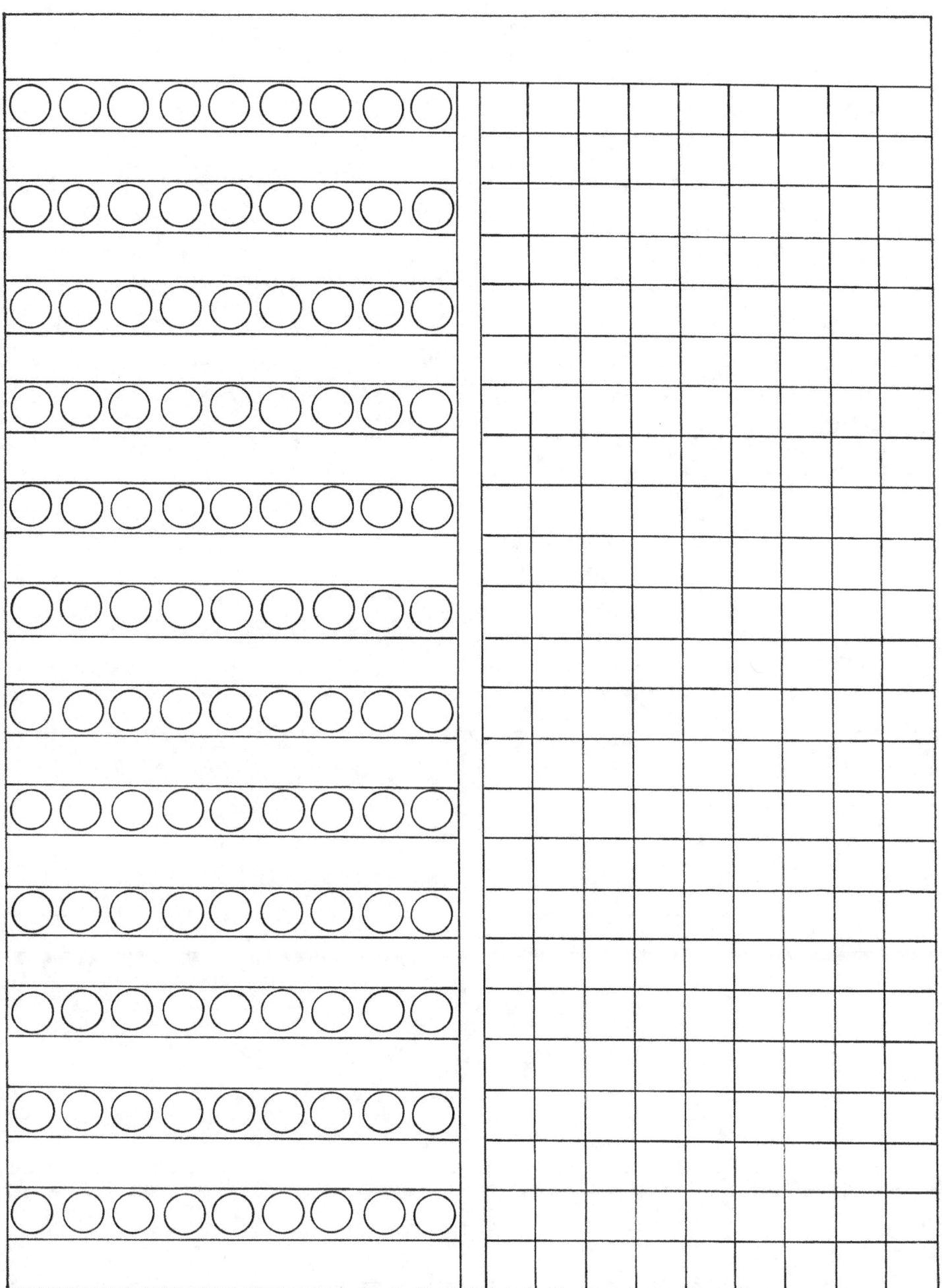

Template 4
8 lines of 37 spaces = total of 296 spaces

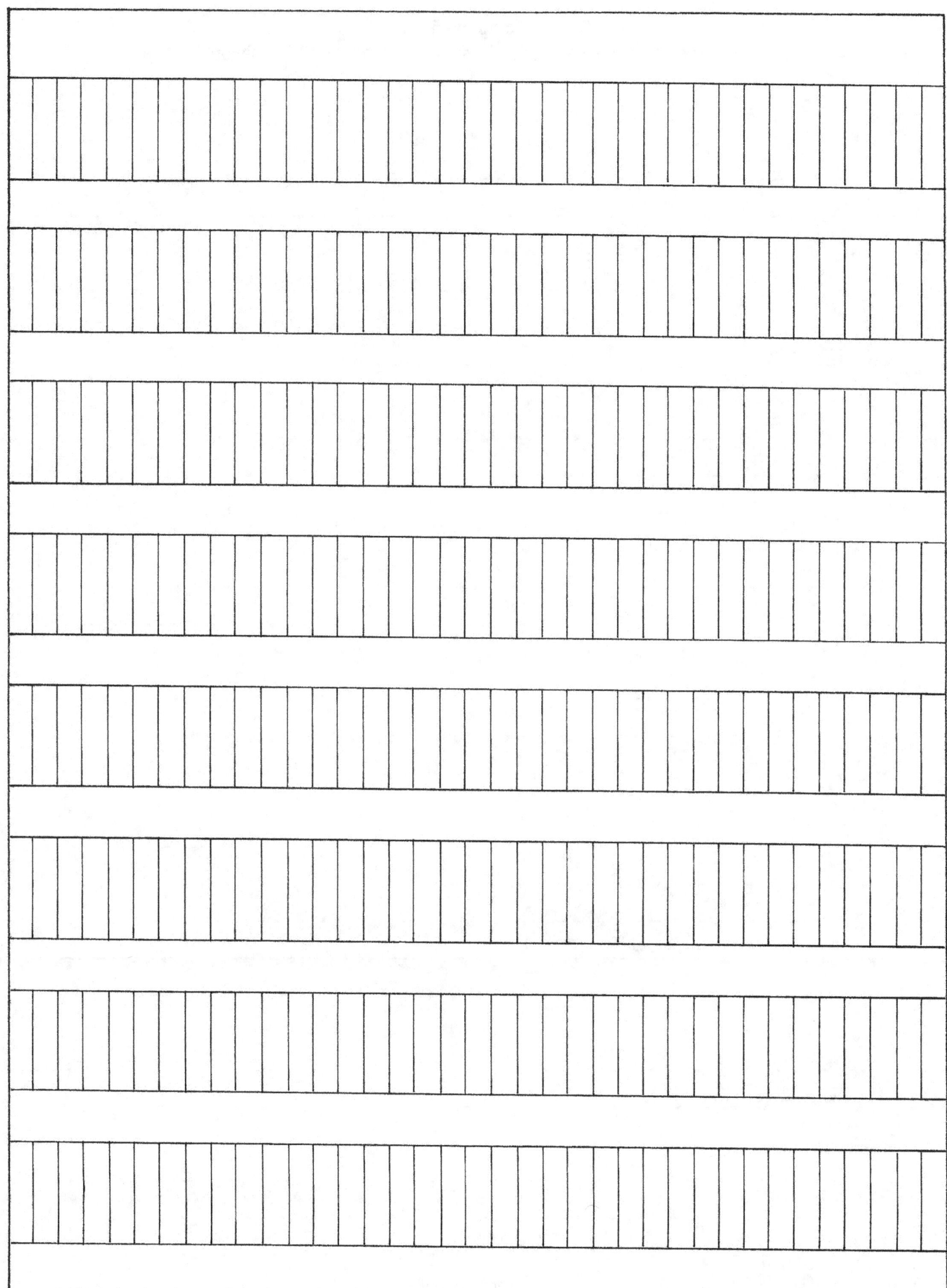

Template 5
8 half color wheel each with 18 spaces = a total of 144 spaces

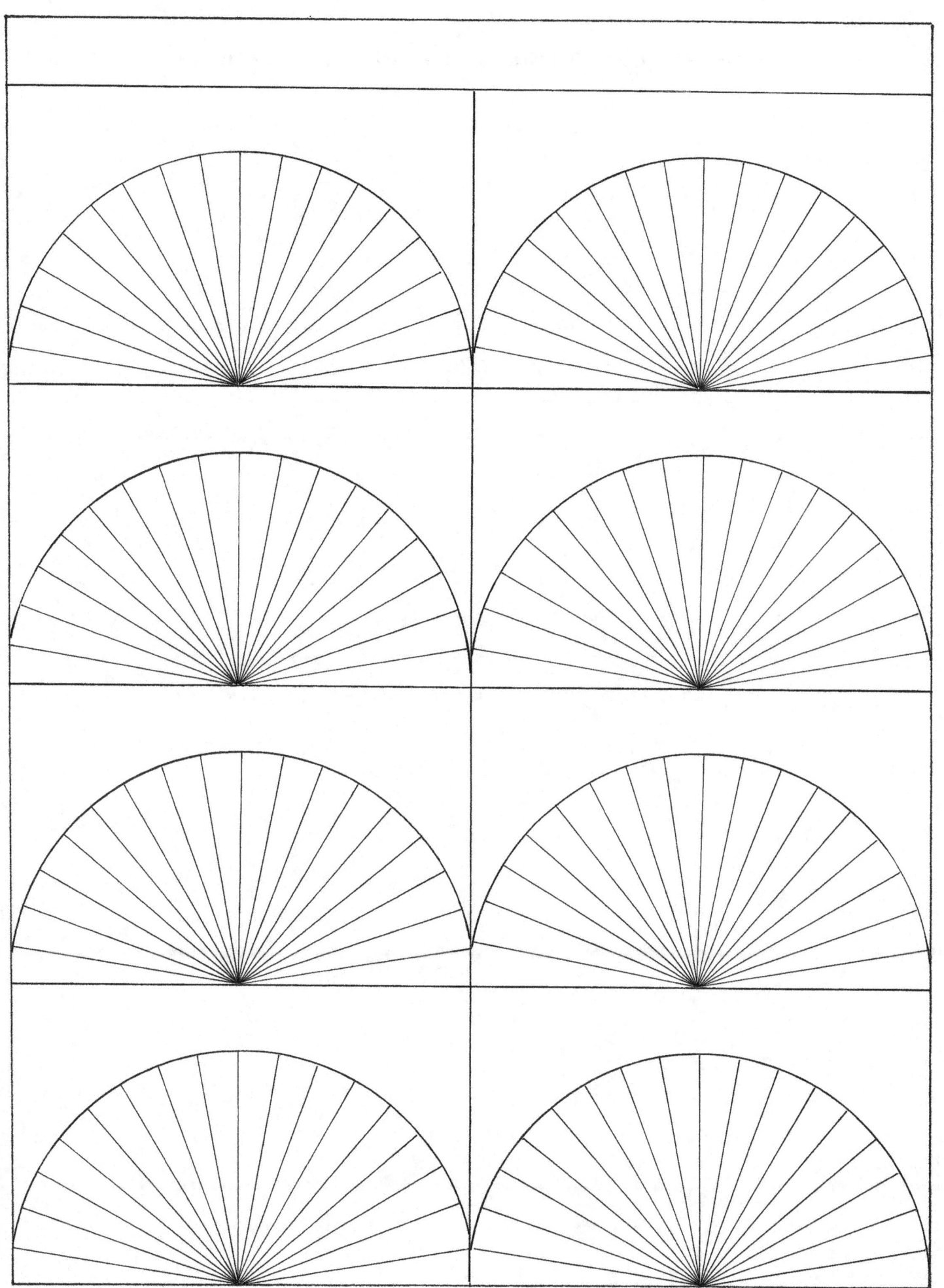

Template 6
6 rows of 8 circles = 48 circles x 8 spaces each = a total of 384 spaces

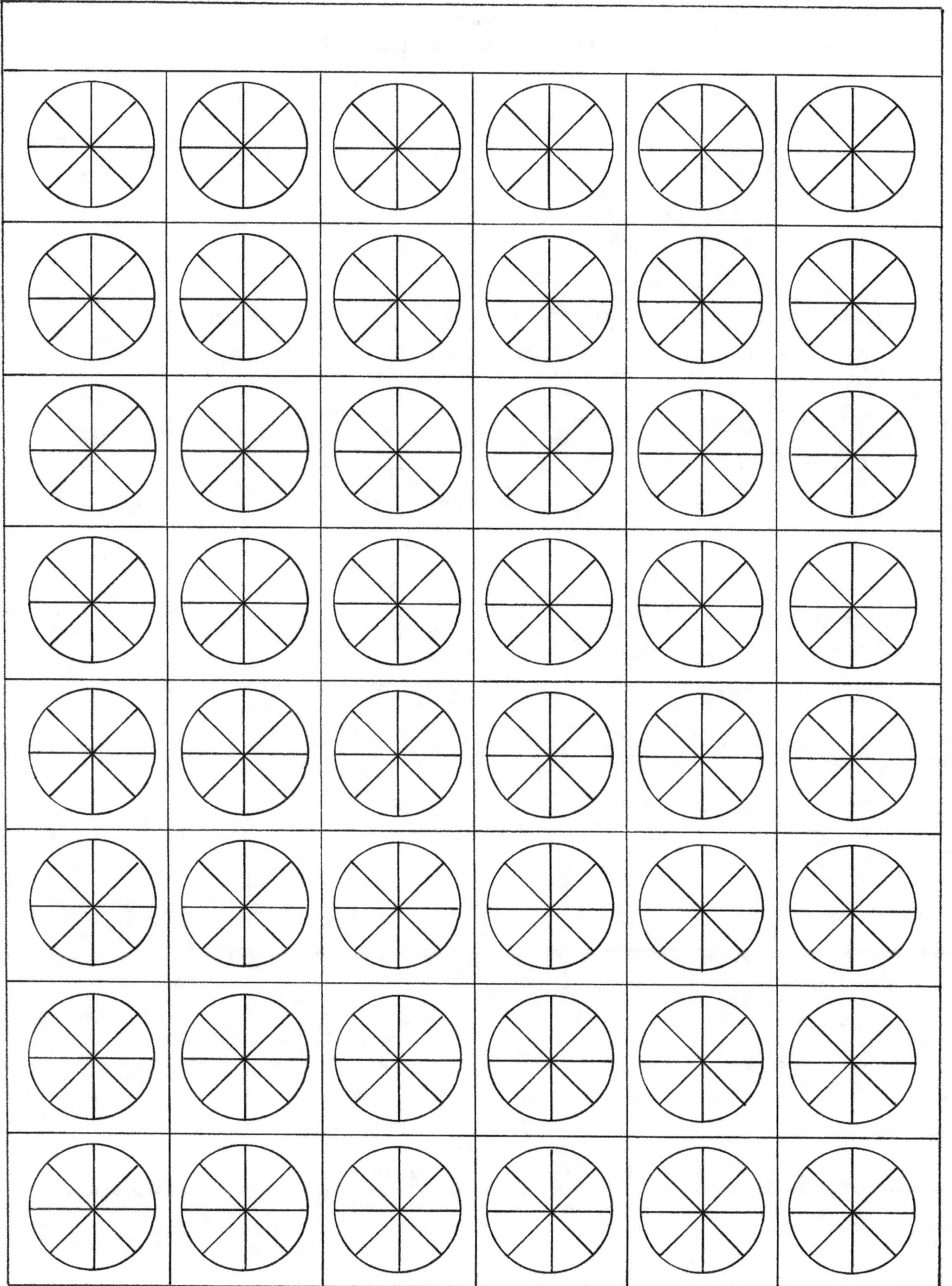

Template 7
8 lines of 24 triangular spaces = a total of 192 spaces

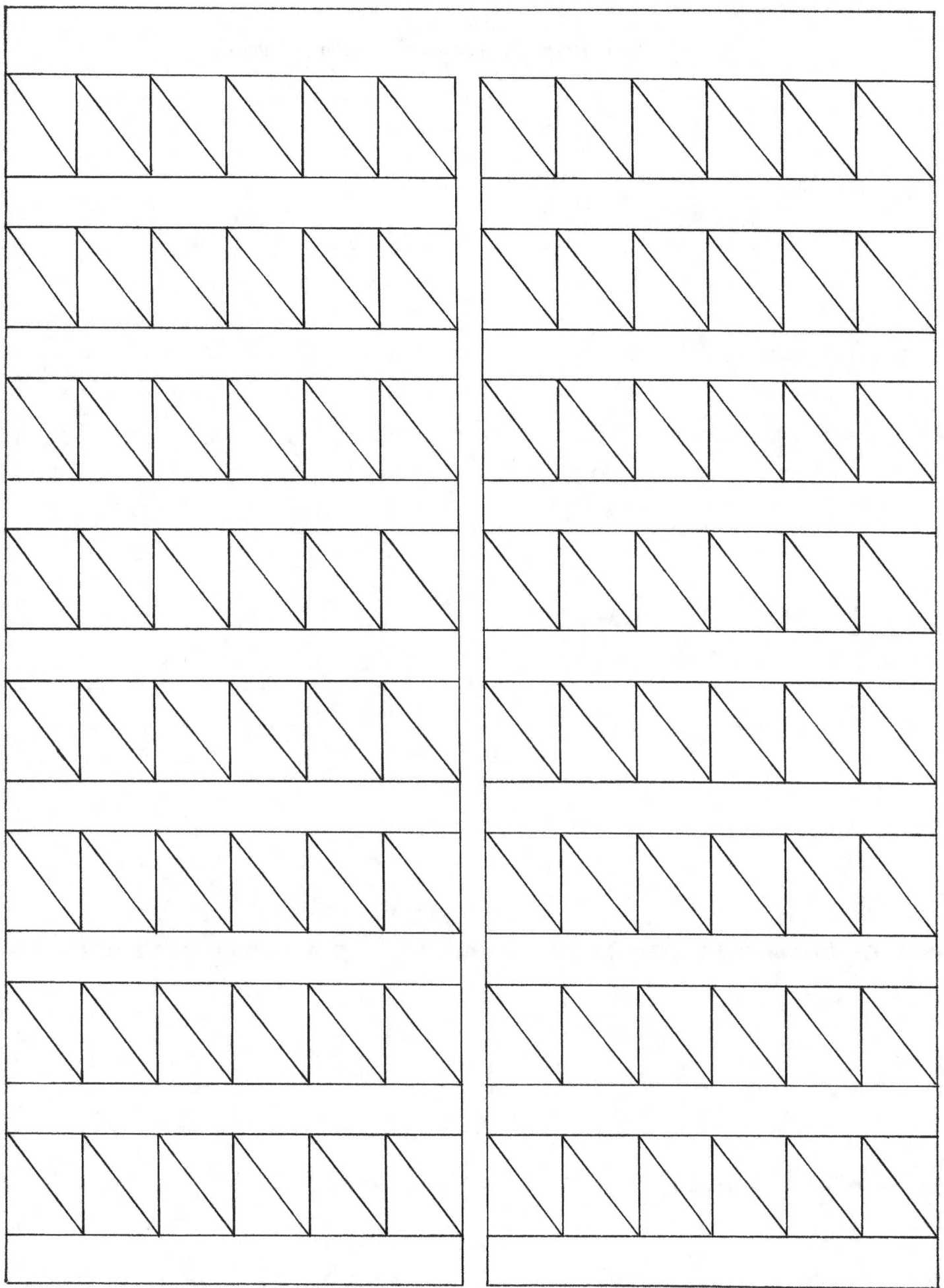

Template 8
3 rows of 2x48 spaces = 96 spaces x 3   a total of 288 spaces

Template 9
Big Color wheel 4 sections of 36 spaces = a total of 144 spaces

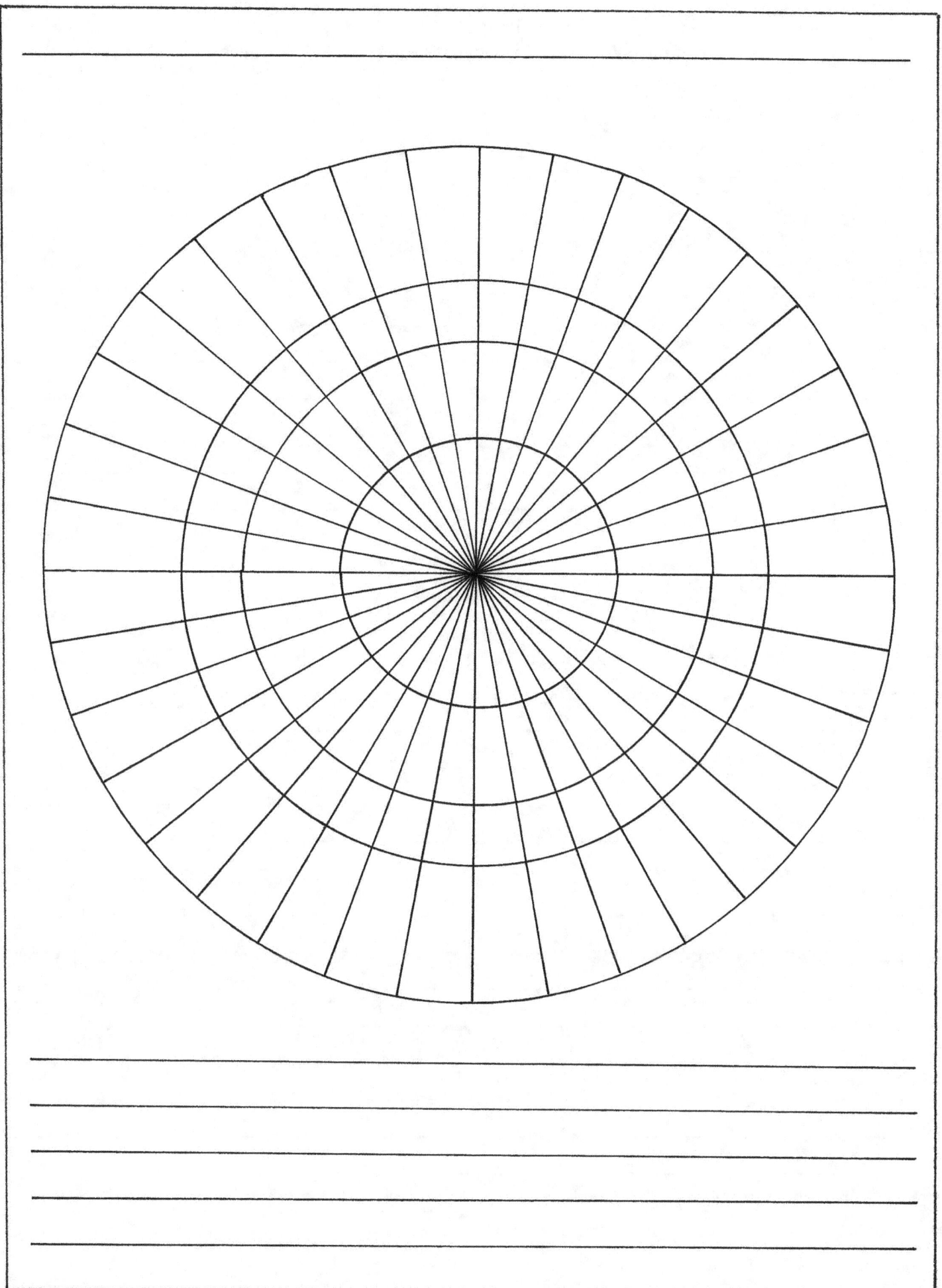

Template 10
4 half Color Wheels of 2x 18 spaces = a total of 144 spaces

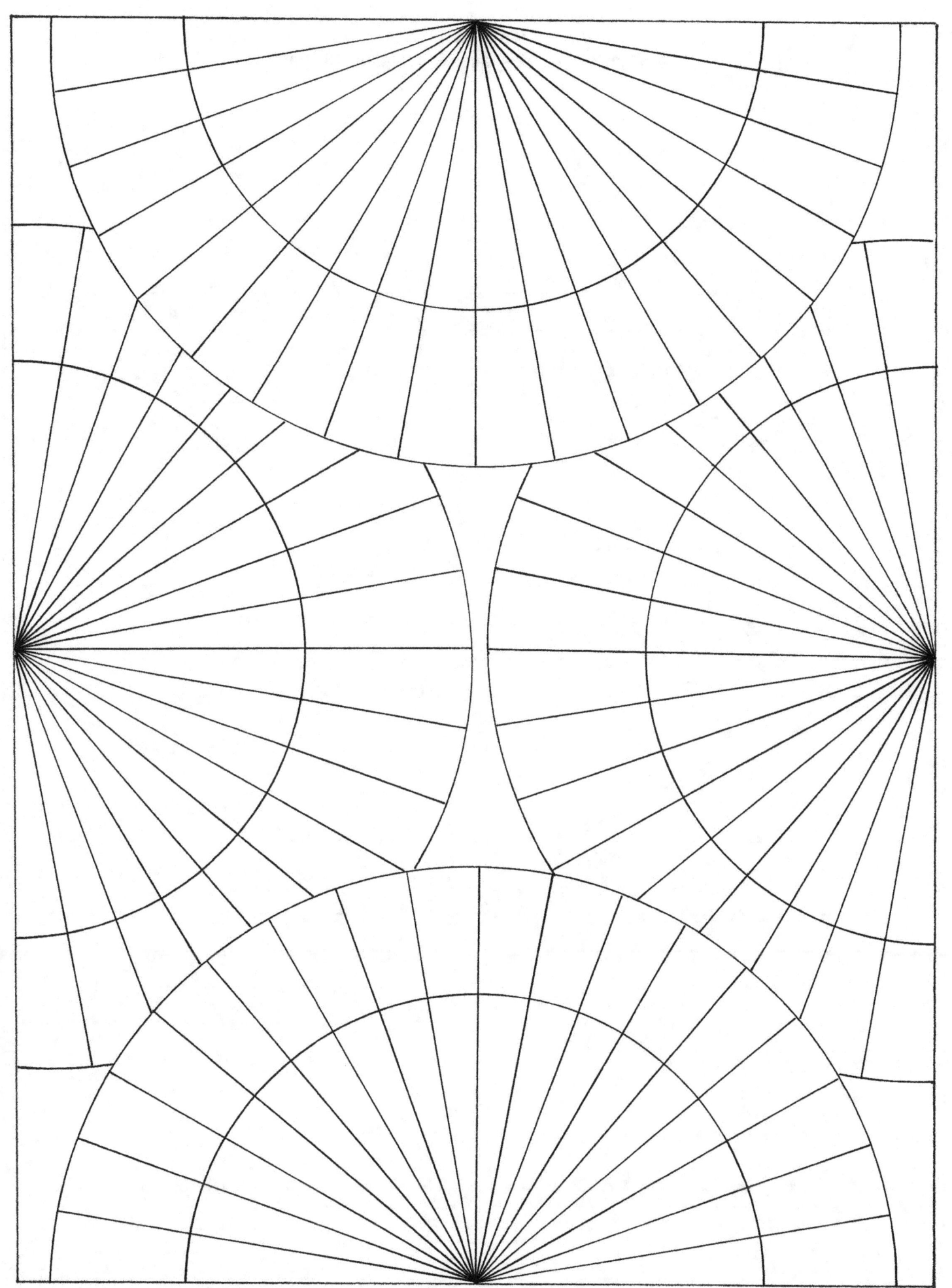

Template 11
Color Wheels of 4x 12 spaces = a total of 48 spaces

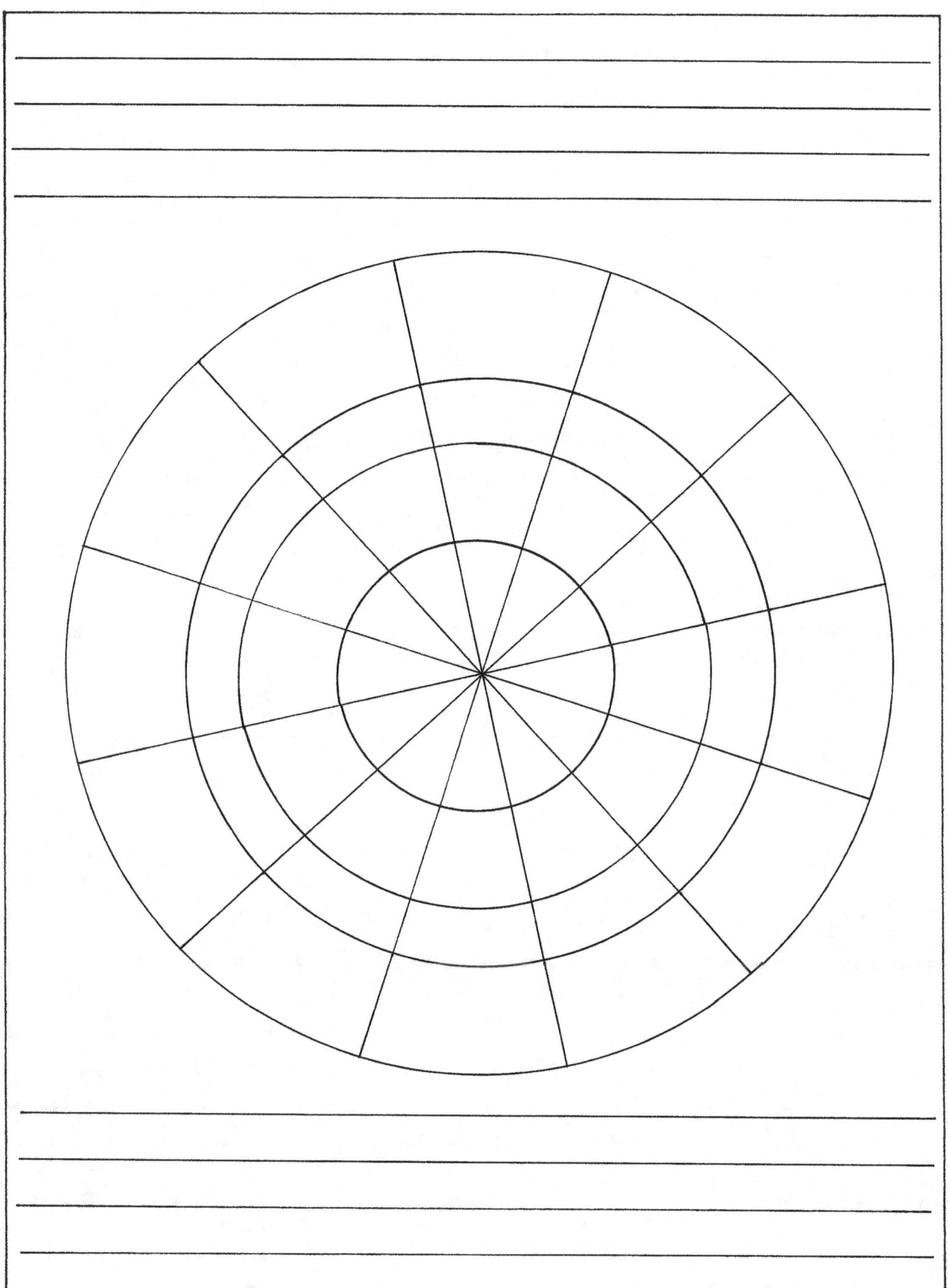

Template 12
24 circles of 3 spaces = a total of 72 spaces

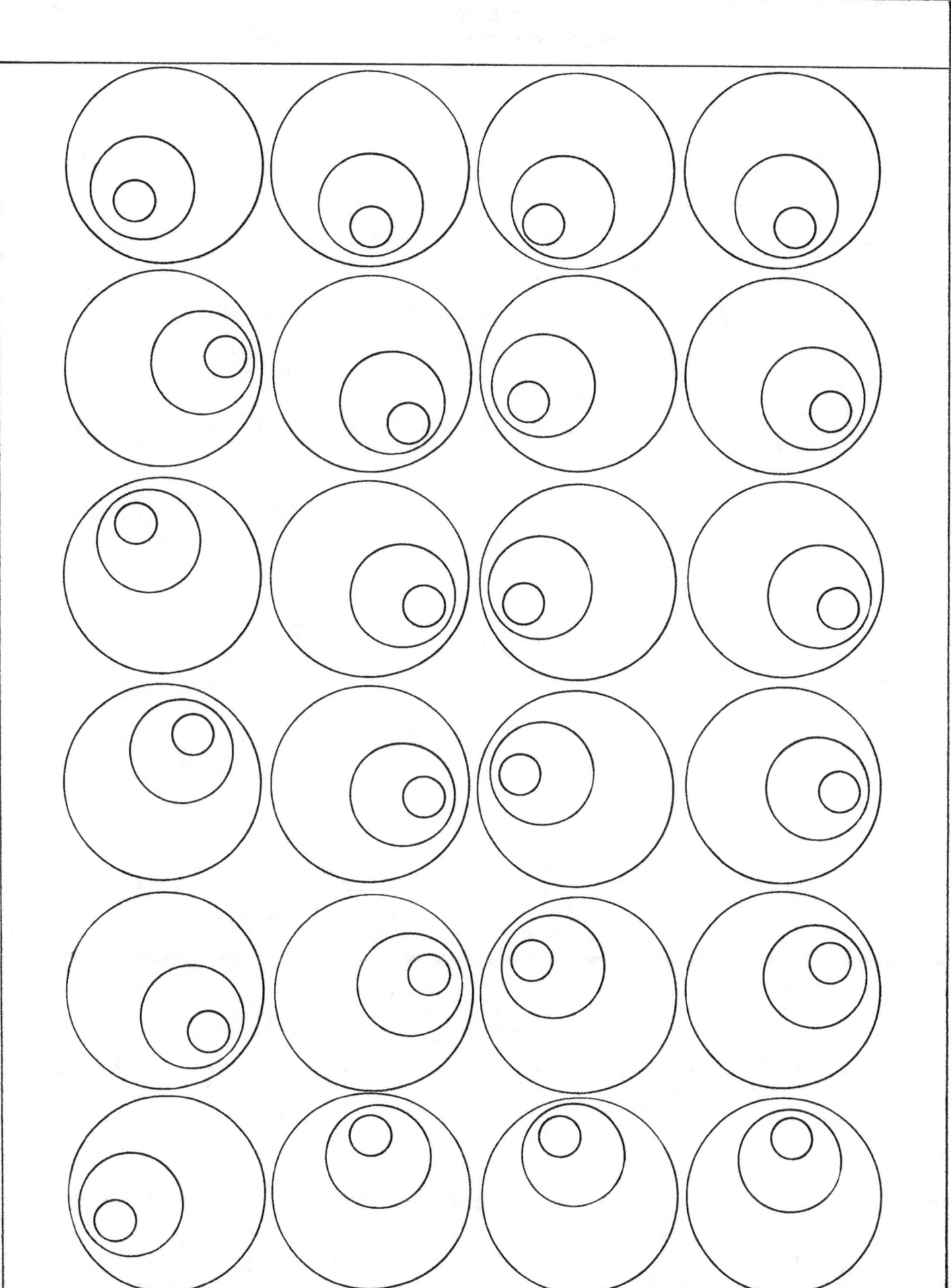

Template 13
2 Color Wheels of 4x12 spaces = a total of 96 spaces

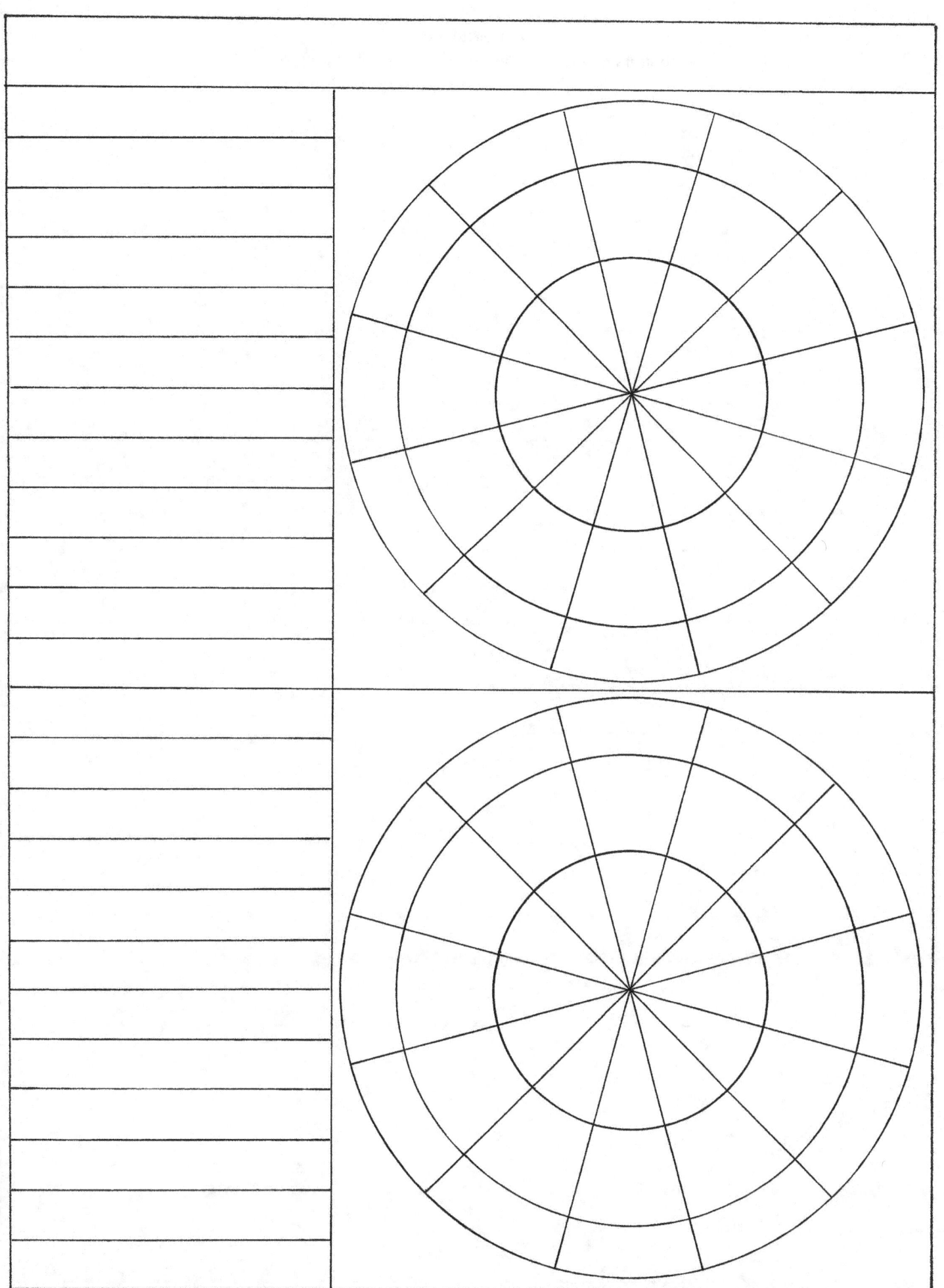

Template 14
8 lines of 2x37 spaces = a total of 592 spaces

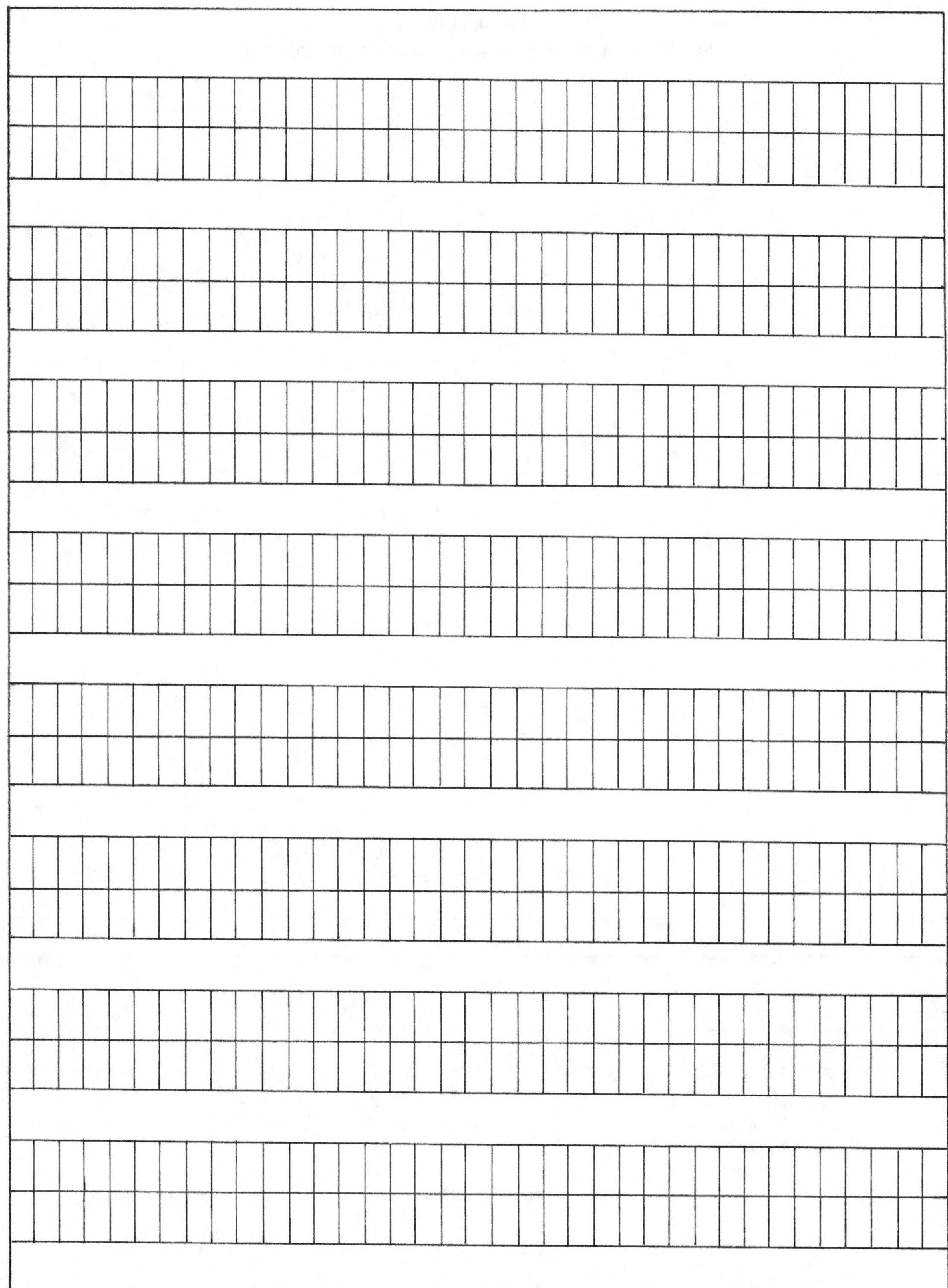

Template 15
8 half Color Wheels of 2x 18 spaces = a total of 288 spaces

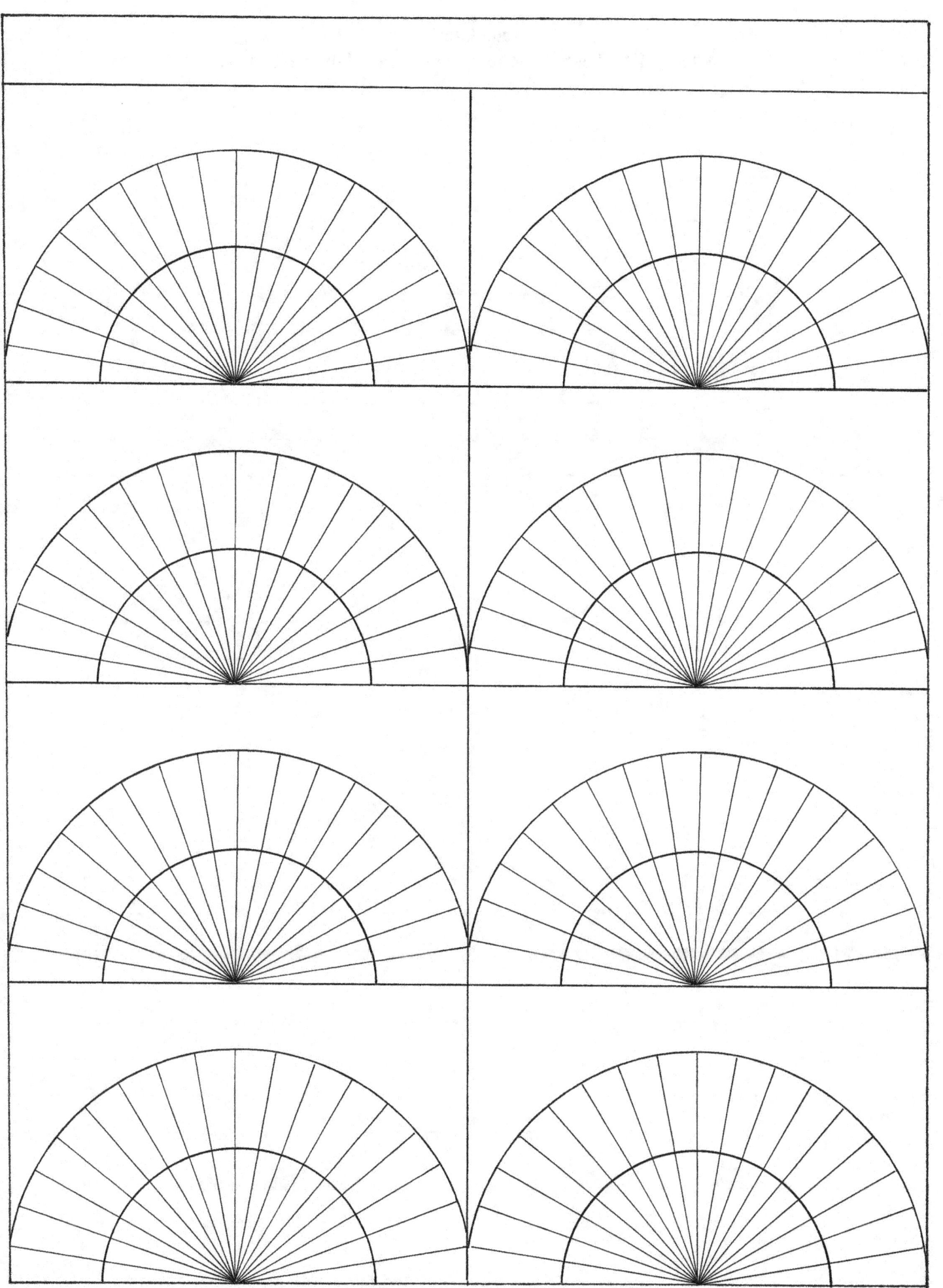

Template 16
4 half Color Wheels of 3x 18 spaces = a total of 216 spaces

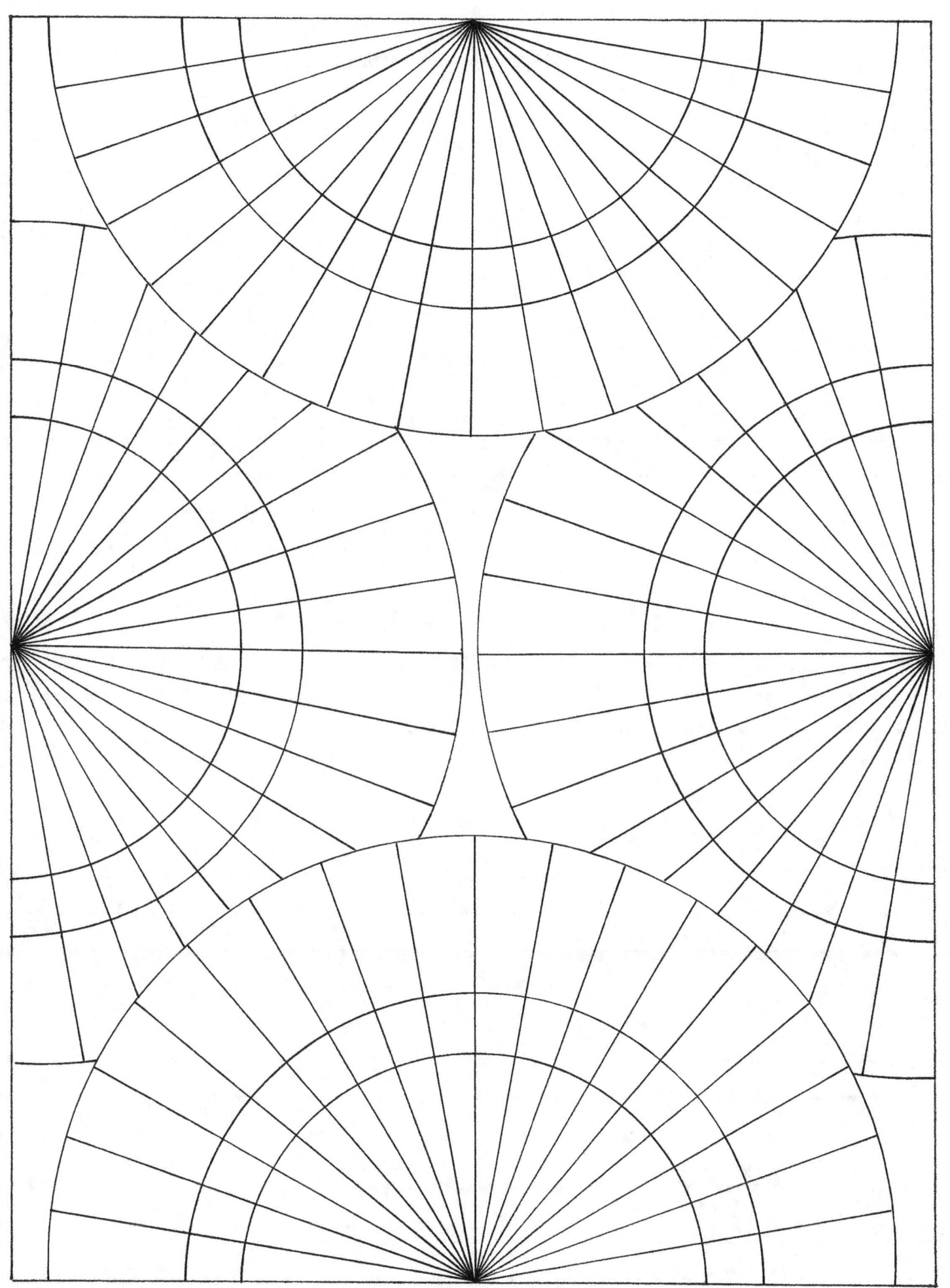

Template 17
3 rows of 4x48 spaces = a total of 576 spaces

Template 18
8 lines of 4x37 spaces = a total of 1184 spaces

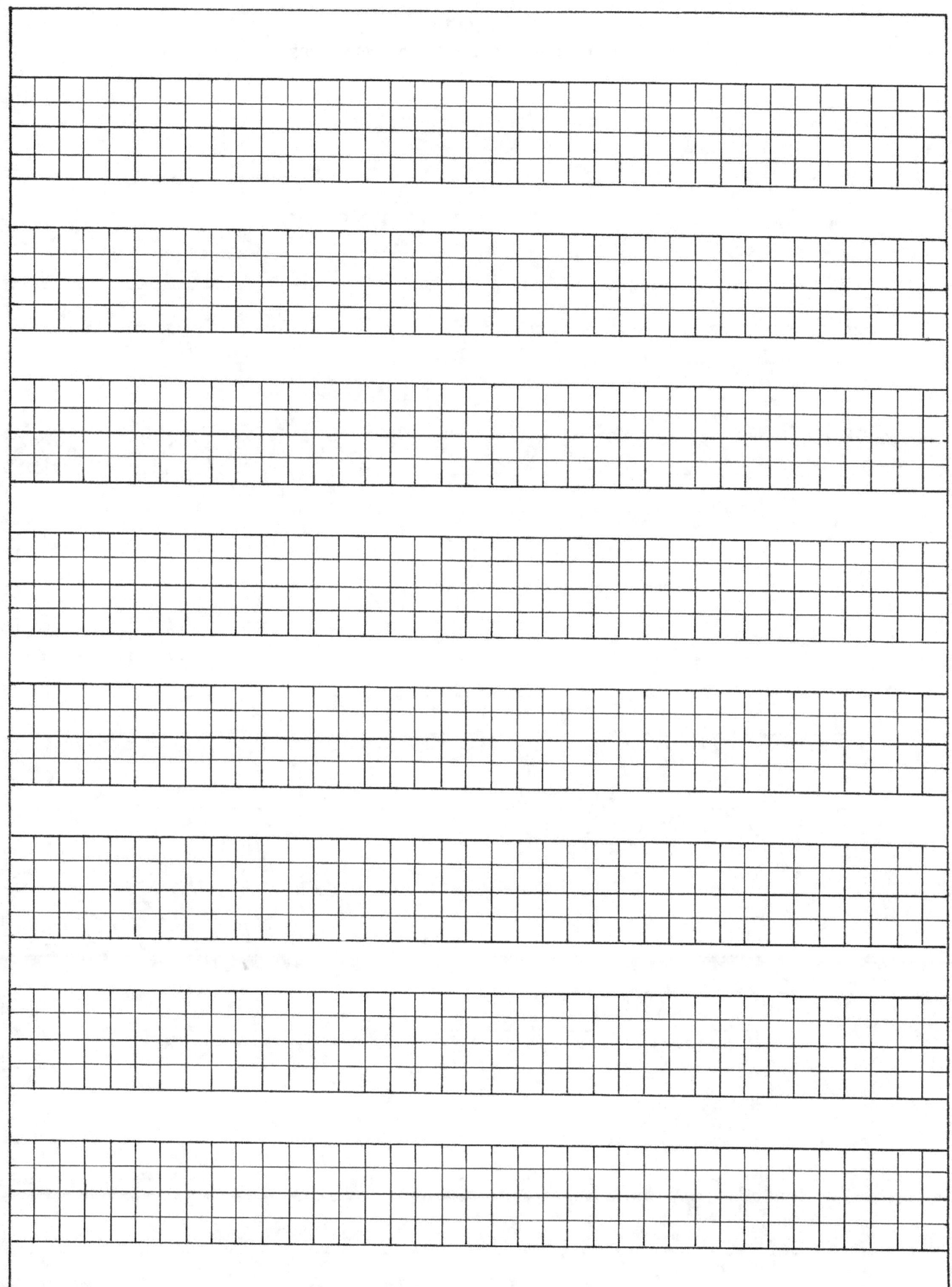

Template 19
8 lines of 12x4 spaces = a total of 384 spaces

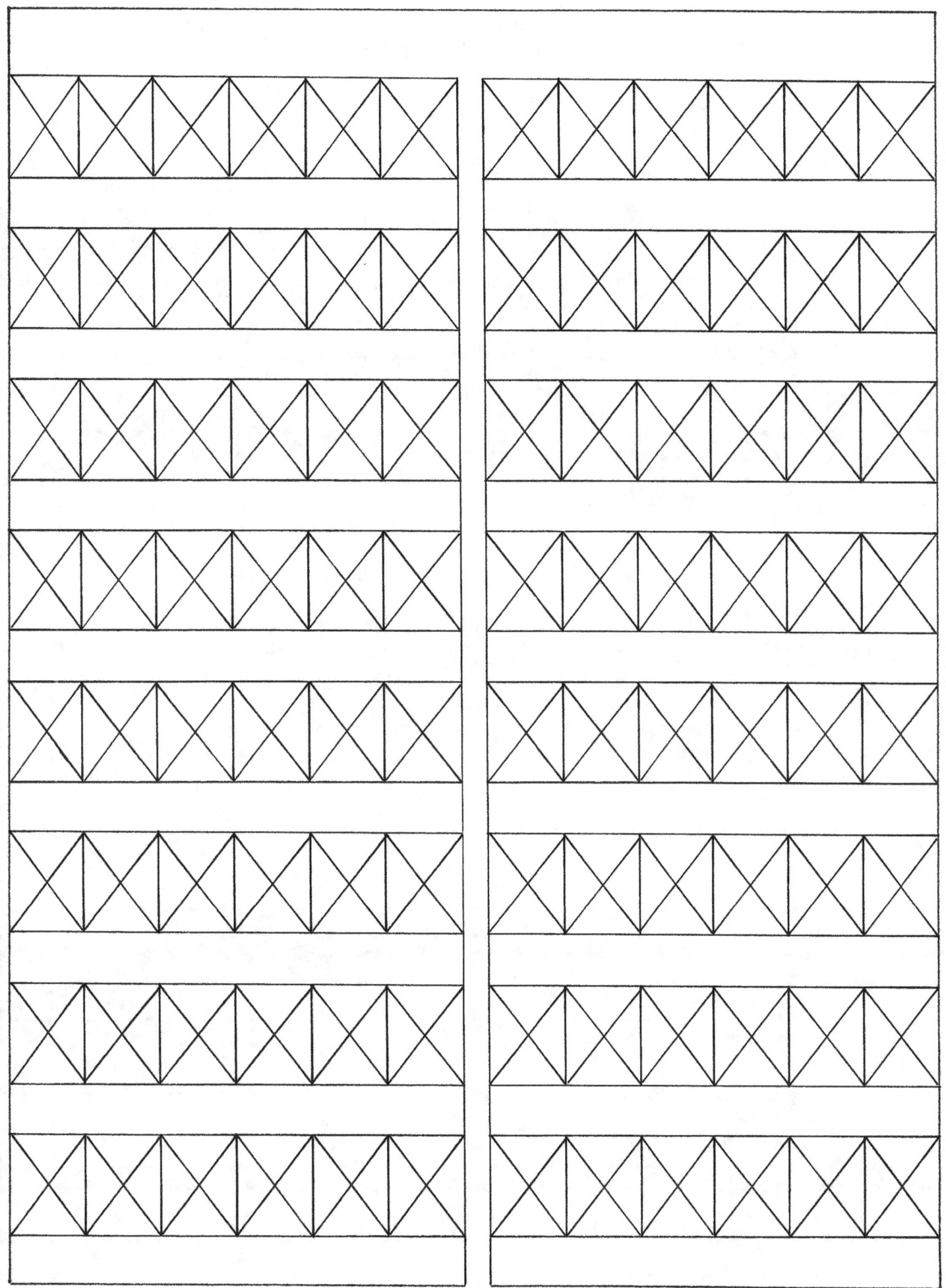

Template 20
Color Wheel with 36 spaces

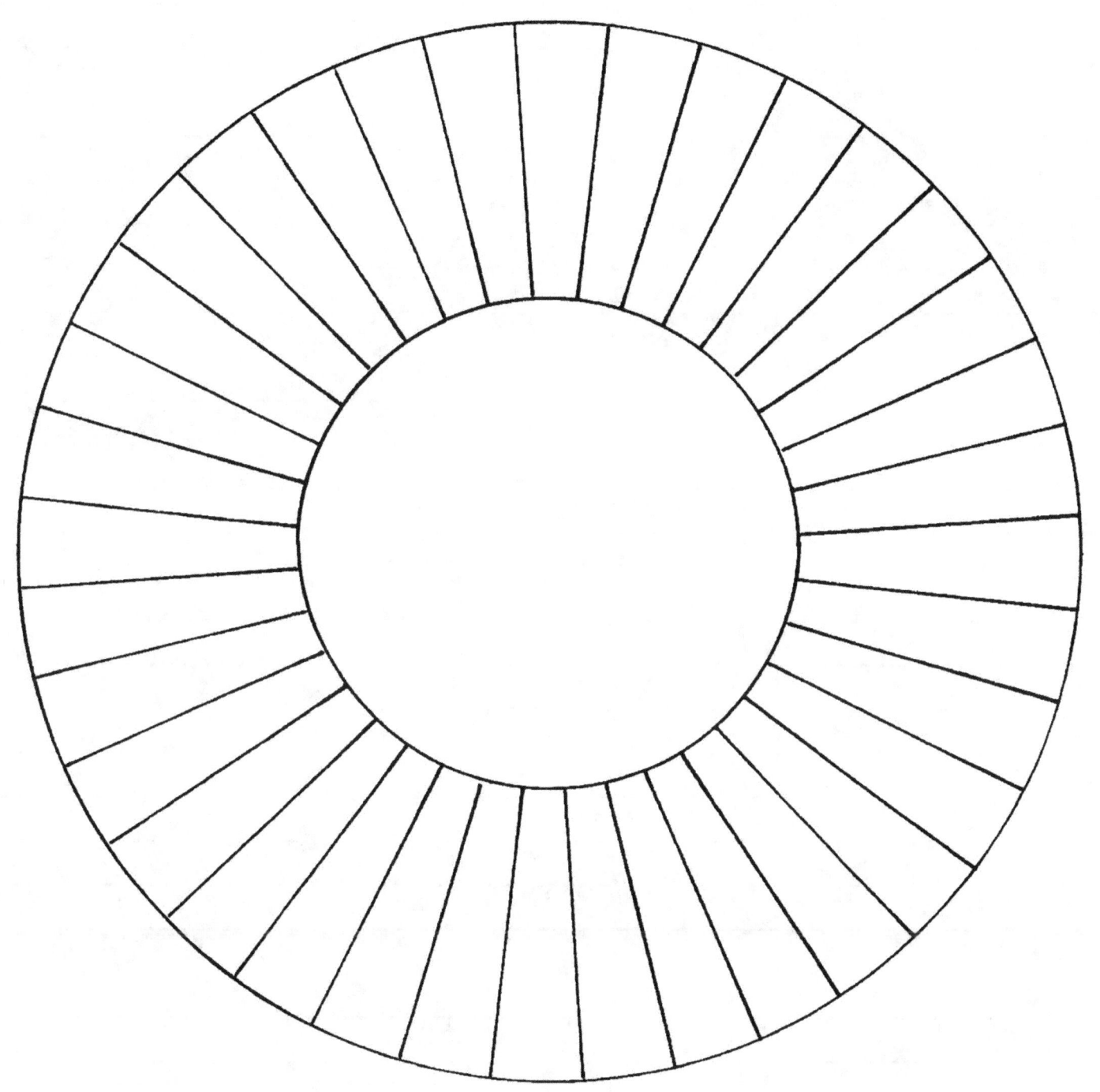

Template 21
Circle explosion of 16x 7 circles = 112 circles

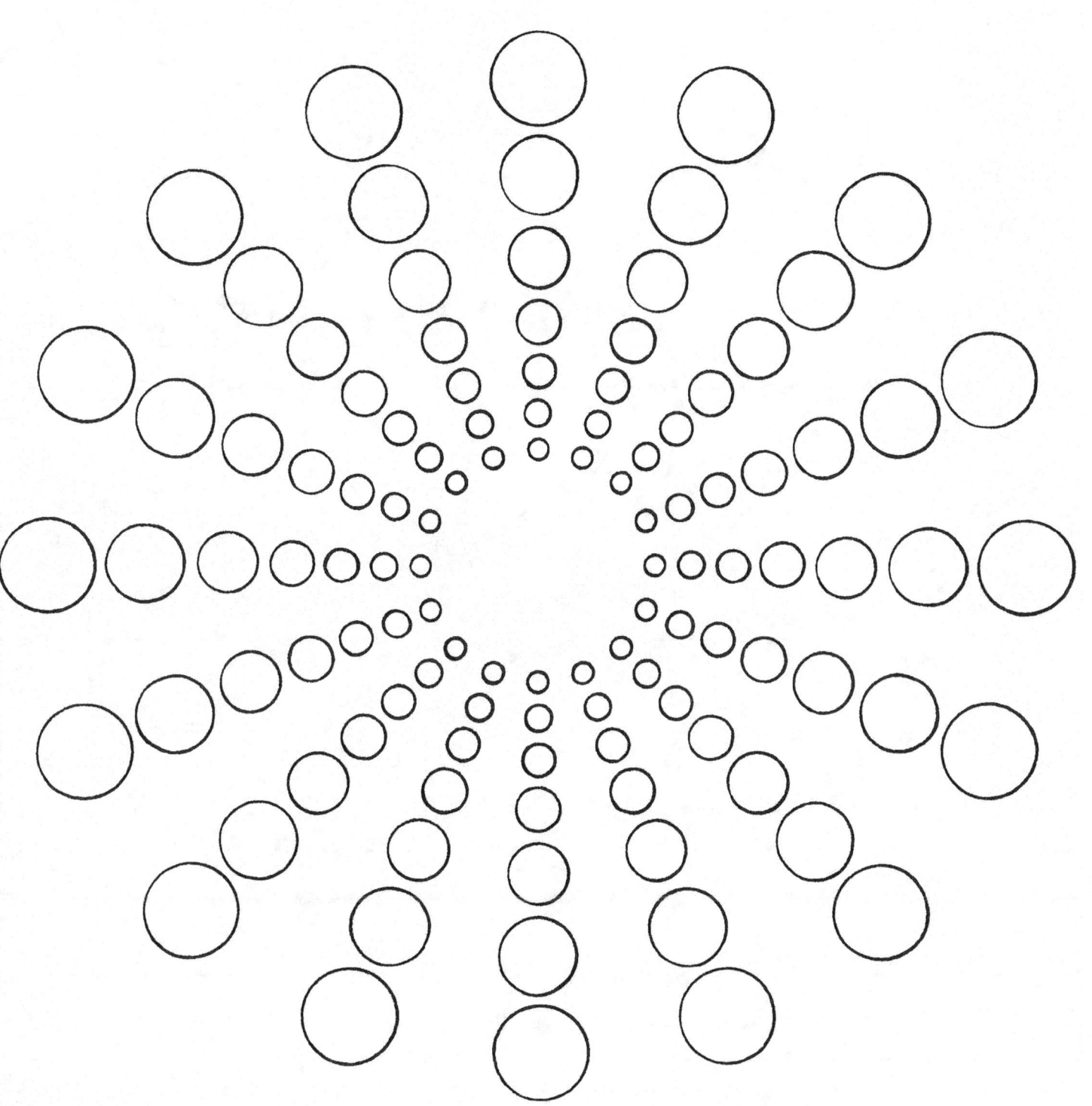

Template 22
Color flowe 16x9 spaces = a total of 144 spaces

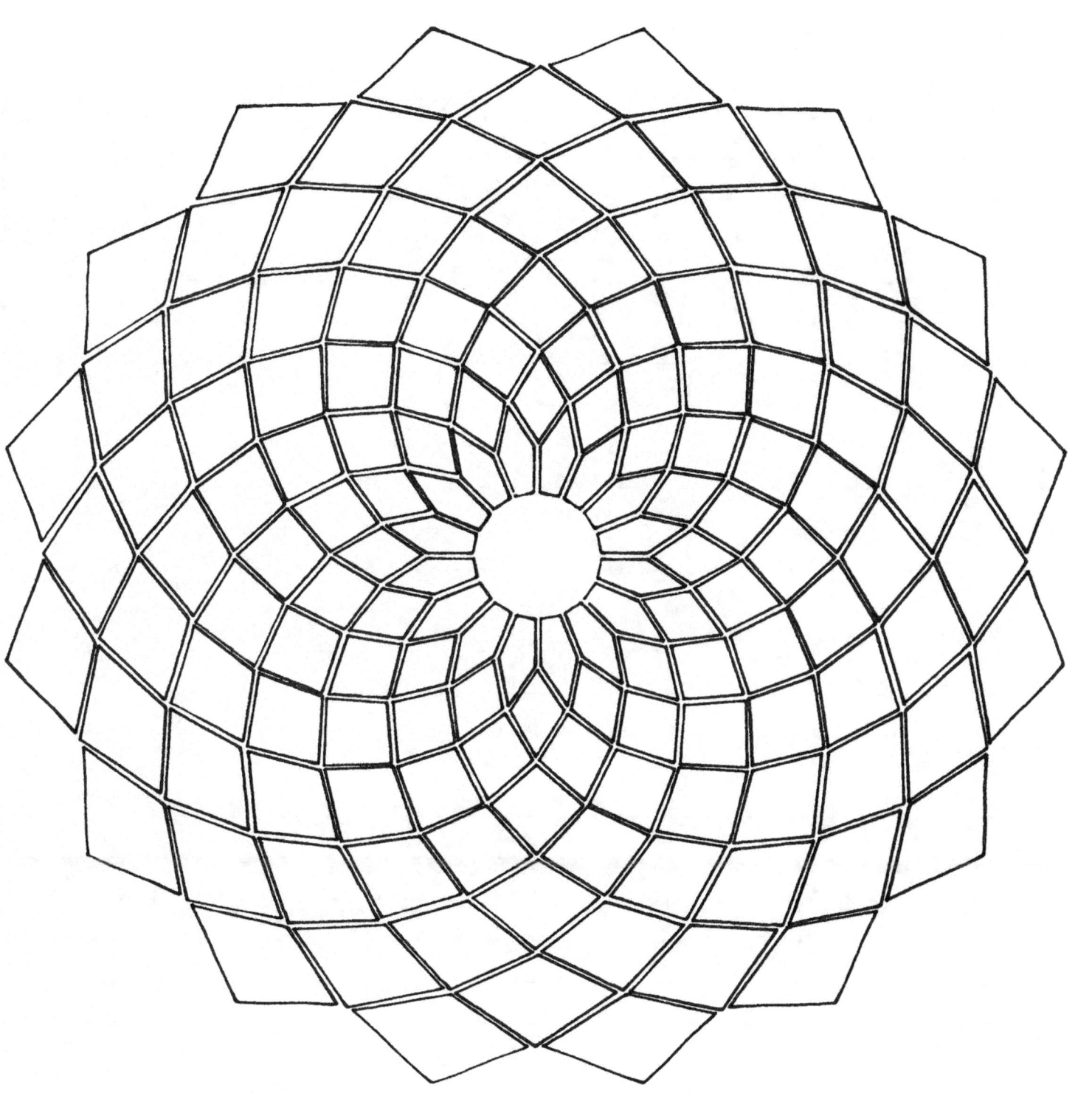

Template 23
1 color wheel of 6x 36 spaces = 216 spaces
4 quarter color wheels of 6 x 9 spaces = 216 spaces
A grand total of 432 spaces

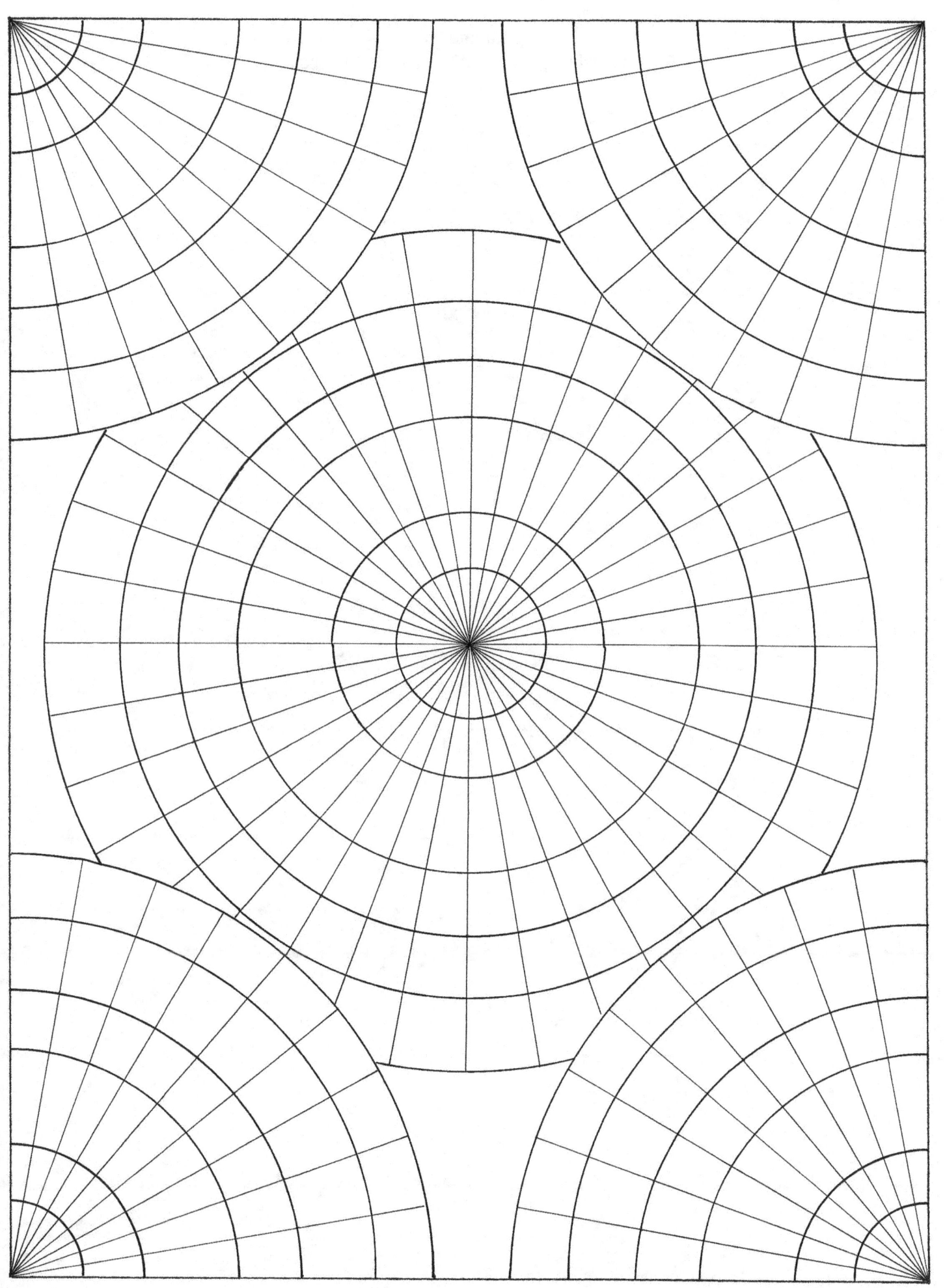

Template 24
Great wheel of colors 5x 32 spaces = 160 spaces

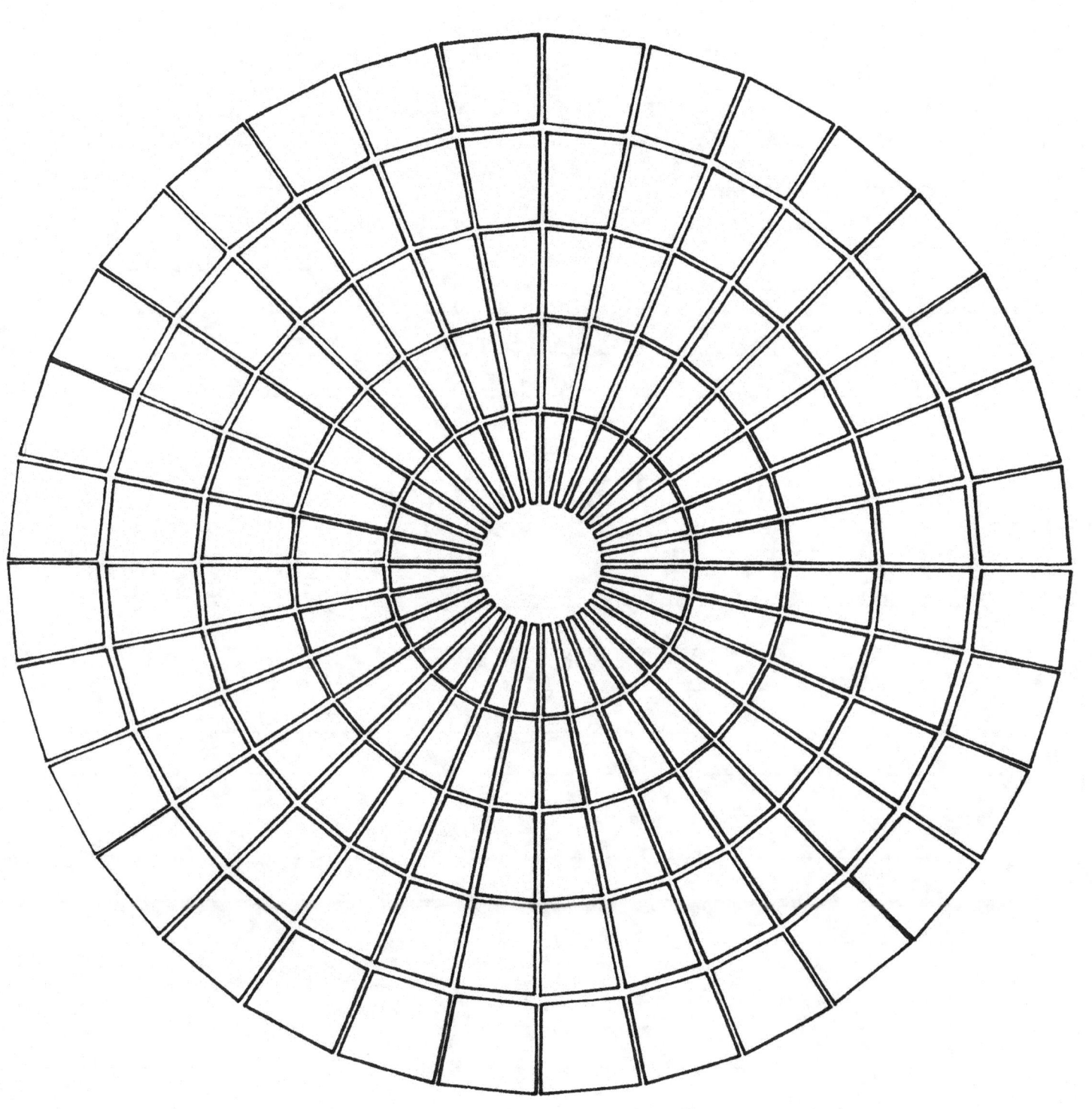

Template 25
8 lines of 12 spaces = a total of 96 spaces

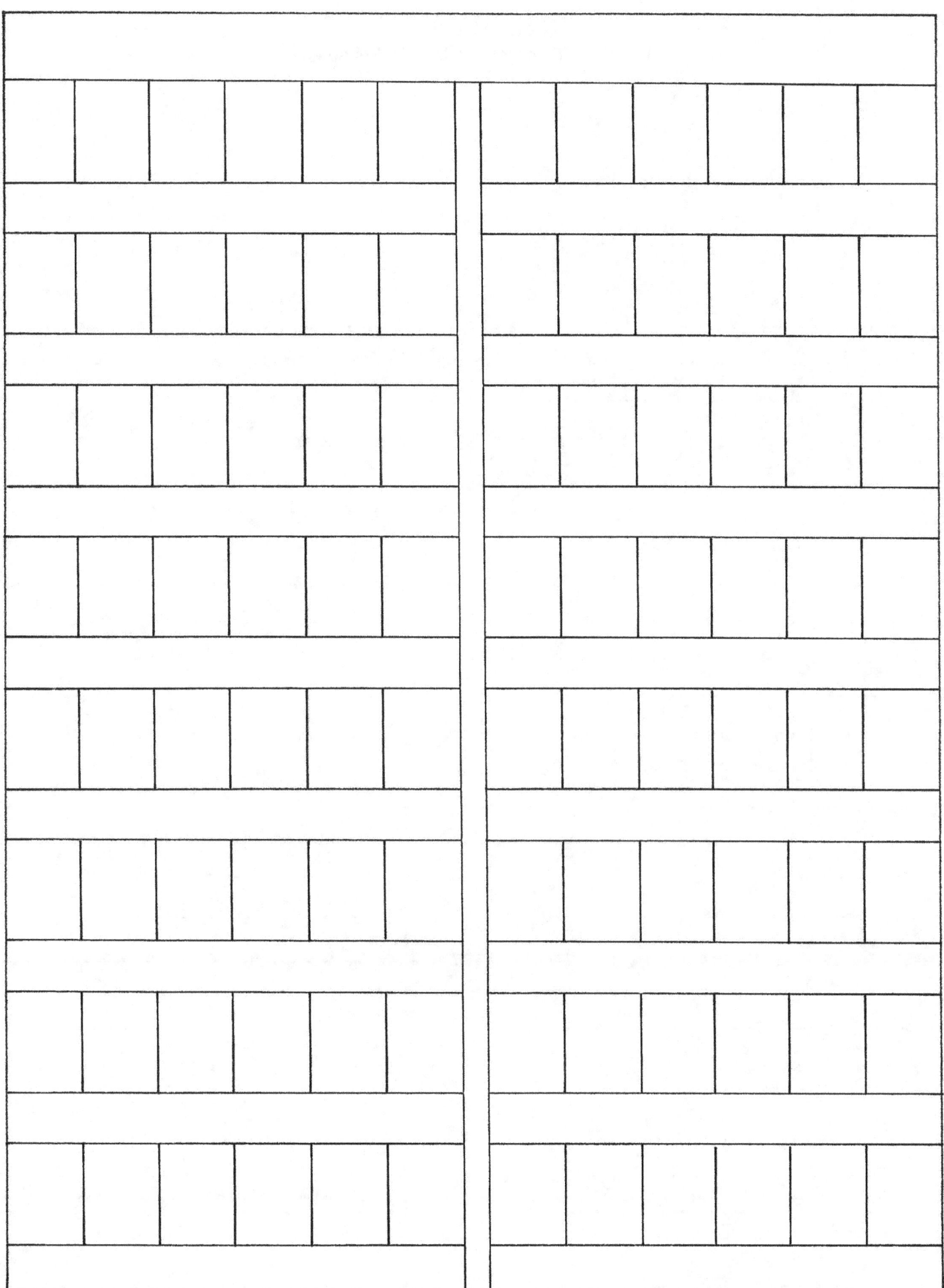

Template 26
3 rows of 48 spaces = a total of 144 spaces

Template 27
Big Color wheel of 36 spaces

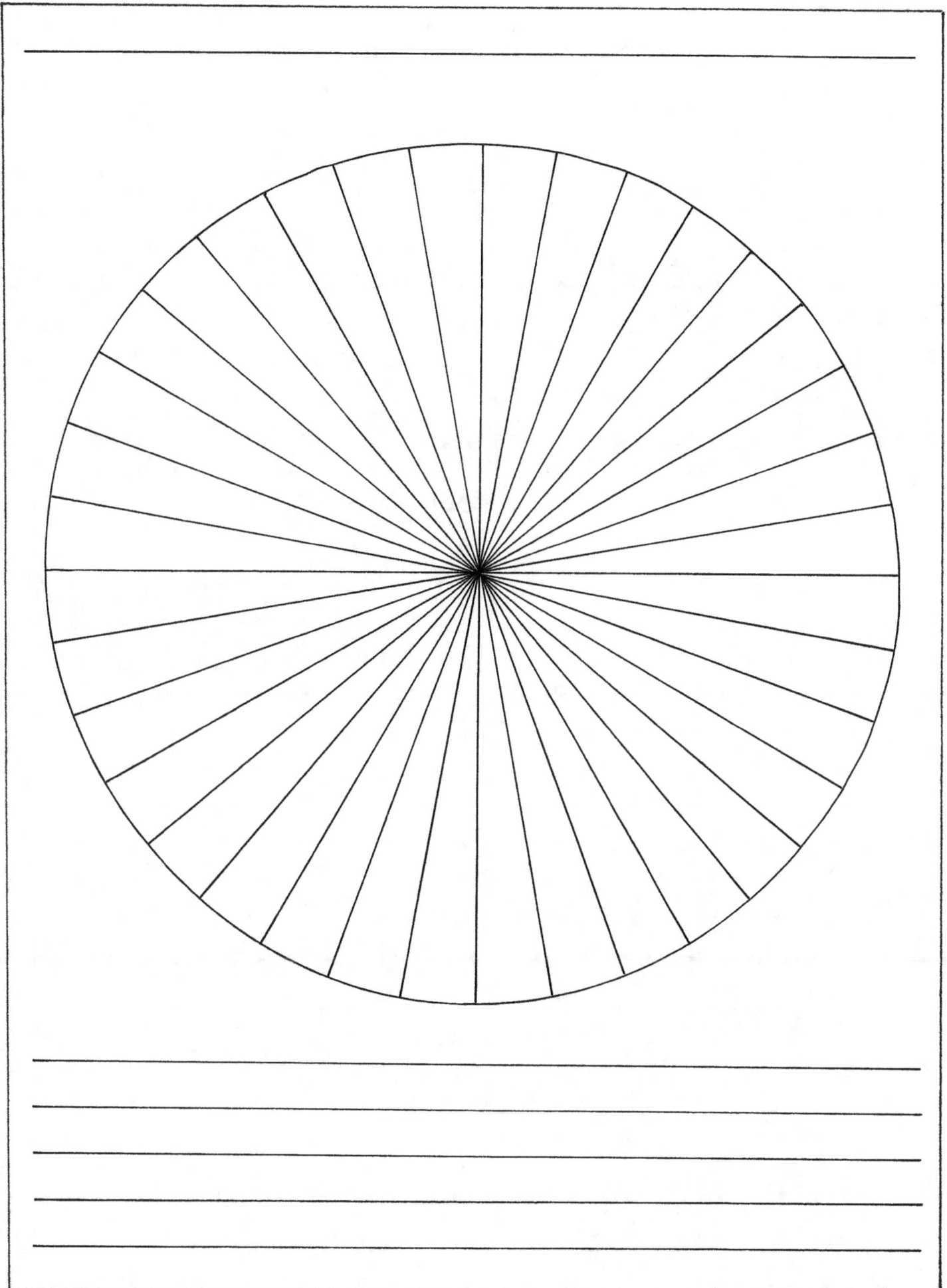

Template 28
4 half color wheels of 18 spaces = a total of 72 spaces

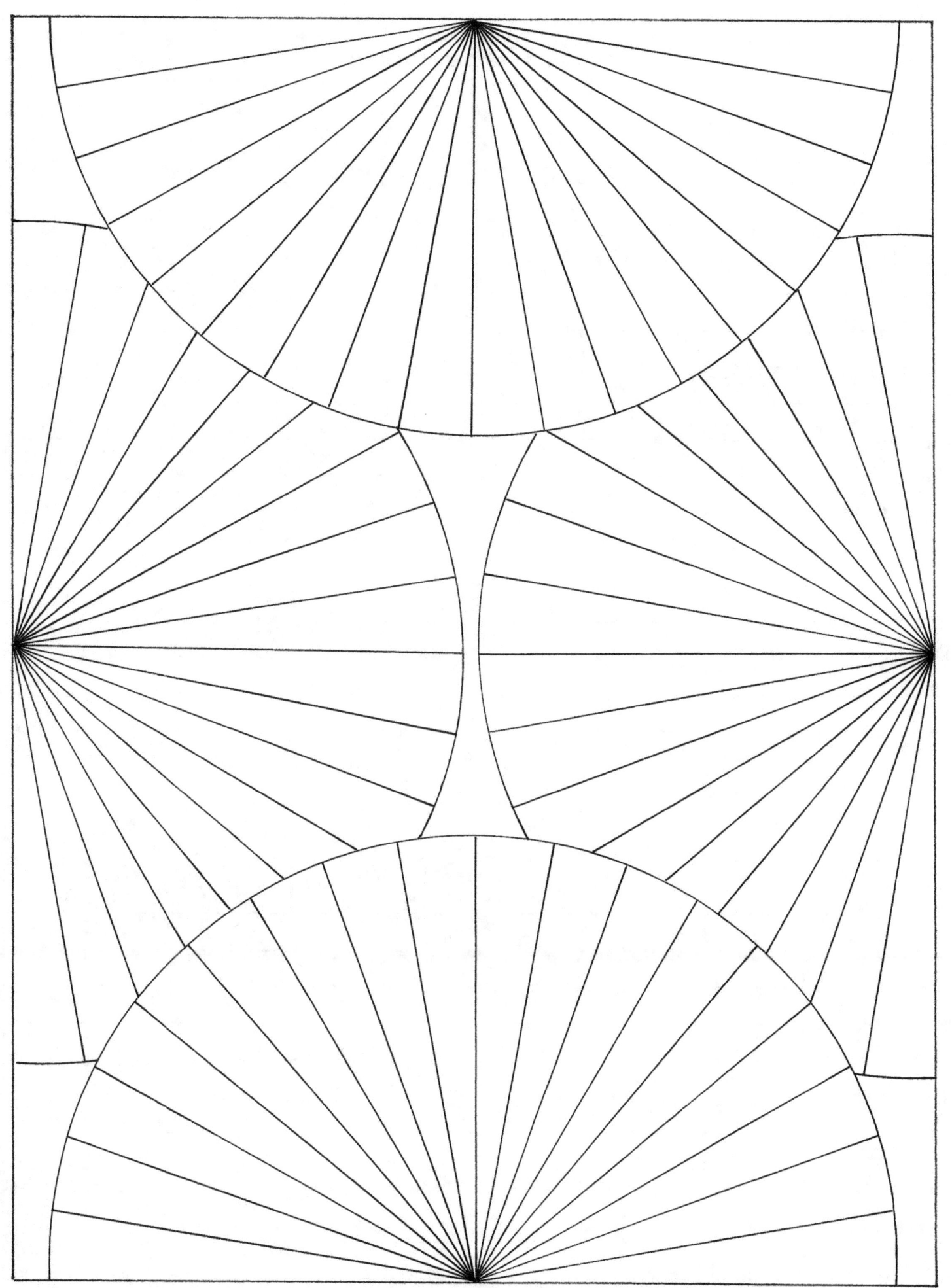

Template 29
10 lines of 9 circles = 90 circles

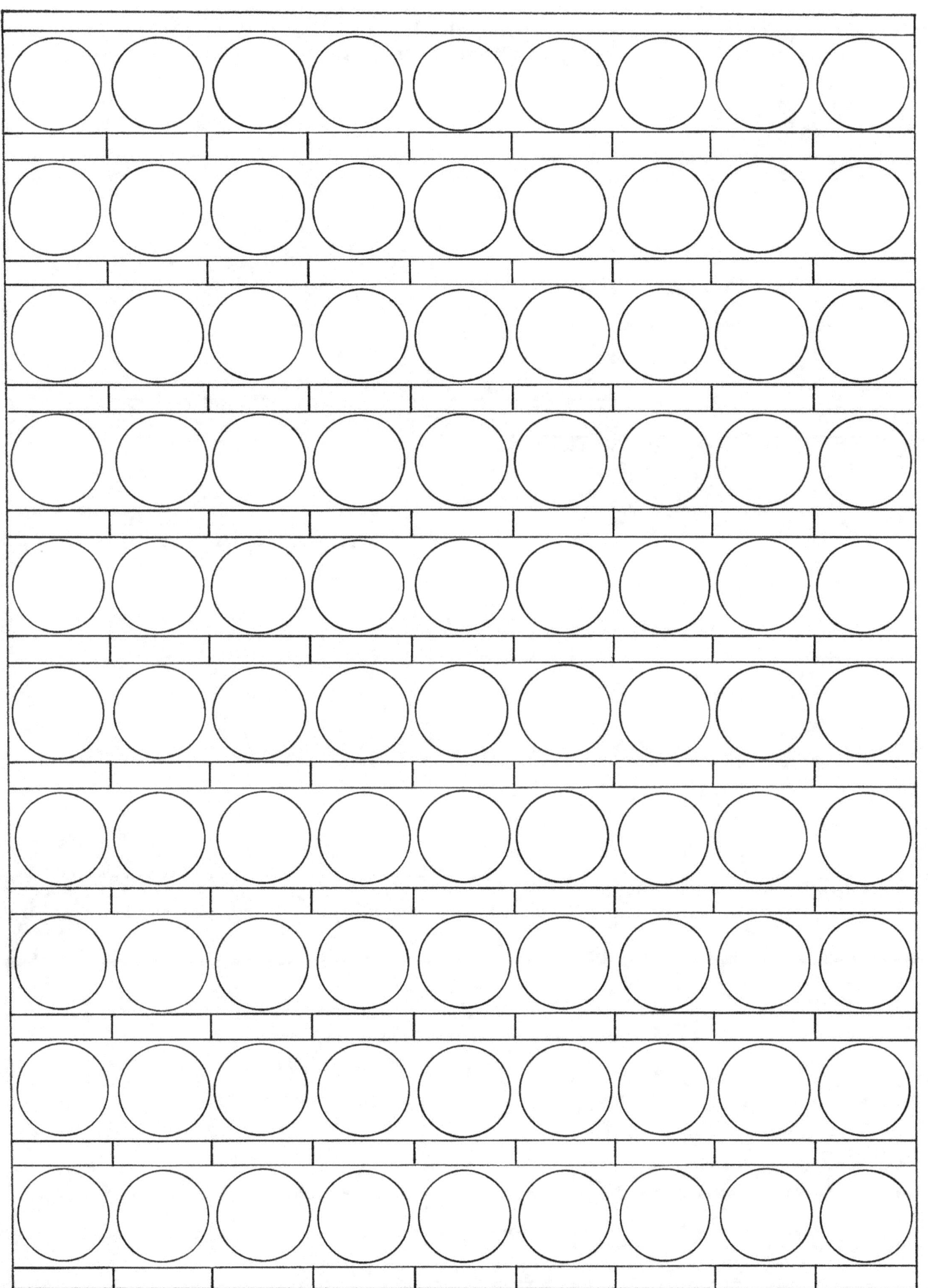

Template 30
Big Color Wheel of 12 spaces

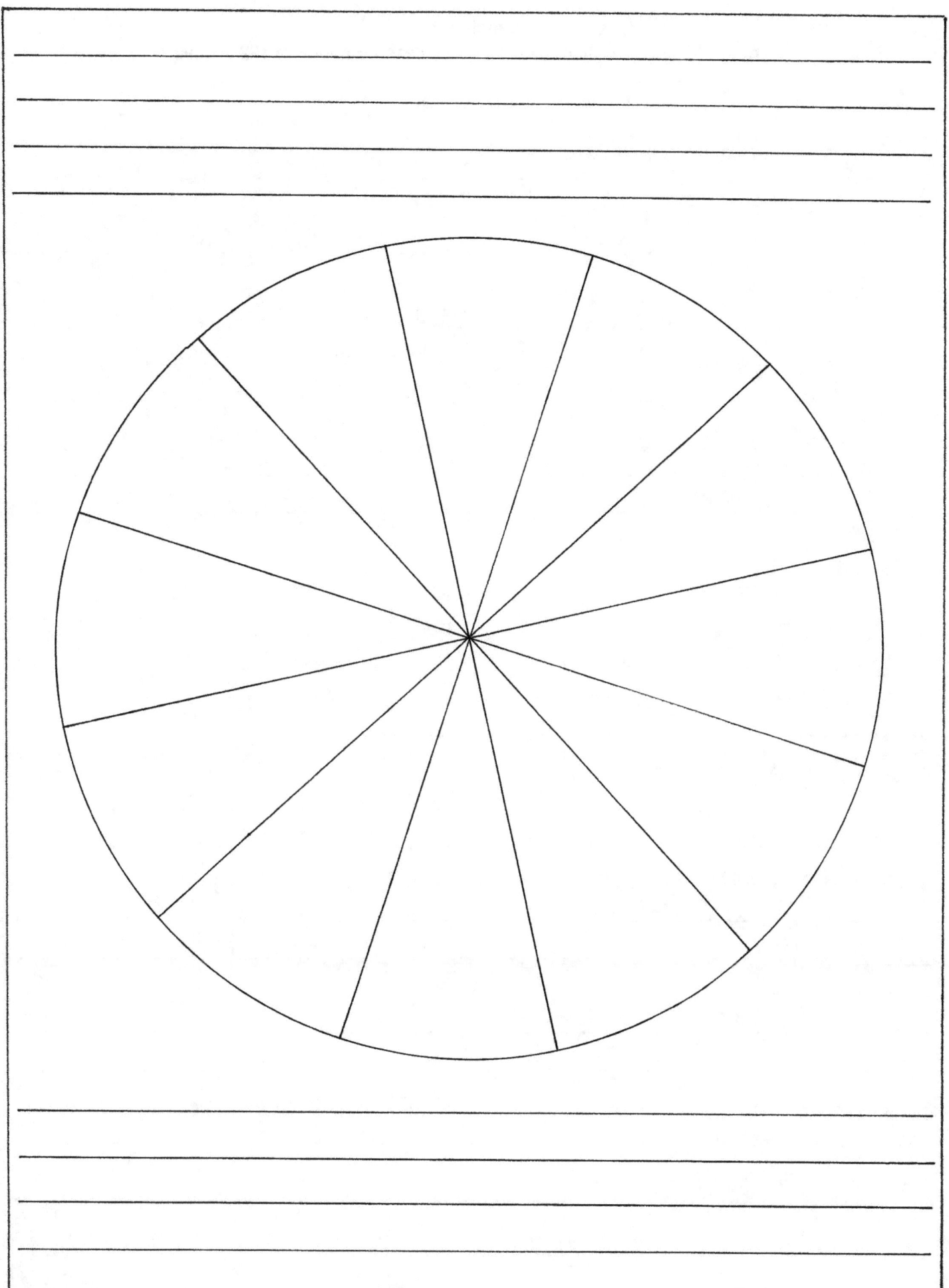

Template 1
6 rows of 8 circles = 48 circles x 4 spaces each = a total of 192 spaces

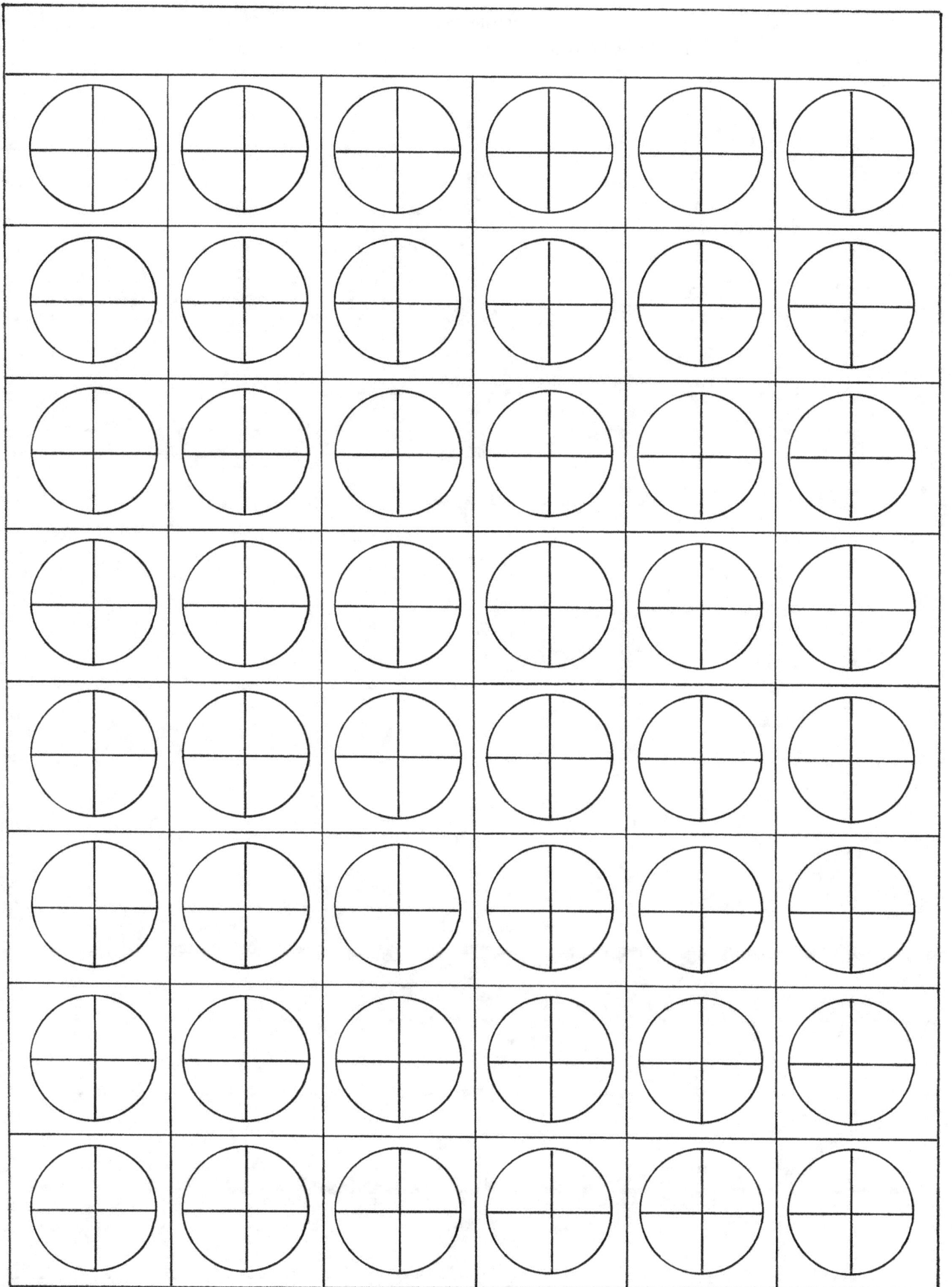

Template 2
2 Color Wheels with each 12 spaces = 24 spaces in total

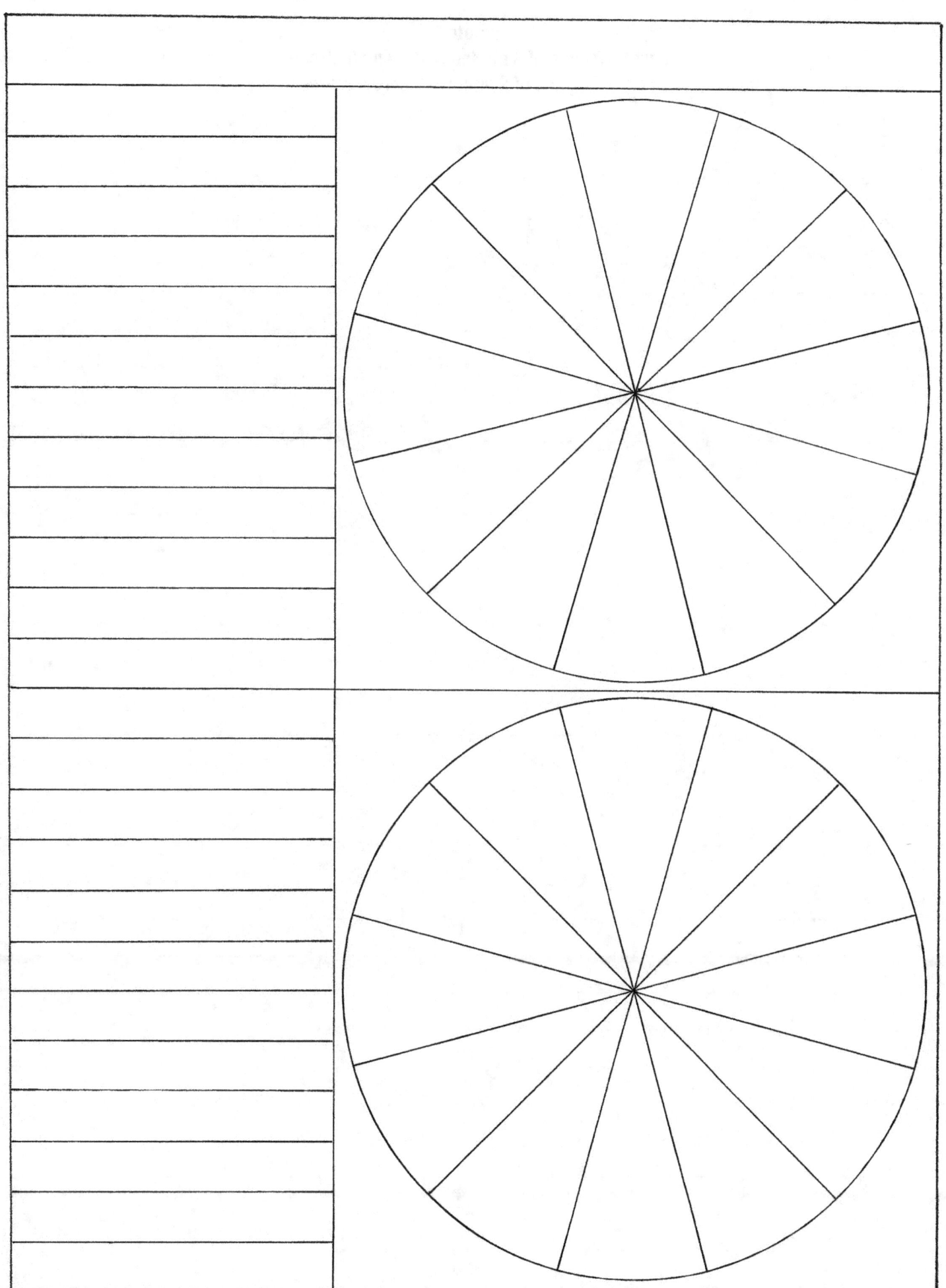

Template 3
Part 1 12 lines of 9 circles = 108 small circles
Part 2 24 lines of 9 squares = 216 squares

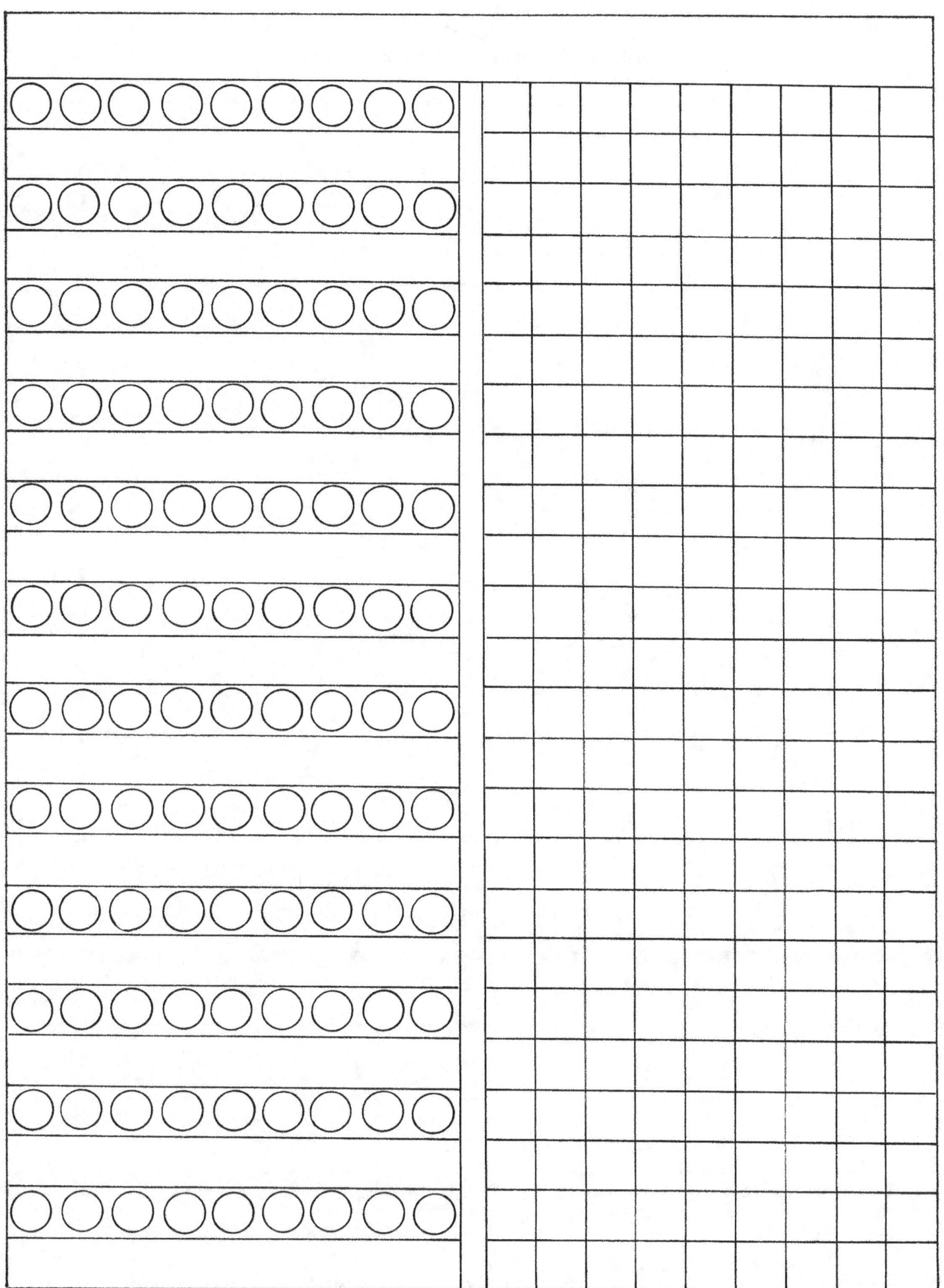

Template 4
8 lines of 37 spaces = total of 296 spaces

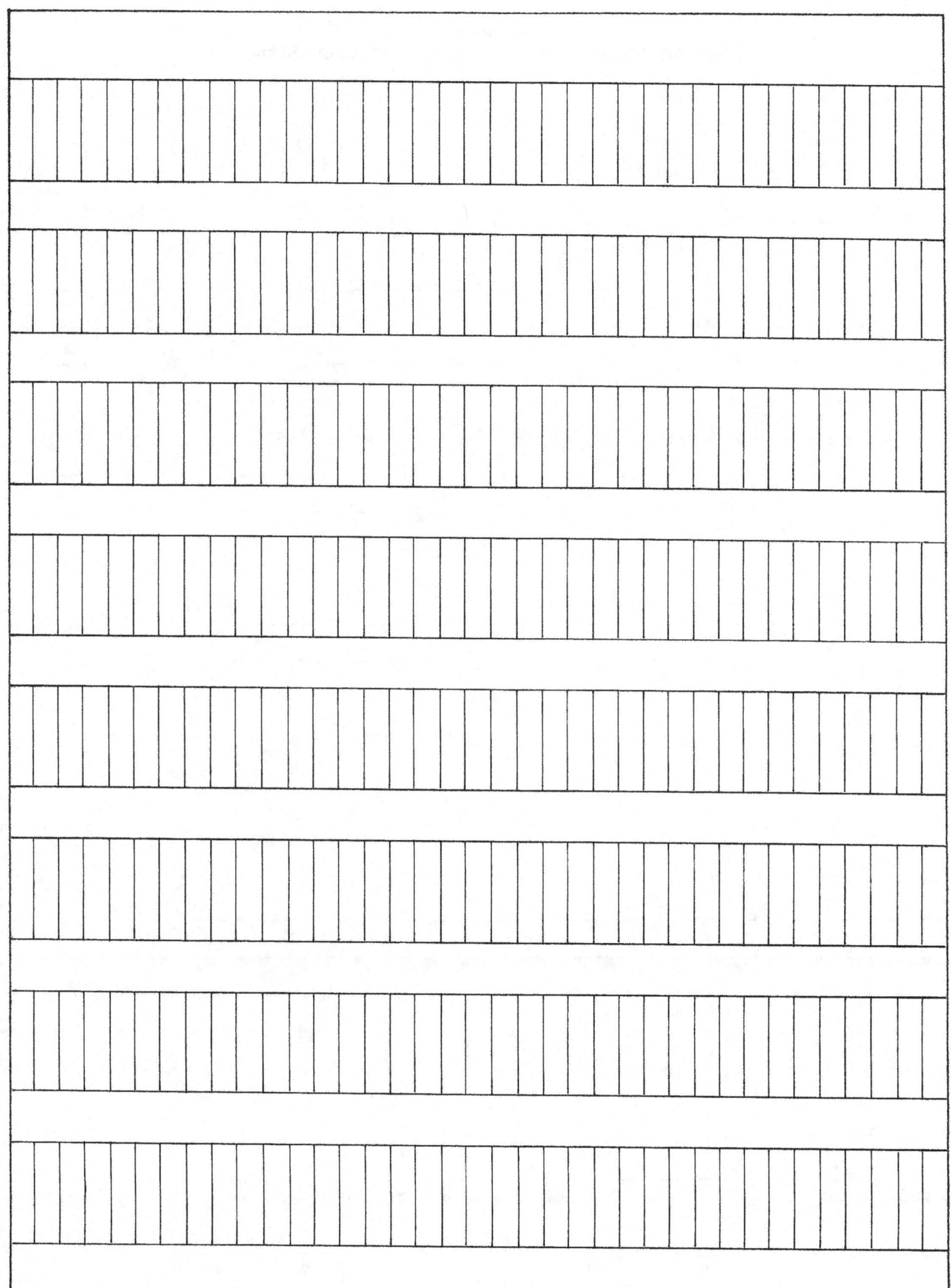

Template 5
8 half color wheel each with 18 spaces = a total of 144 spaces

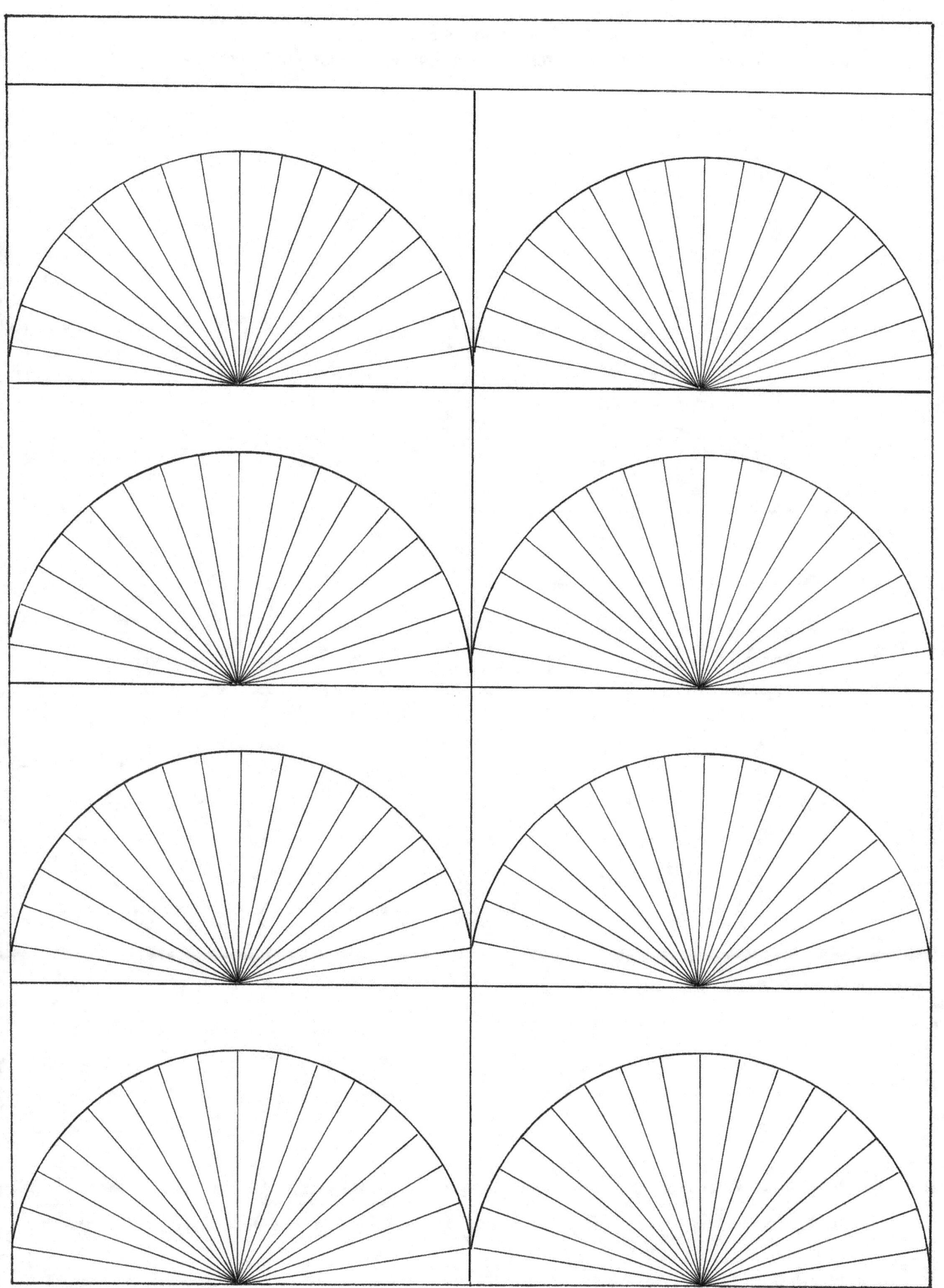

Template 6
6 rows of 8 circles = 48 circles x 8 spaces each = a total of 384 spaces

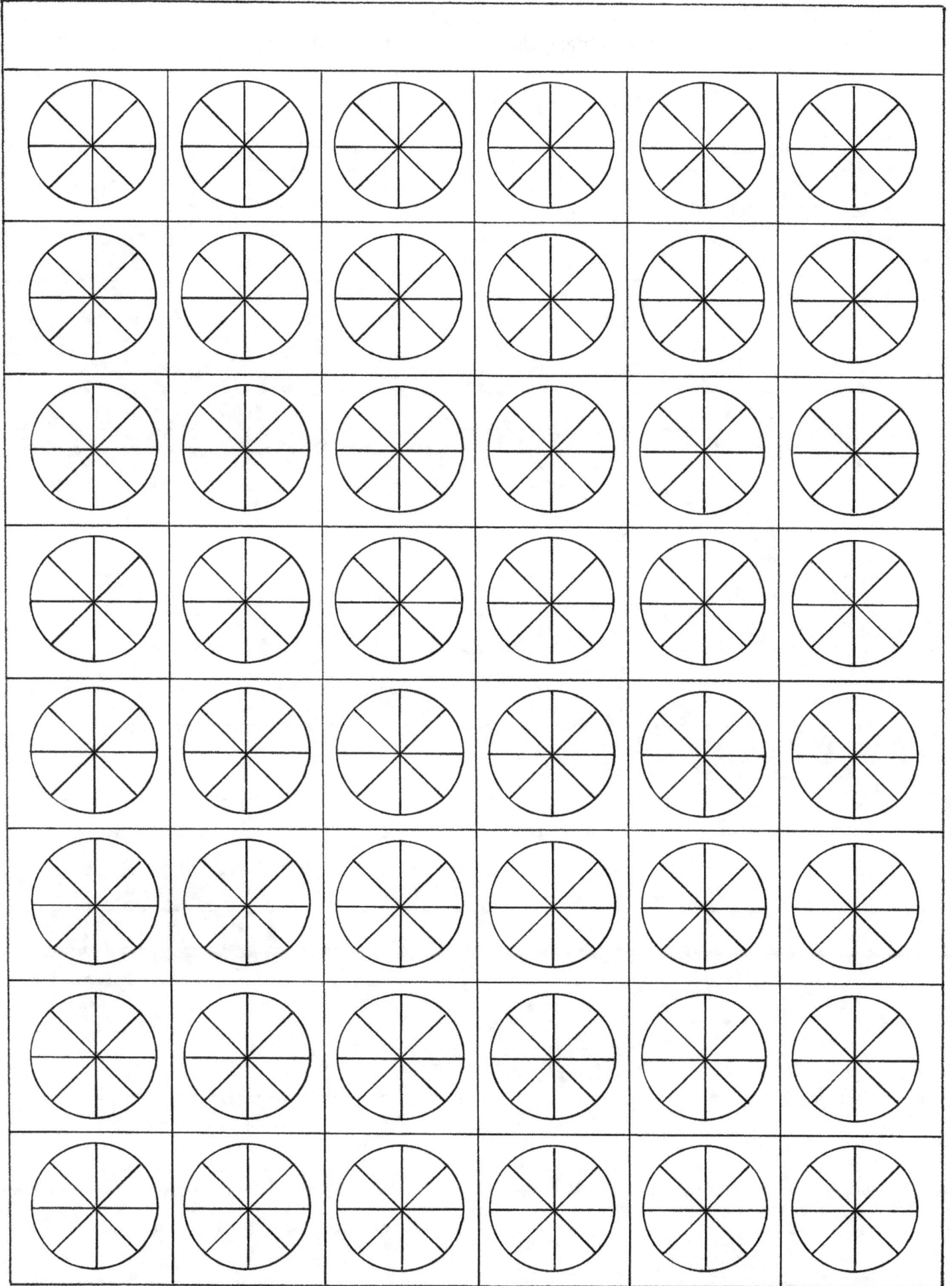

Template 7
8 lines of 24 triangular spaces = a total of 192 spaces

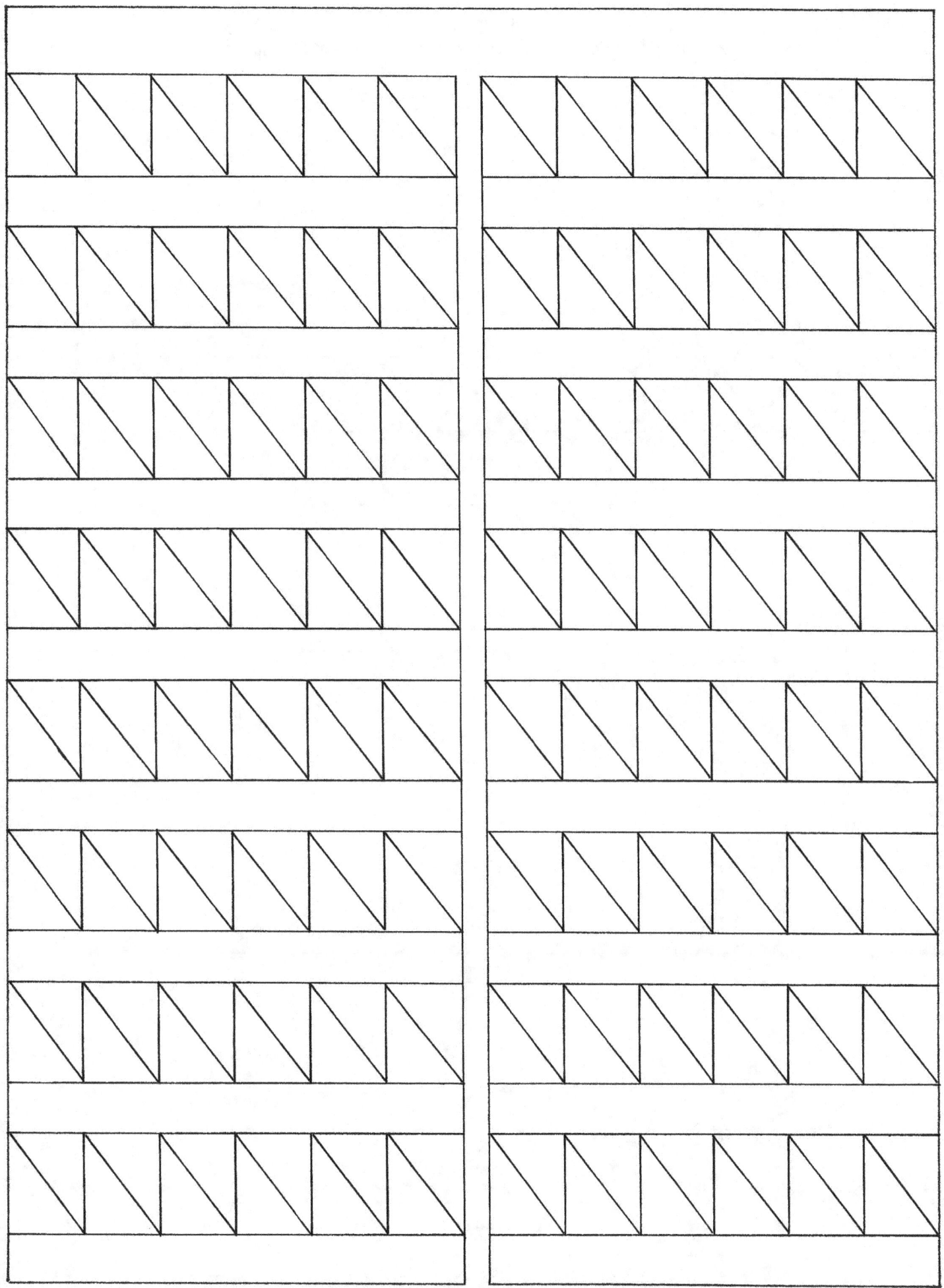

Template 8
3 rows of 2x48 spaces = 96 spaces x 3   a total of 288 spaces

Template 9
Big Color wheel 4 sections of 36 spaces = a total of 144 spaces

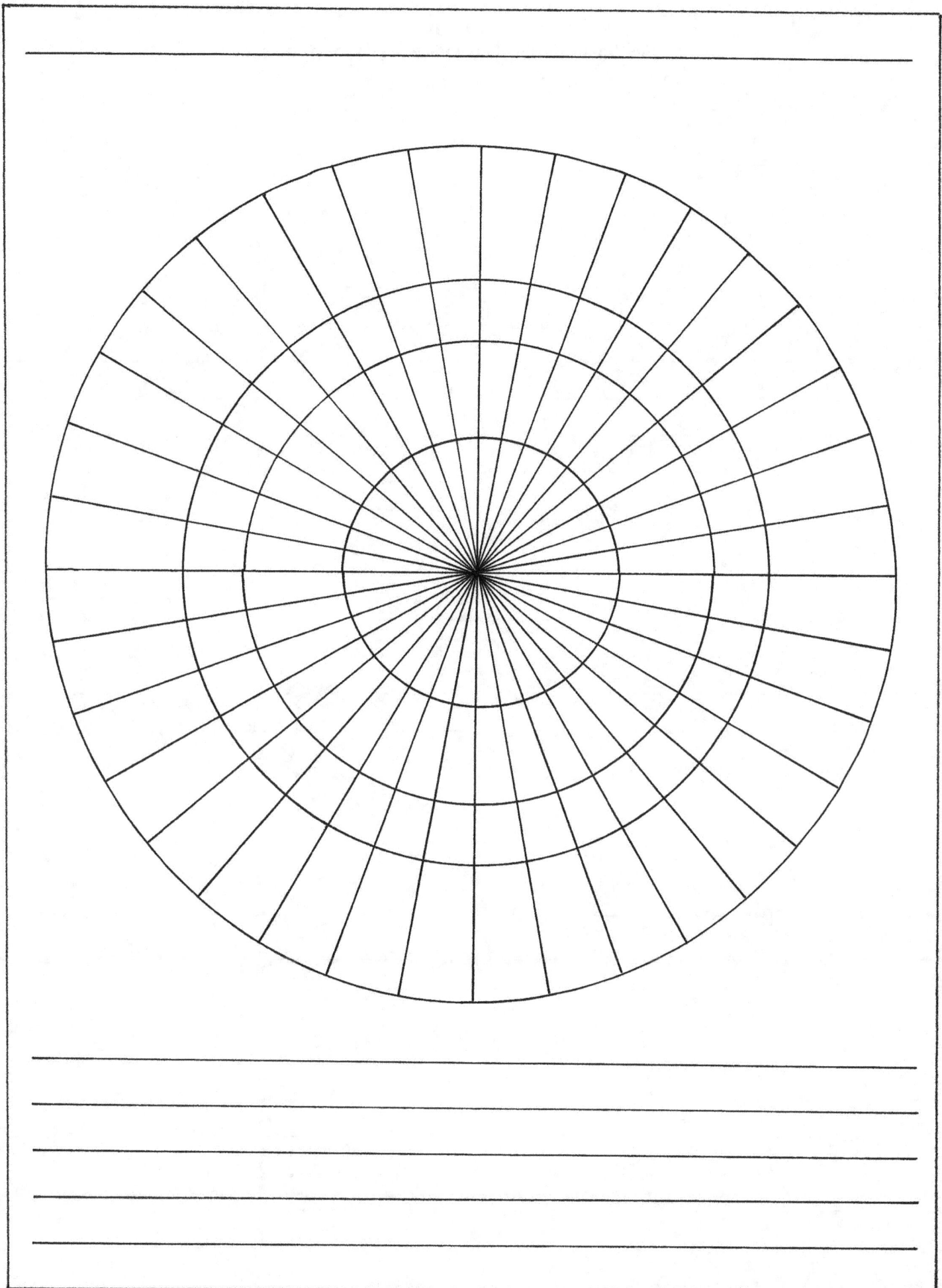

Template 10
4 half Color Wheels of 2x 18 spaces = a total of 144 spaces

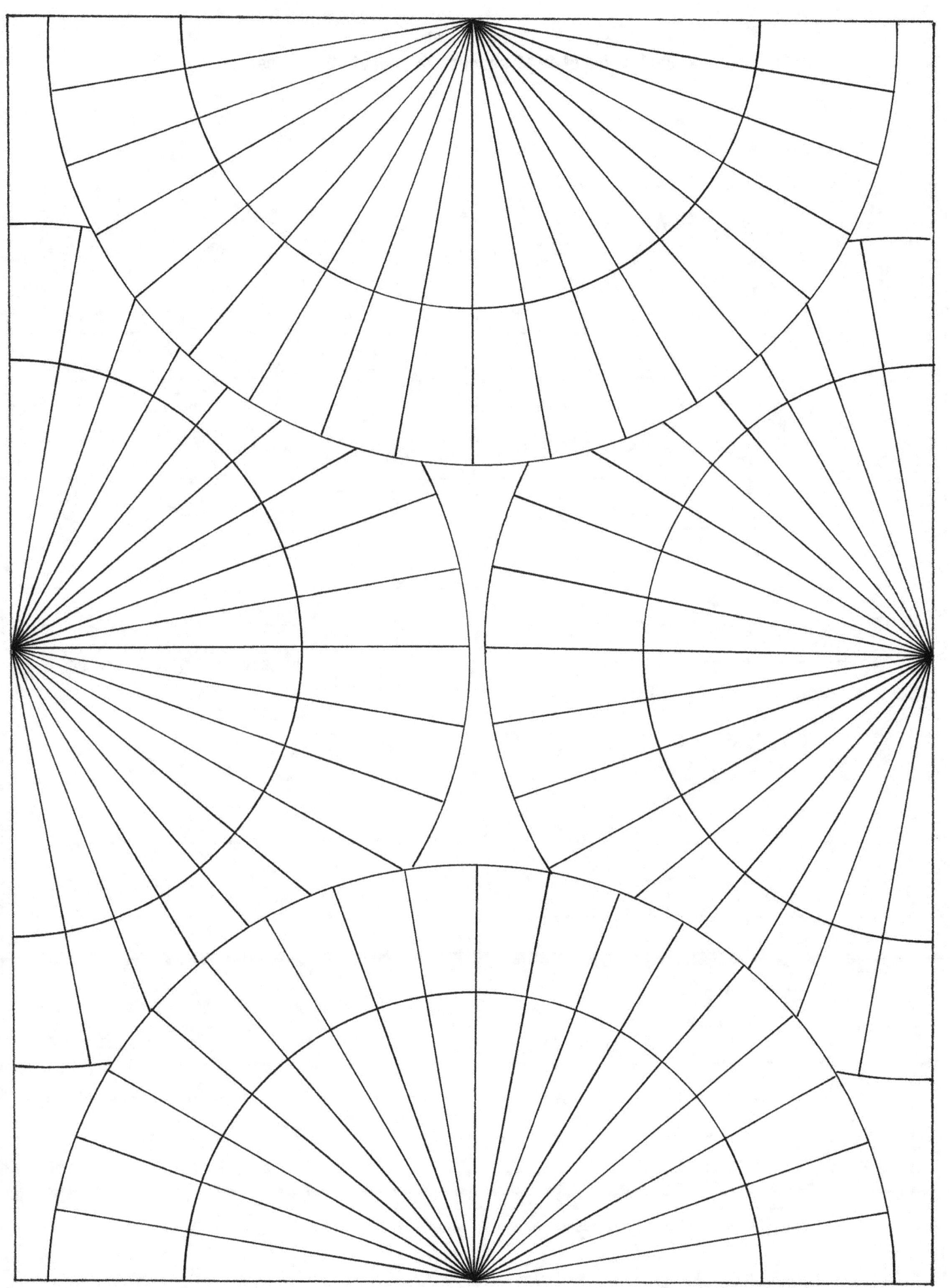

Template 11
Color Wheels of 4x 12 spaces = a total of 48 spaces

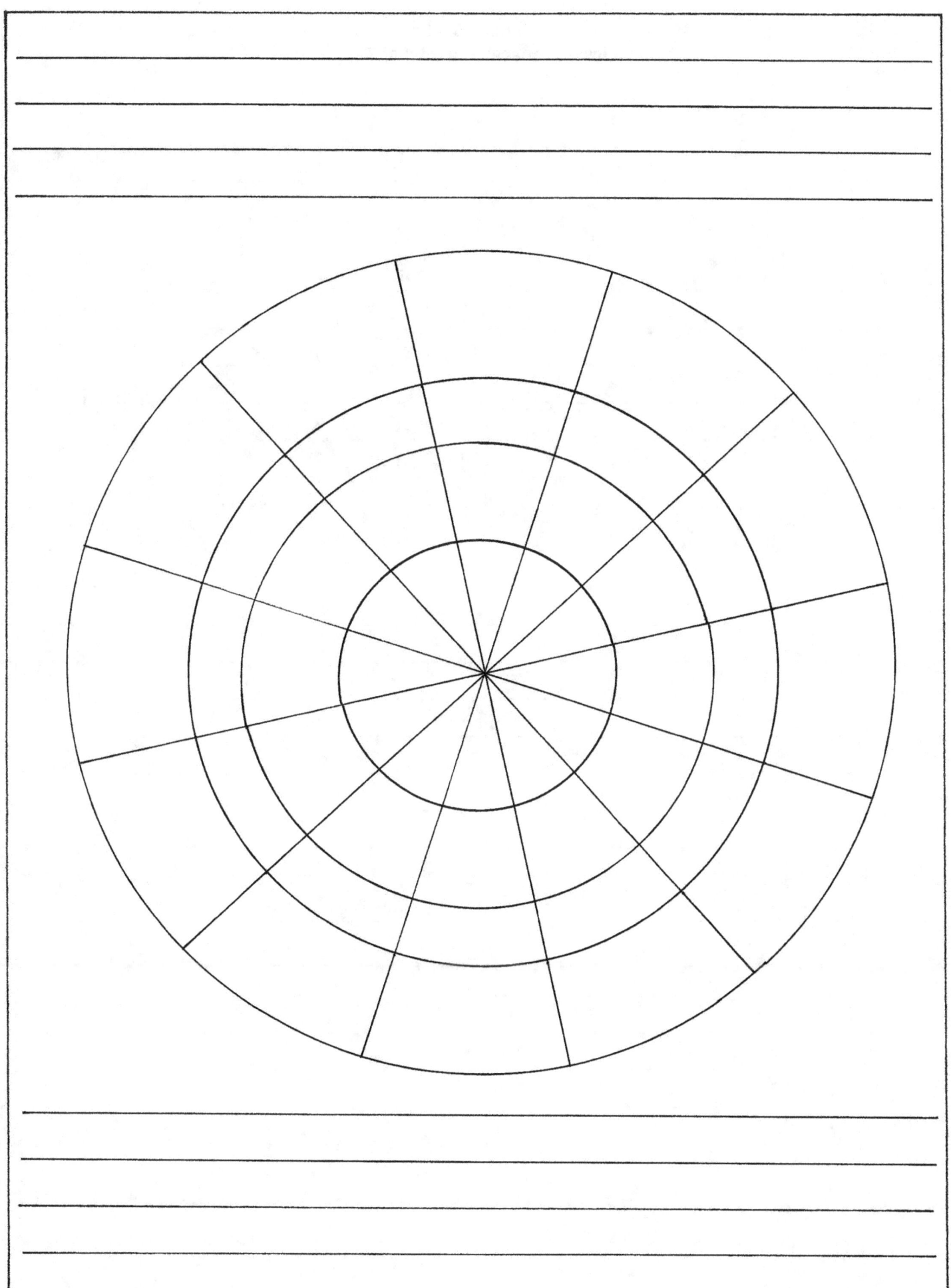

Template 12
24 circles of 3 spaces = a total of 72 spaces

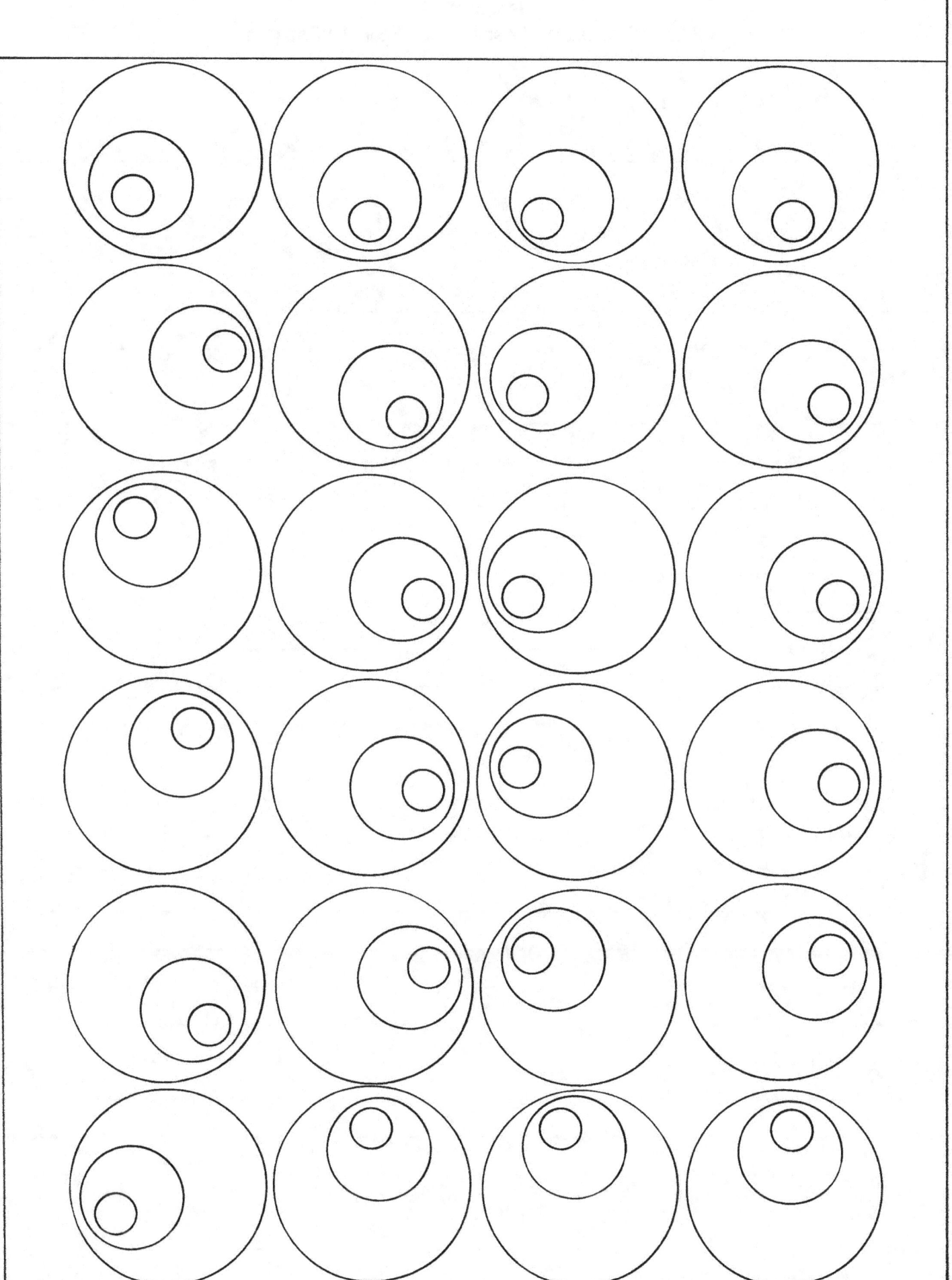

Template 13
2 Color Wheels of 4x12 spaces = a total of 96 spaces

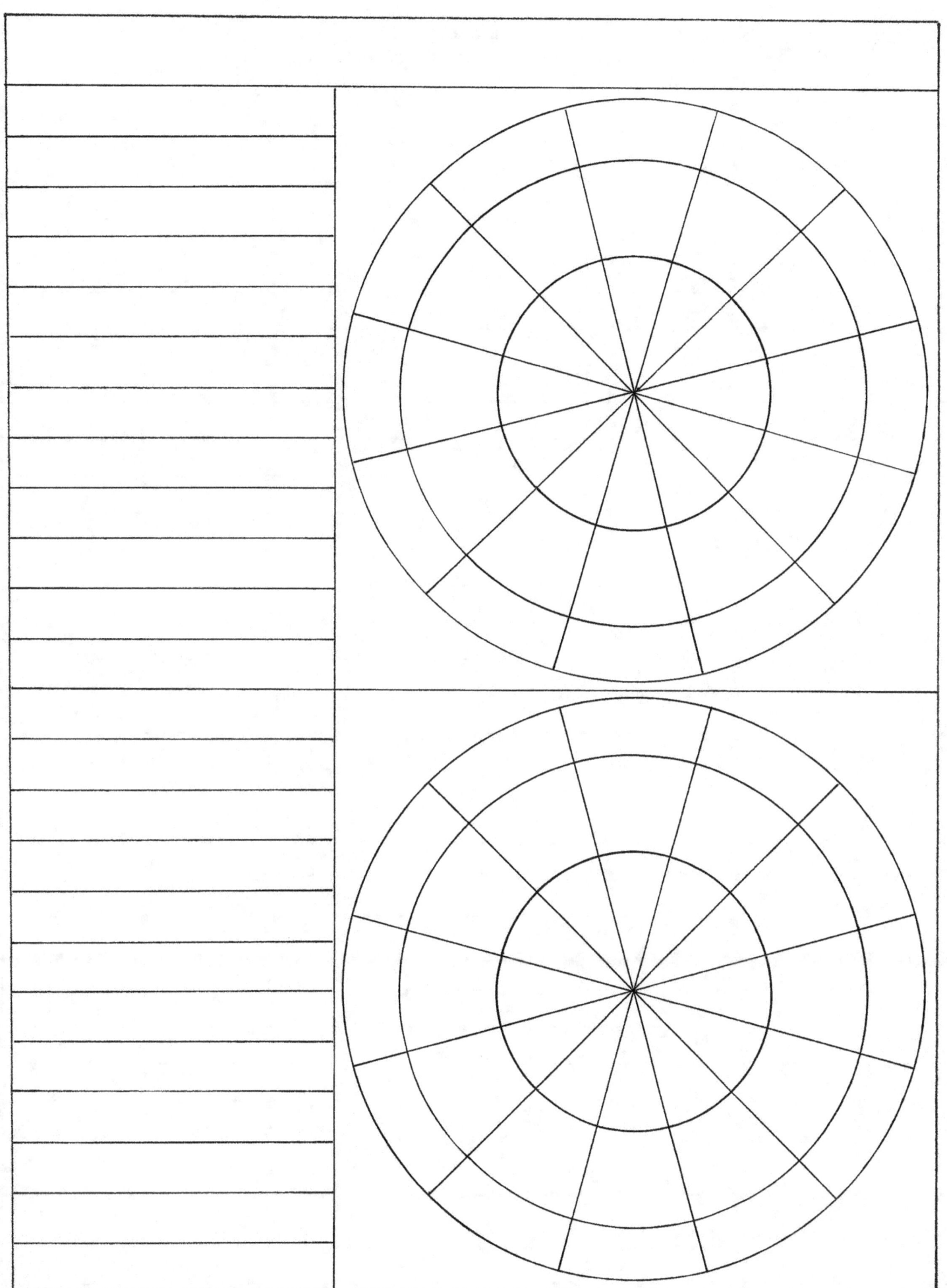

Template 14
8 lines of 2x37 spaces = a total of 592 spaces

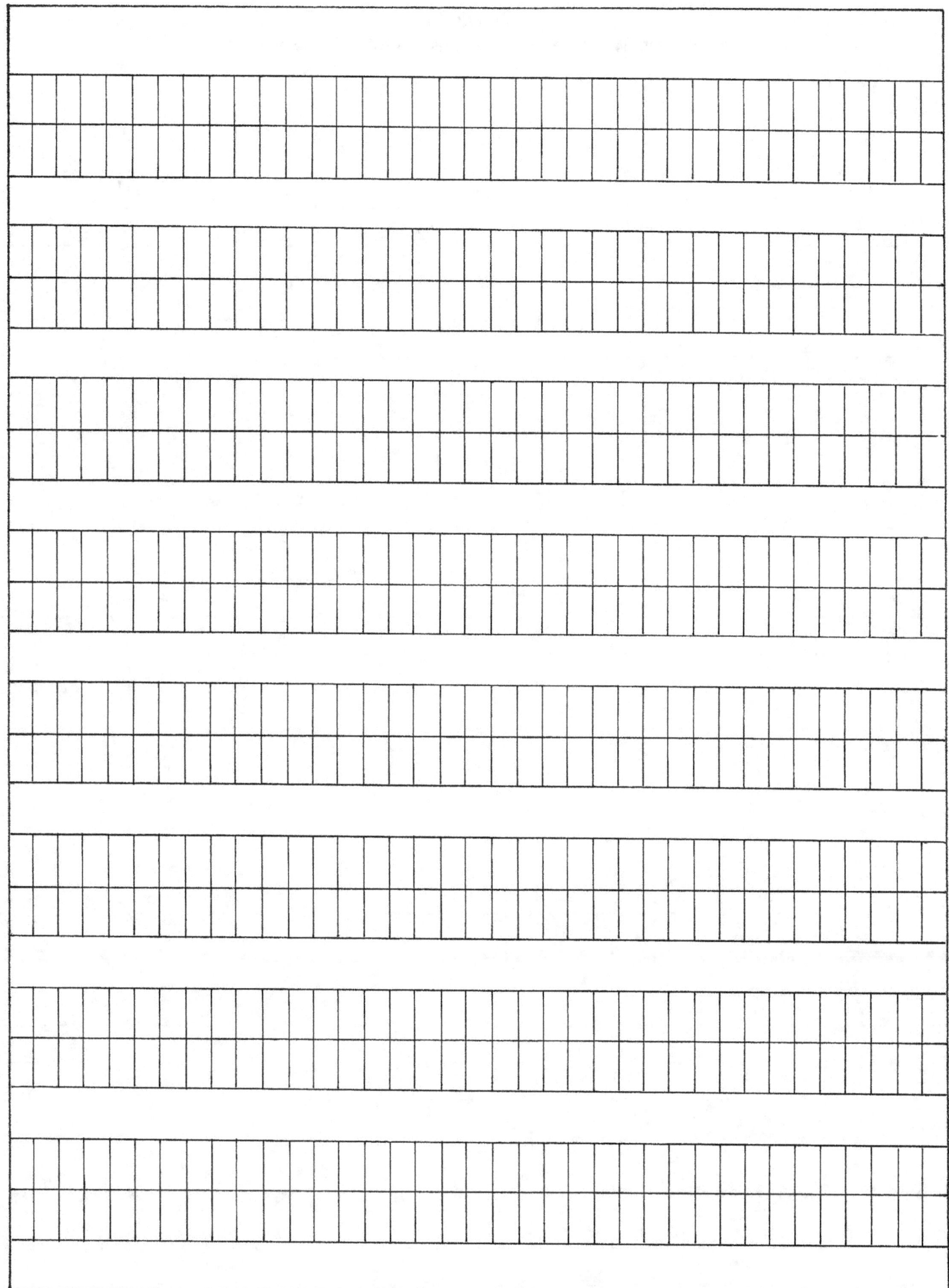

Template 15
8 half Color Wheels of 2x 18 spaces = a total of 288 spaces

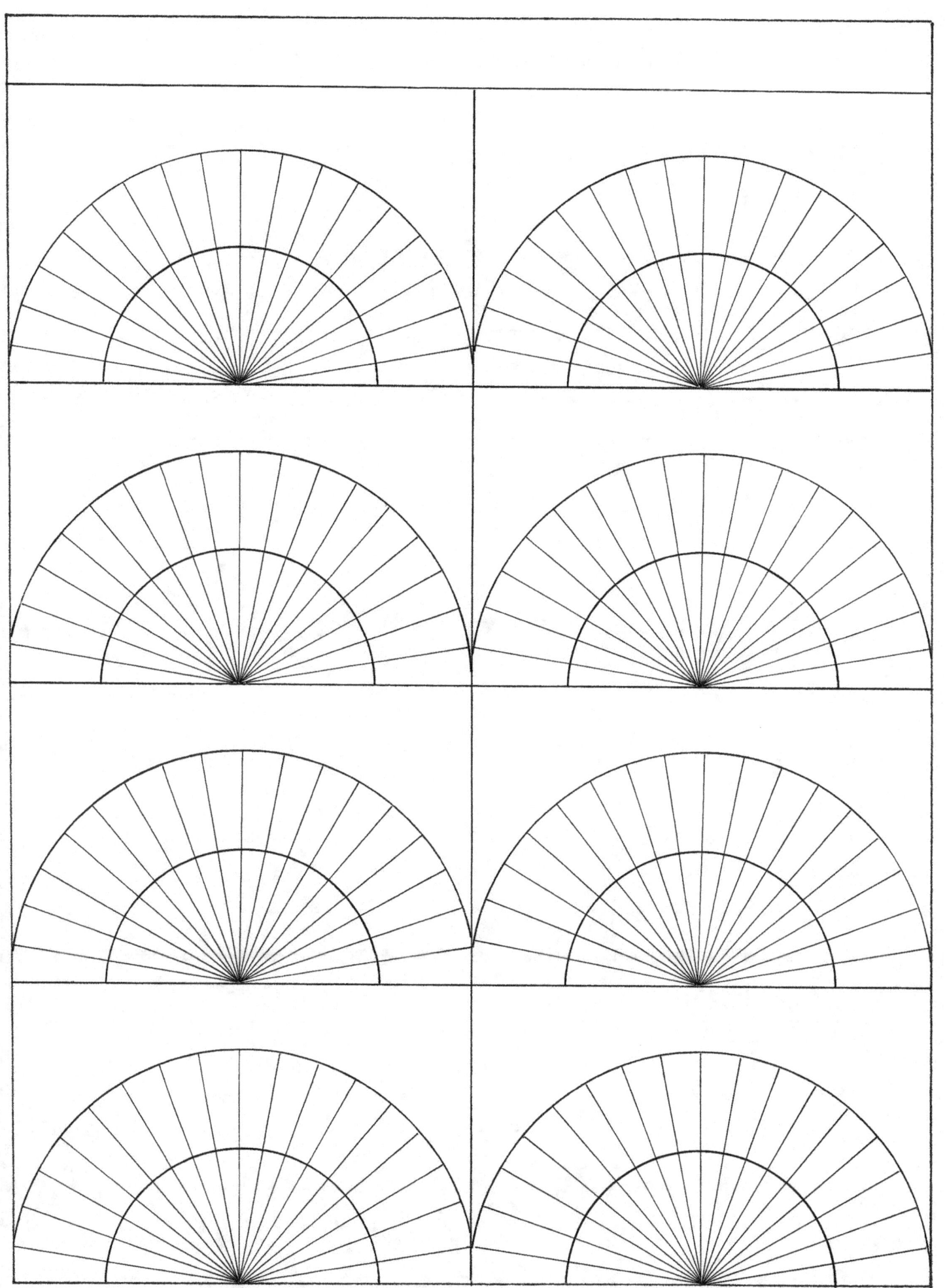

Template 16
4 half Color Wheels of 3x 18 spaces = a total of 216 spaces

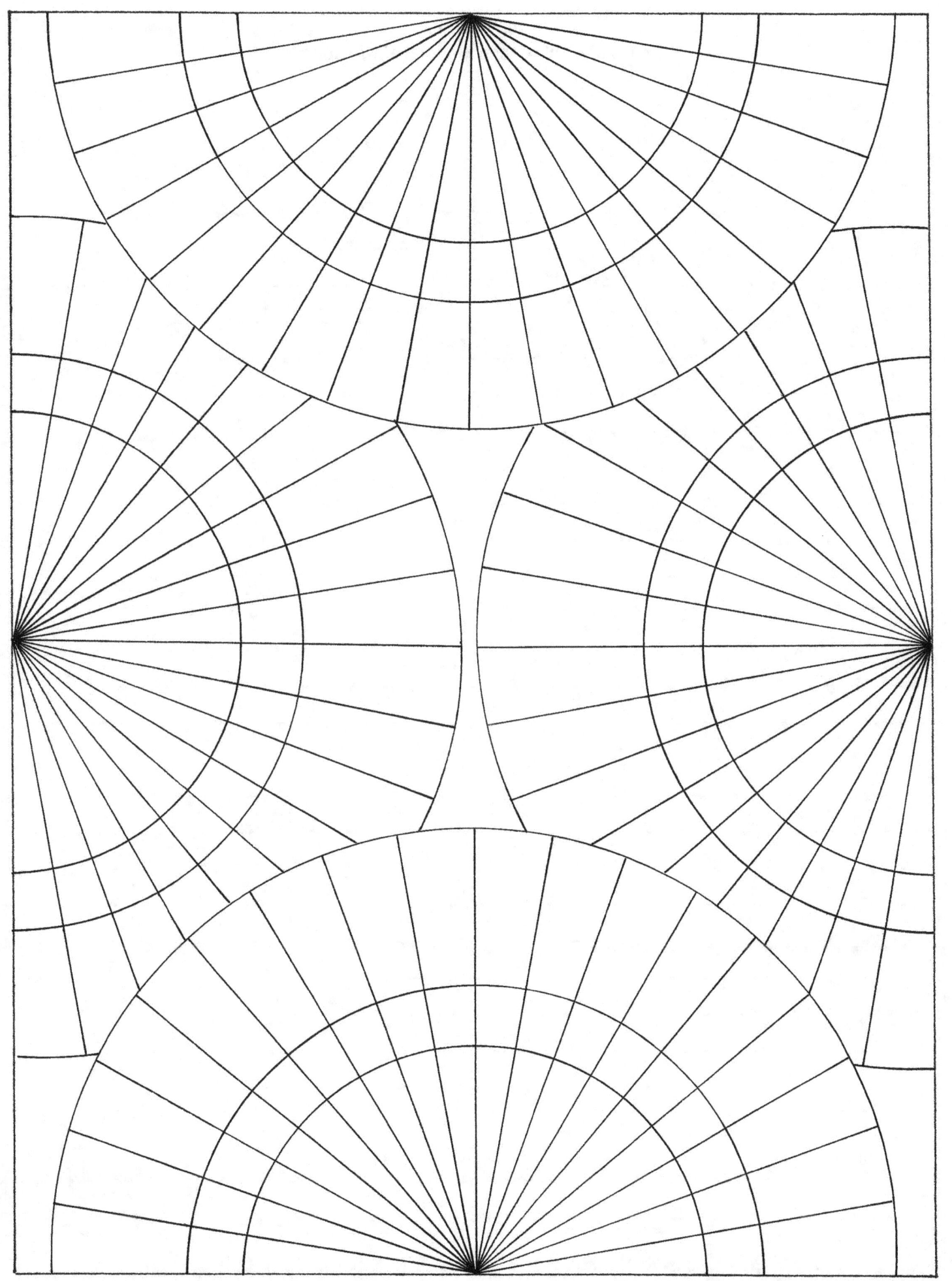

Template 17
3 rows of 4x48 spaces = a total of 576 spaces

Template 18
8 lines of 4x37 spaces = a total of 1184 spaces

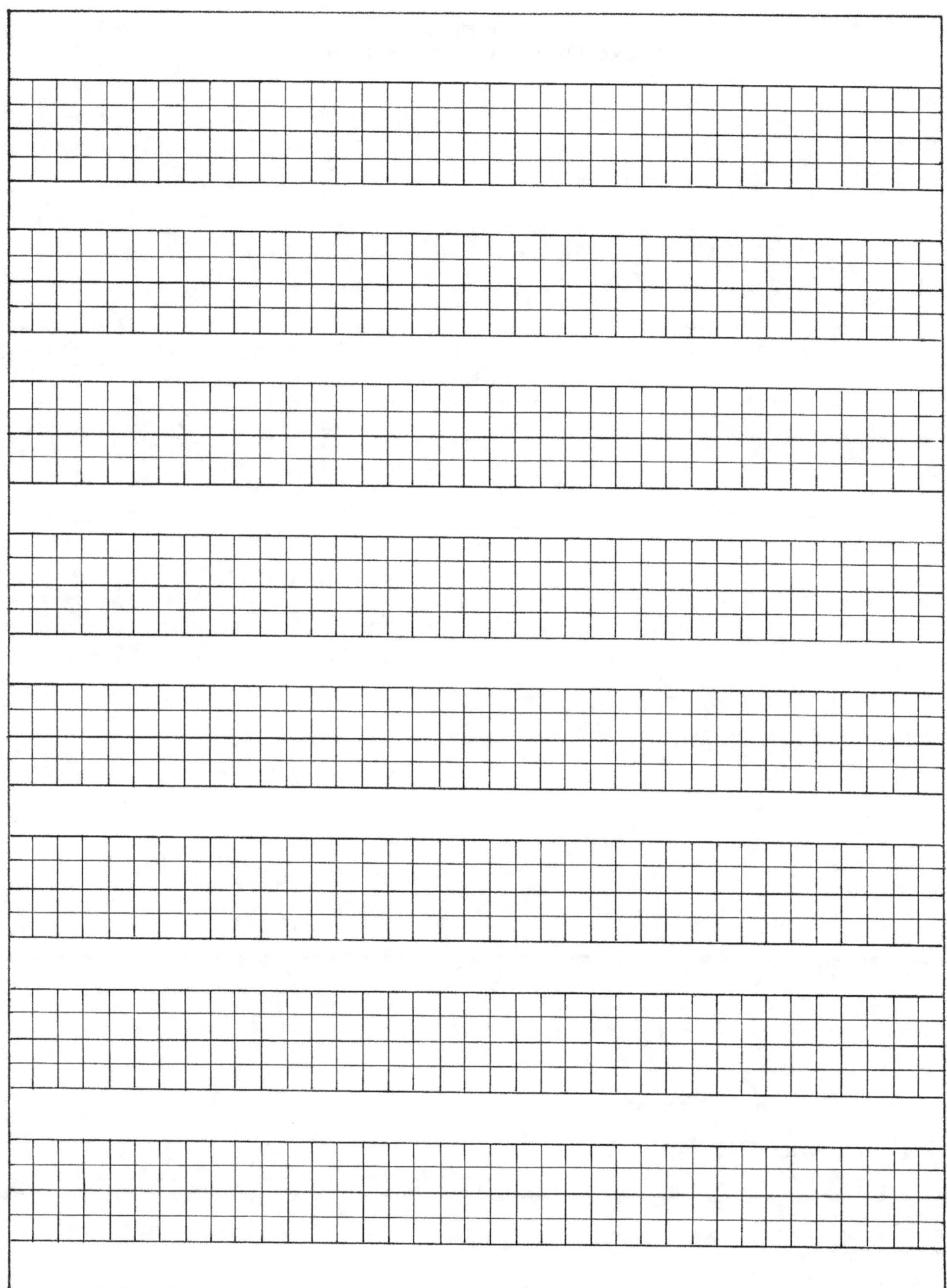

Template 19
8 lines of 12x4 spaces = a total of 384 spaces

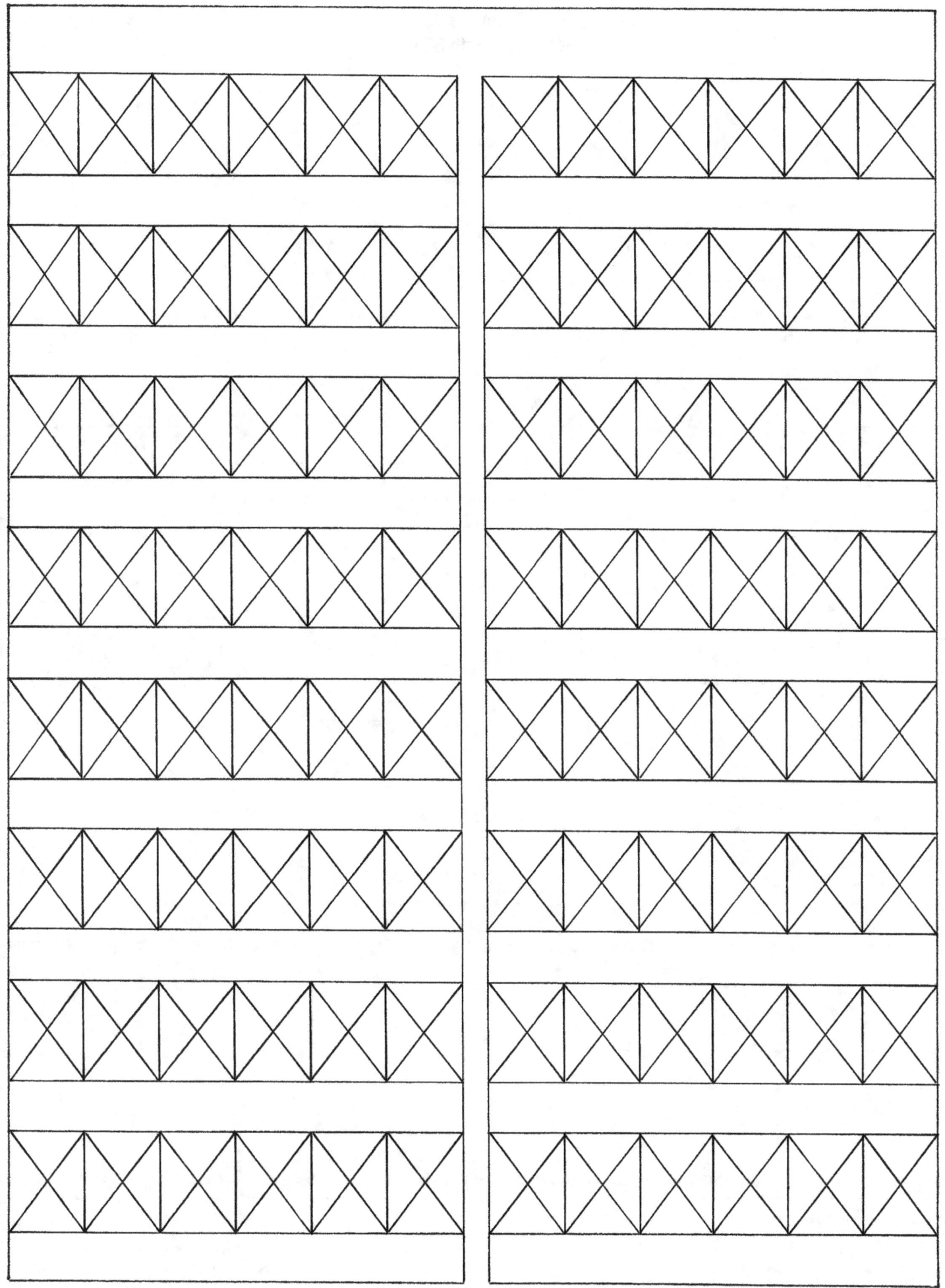

Template 20
Color Wheel with 36 spaces

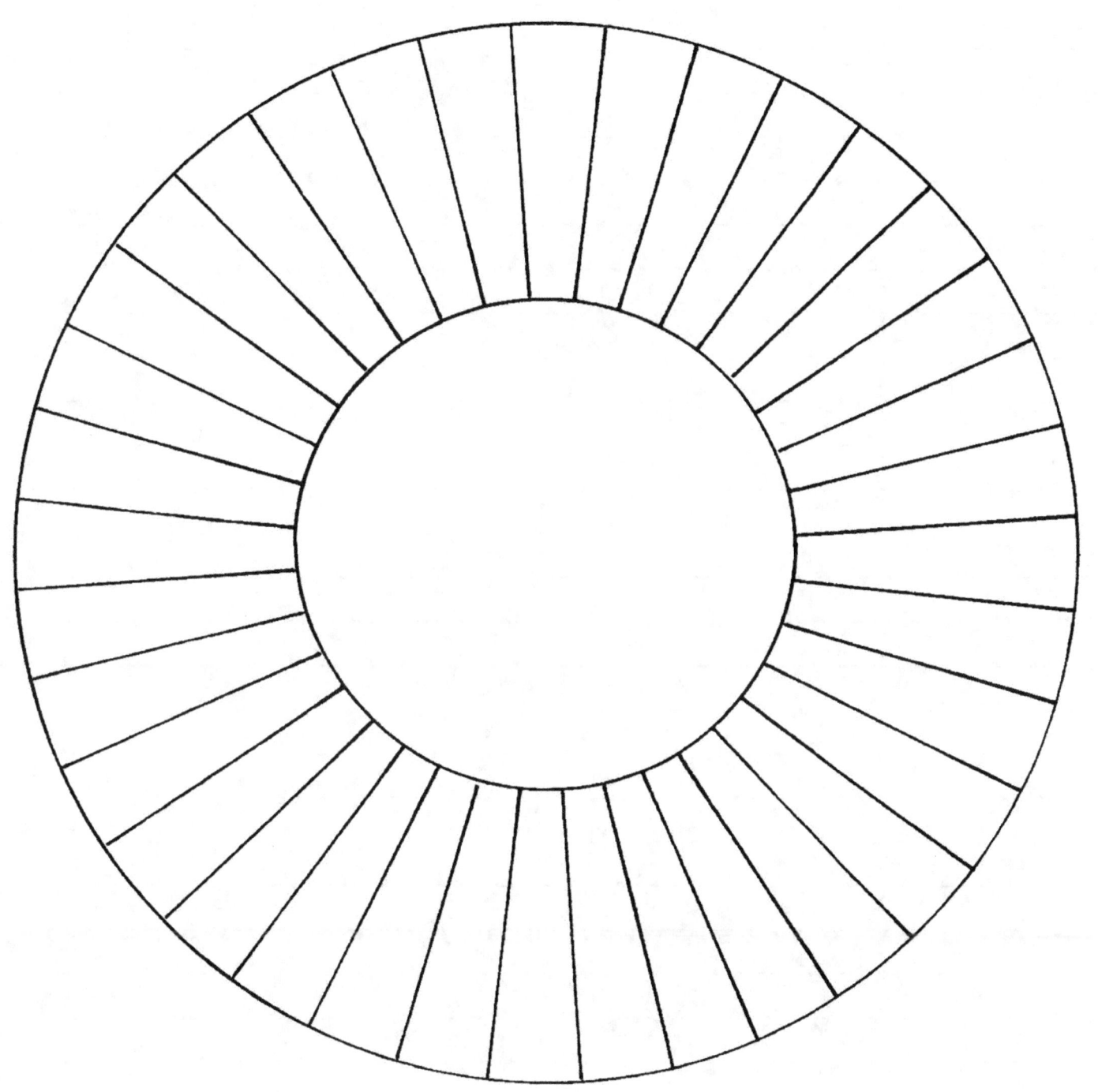

Template 21
Circle explosion of 16x 7 circles = 112 circles

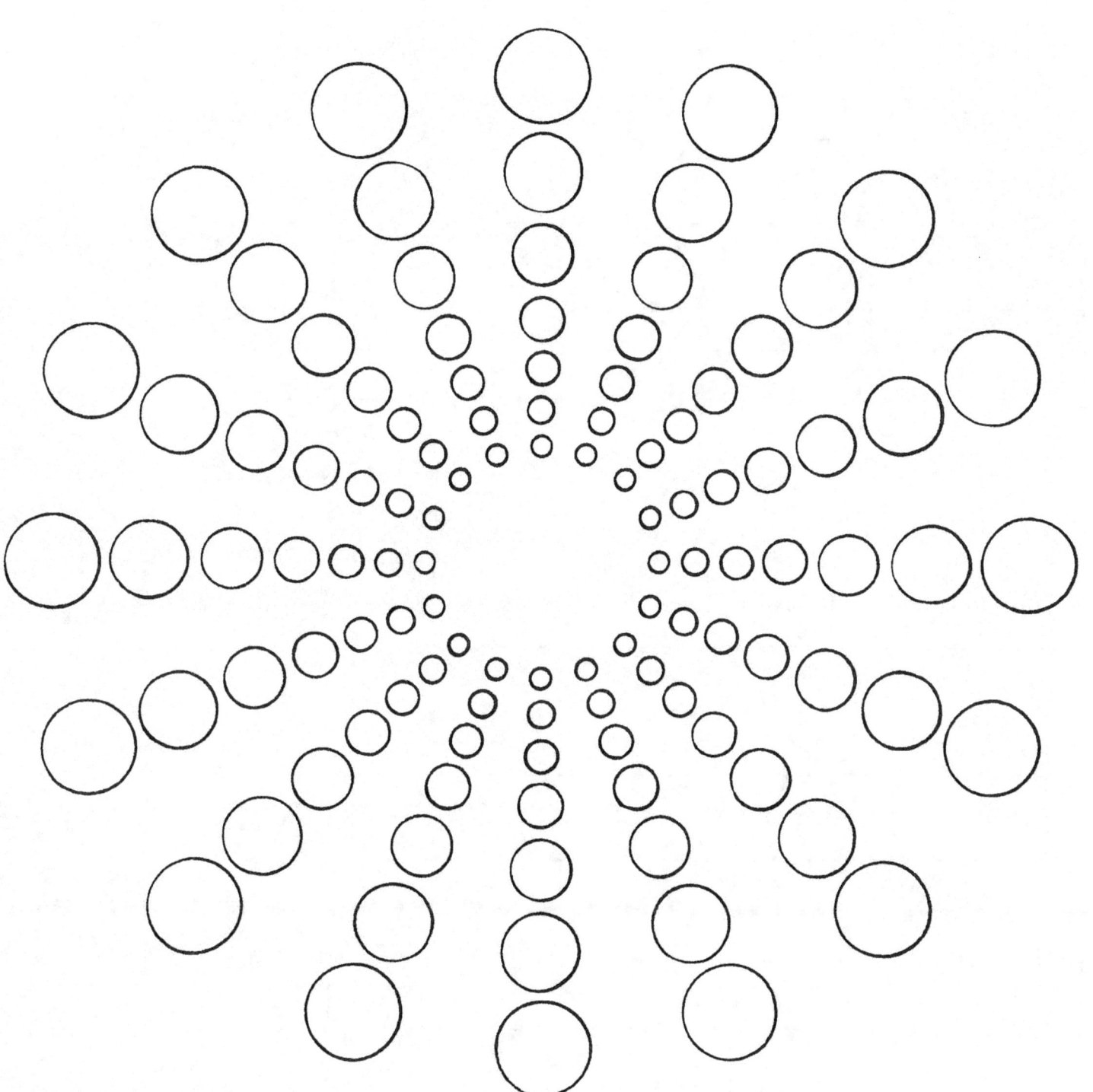

Template 22
Color flowe 16x9 spaces = a total of 144 spaces

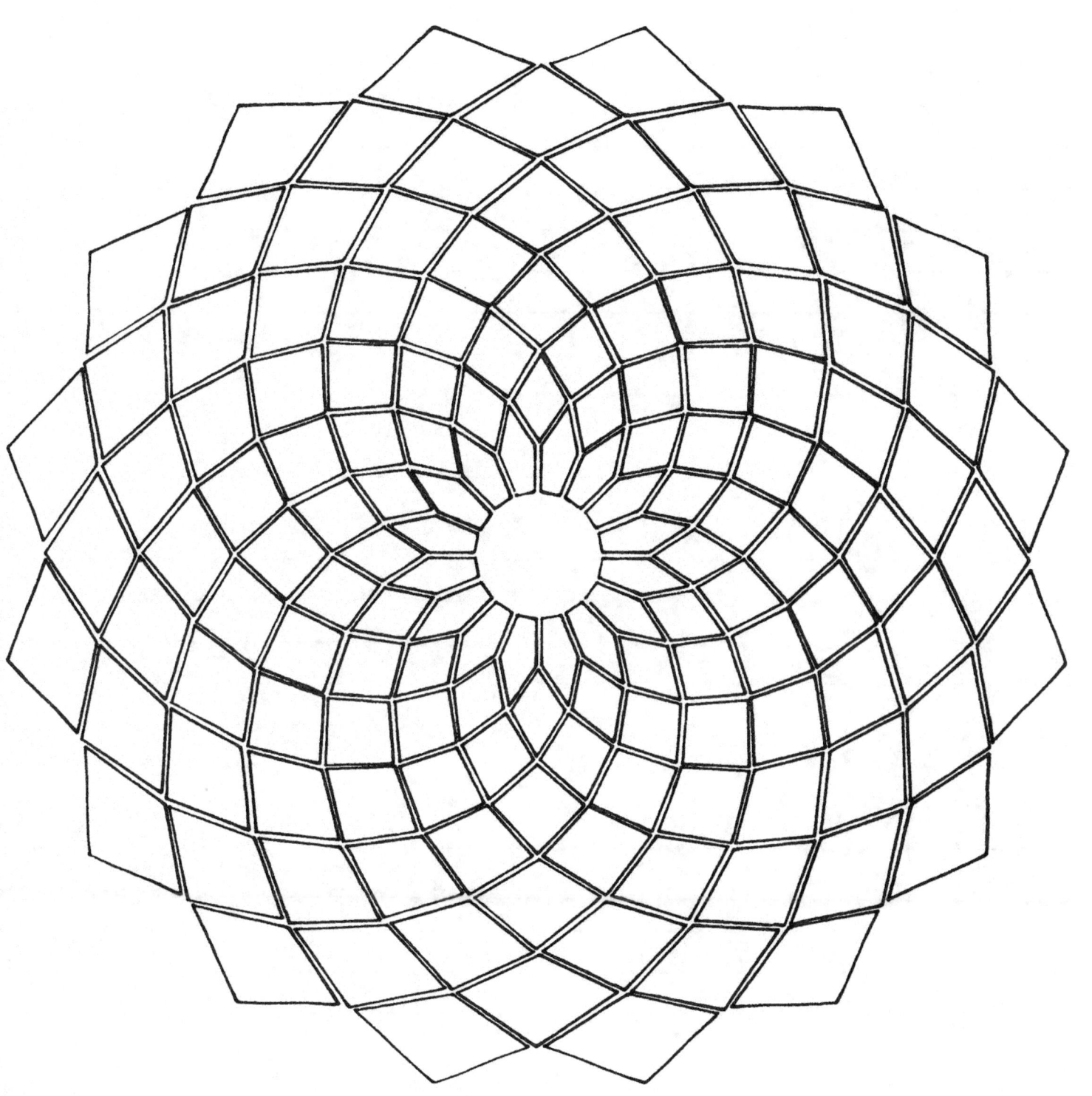

Template 23
1 color wheel of 6x 36 spaces = 216 spaces
4 quarter color wheels of 6 x 9 spaces = 216 spaces
A grand total of 432 spaces

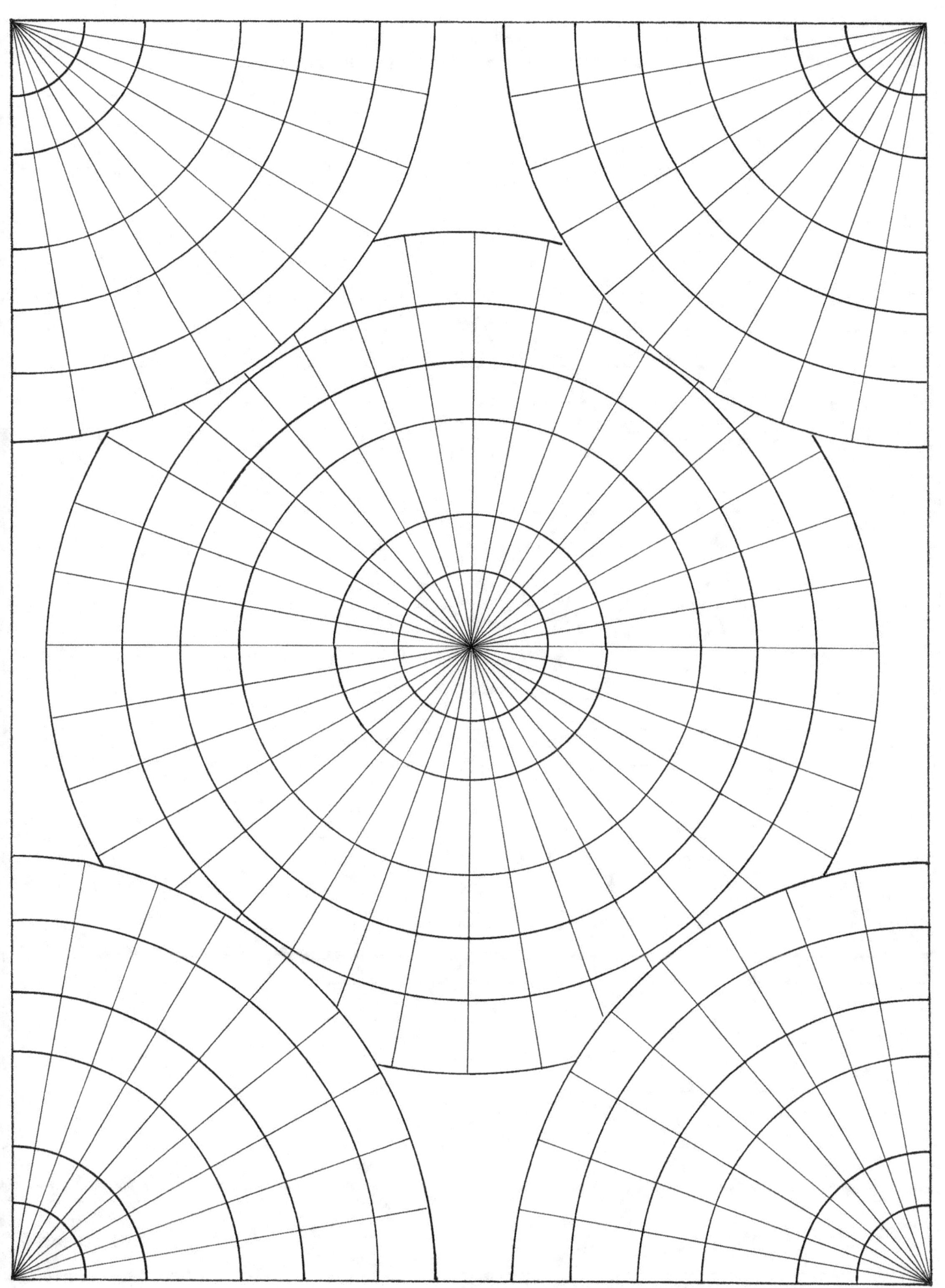

Template 24
Great wheel of colors 5x 32 spaces = 160 spaces

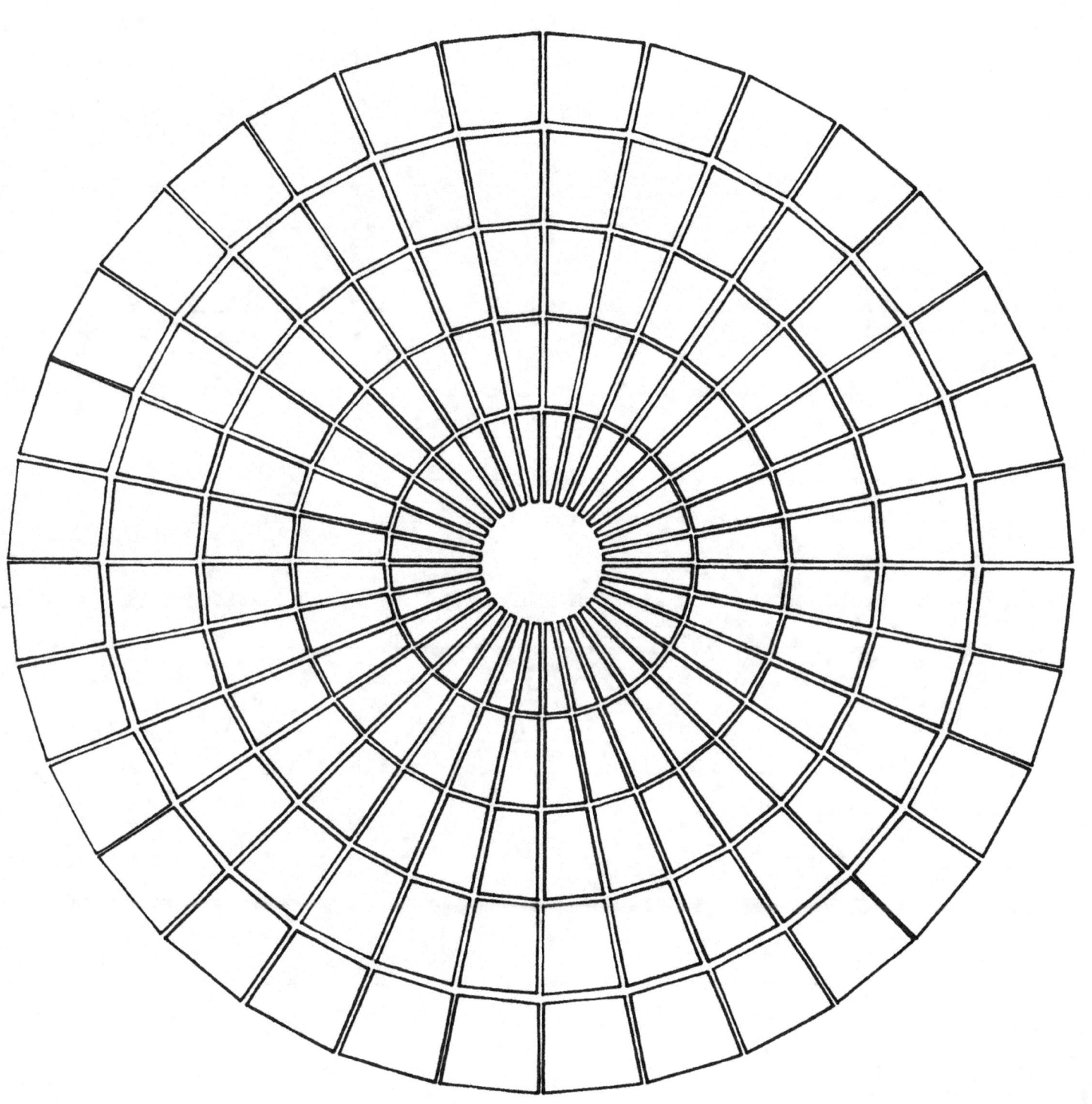

Template 25
8 lines of 12 spaces = a total of 96 spaces

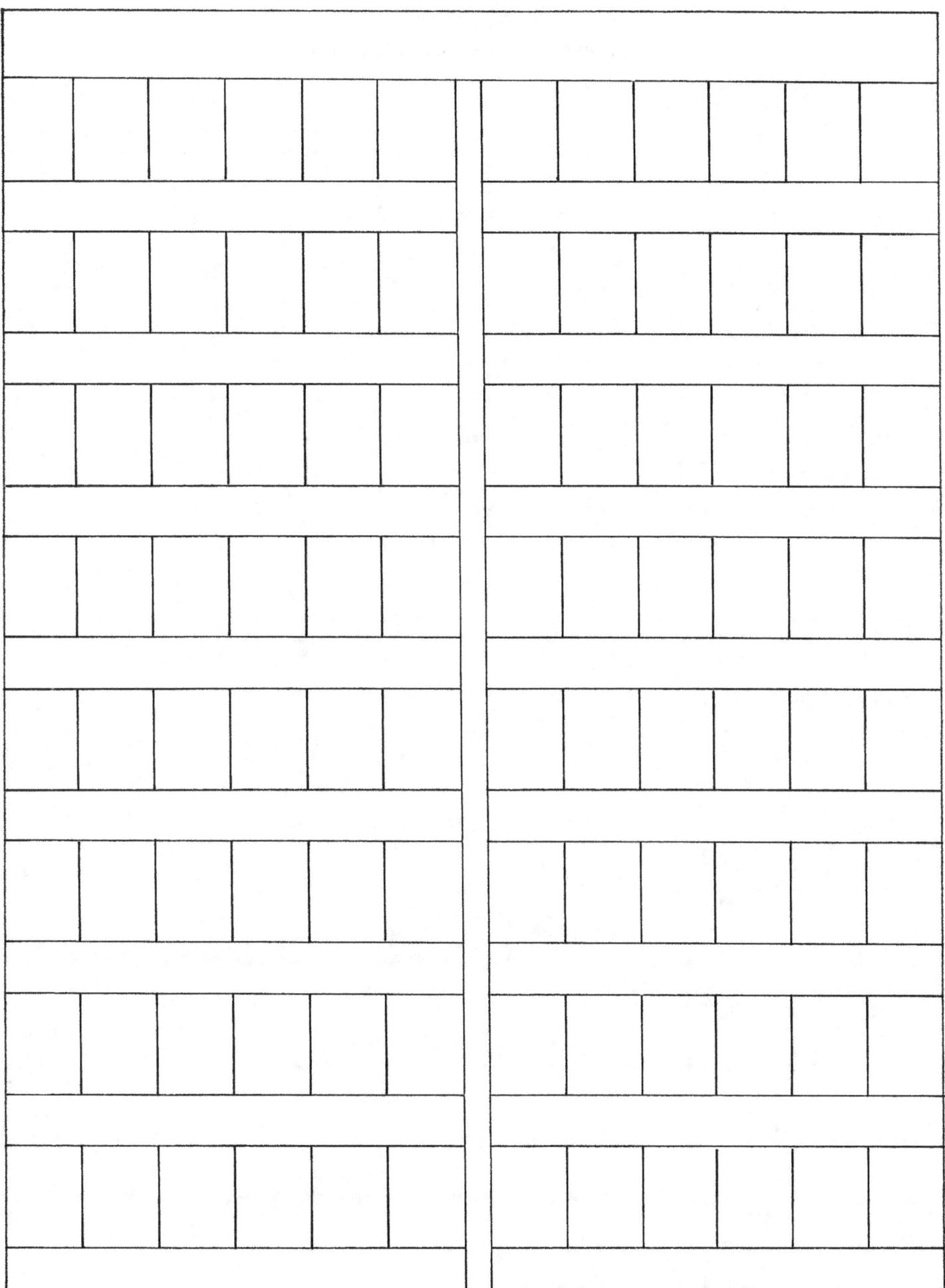

Template 26
3 rows of 48 spaces = a total of 144 spaces

Template 27
Big Color wheel of 36 spaces

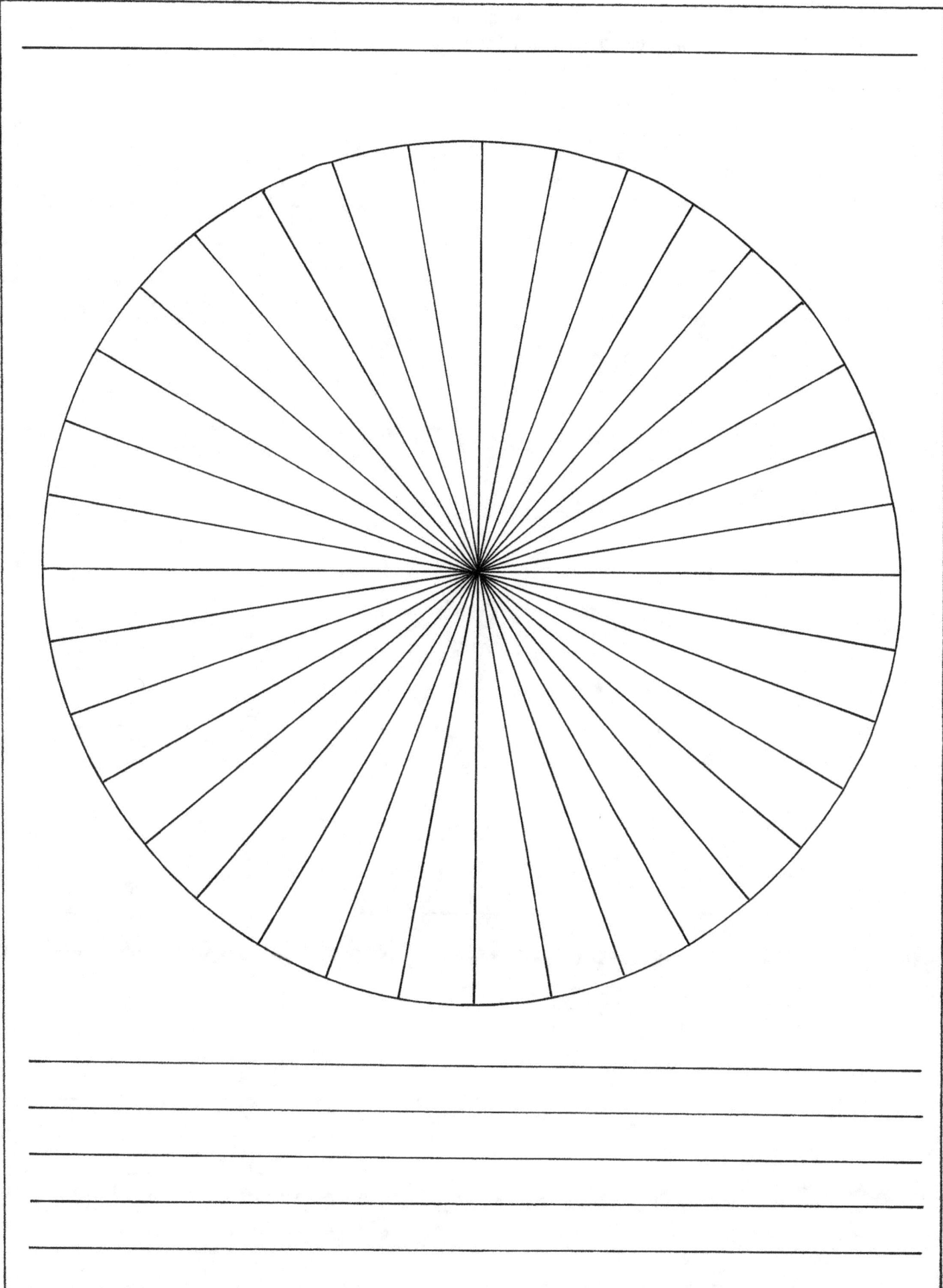

Template 28
4 half color wheels of 18 spaces = a total of 72 spaces

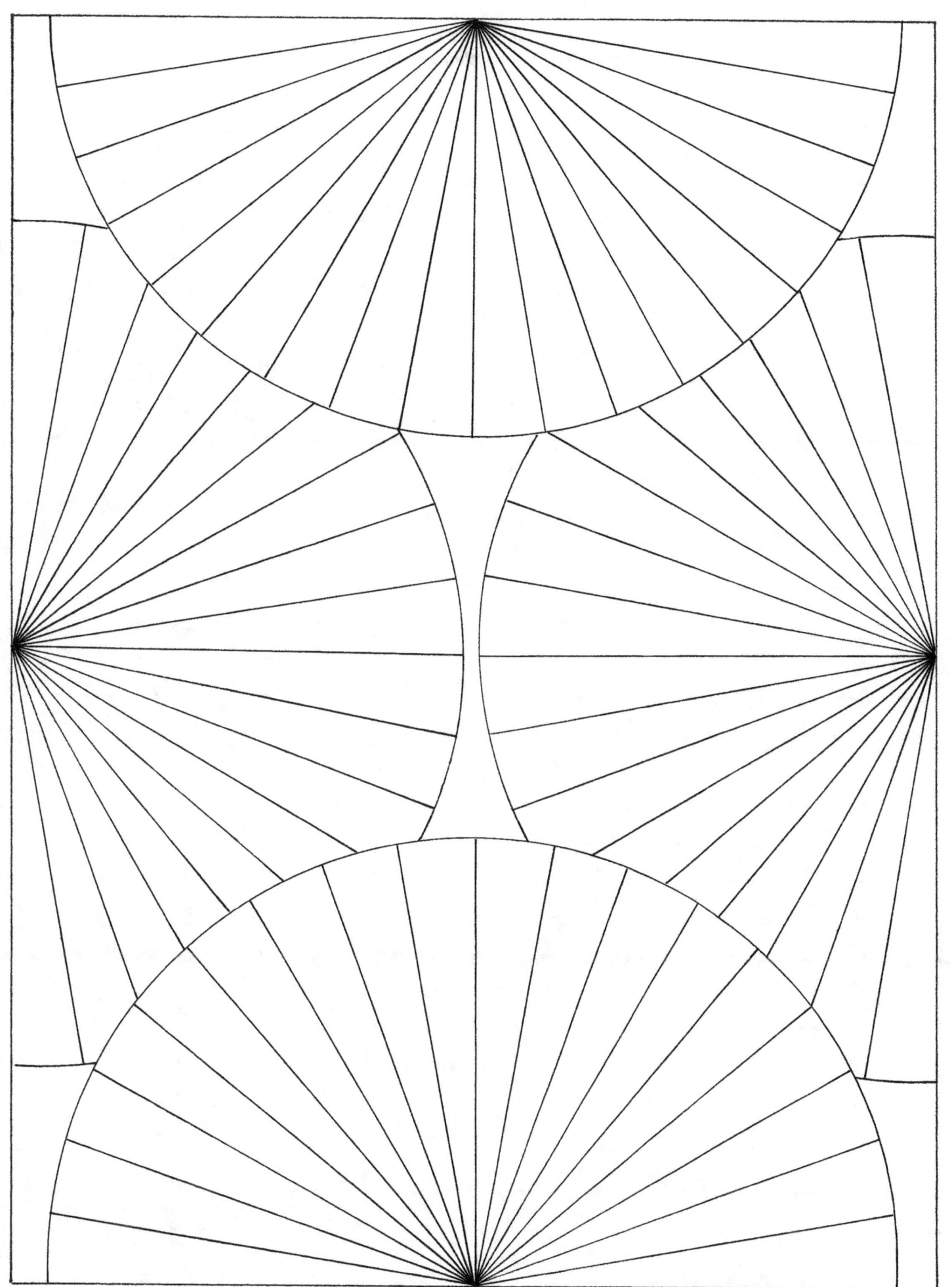

Template 29
10 lines of 9 circles = 90 circles

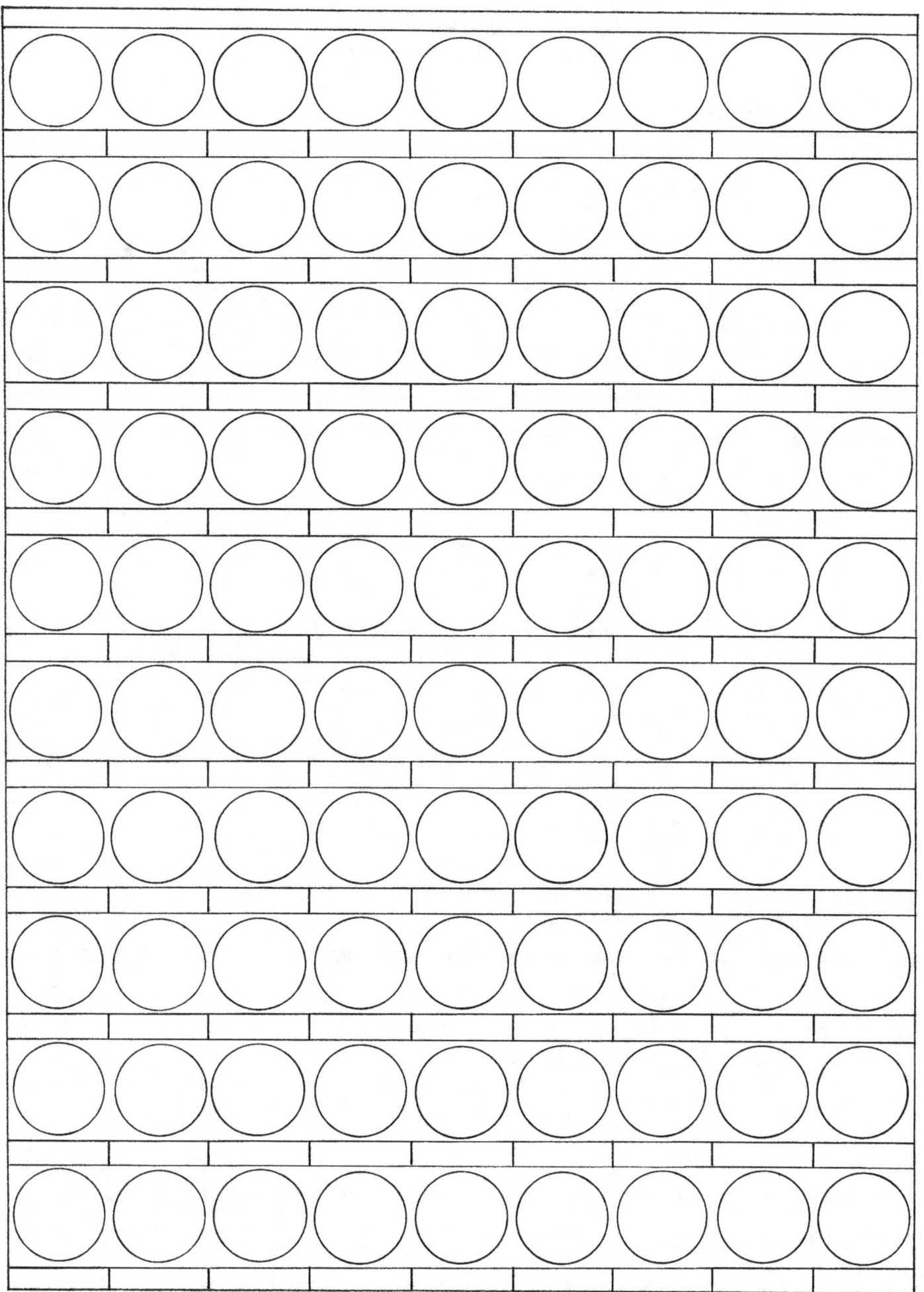

Template 30
Big Color Wheel of 12 spaces

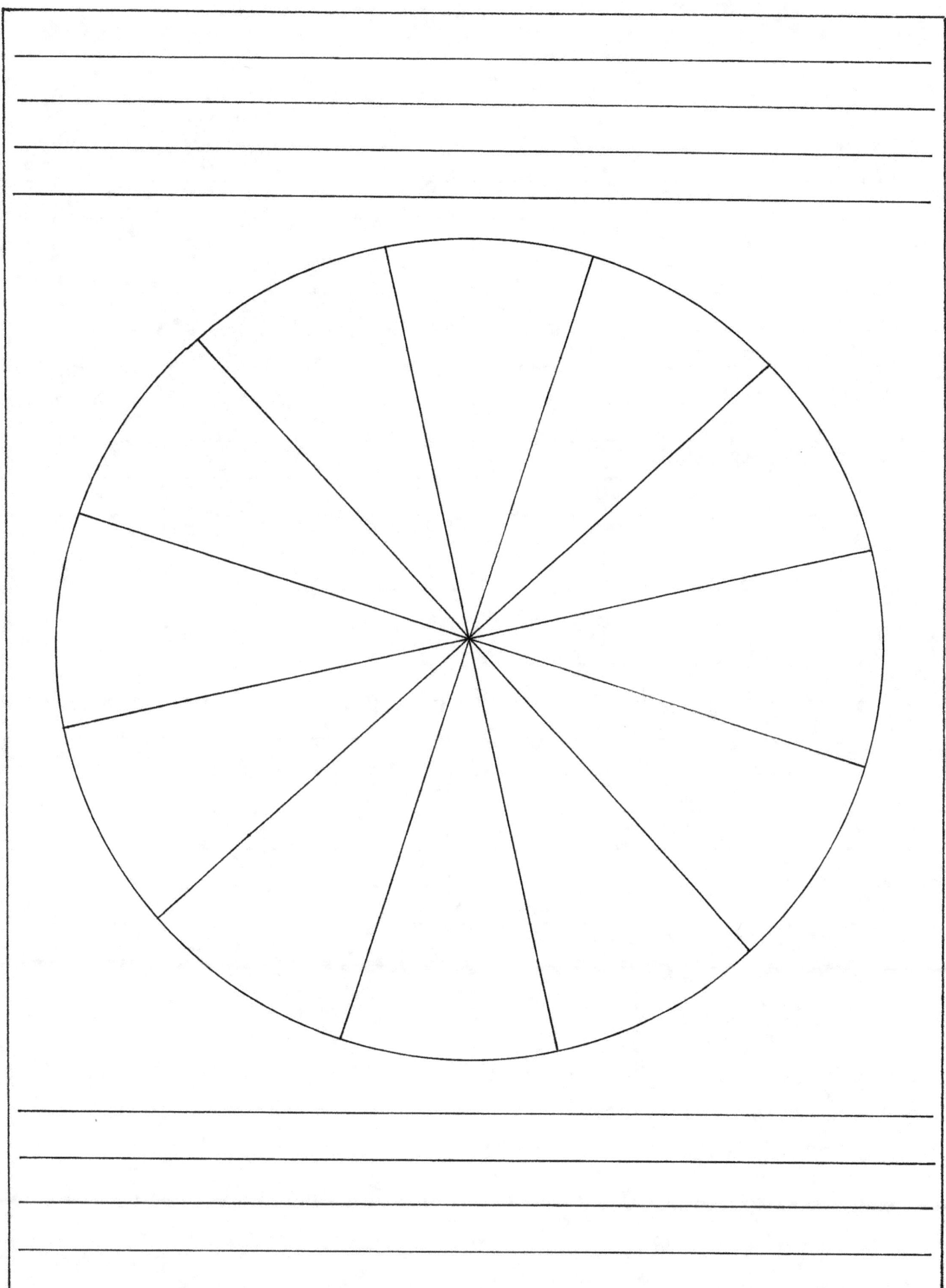

www.ingramcontent.com/pod-product-compliance
Lightning Source LLC
Chambersburg PA
CBHW082324220526
45470CB00008B/2393